NORTH-EASTERN FRONTIER OF INDIA
Structural Imperatives and Aspects of Change

By the same author

1. Politics of Sikkim, 1975, 1994
2. Studies on the Himalayan Communities, 1983
3. Bhutan: Ethnic Identity and National Dilemma, 1991, 1994
4. Beyond the Trees, Tigers and Tribes, 1993
5. Hill Cities of the Eastern Himalaya: Ethnicity, Land Relations and Urbanisation, 1993

NORTH-EASTERN FRONTIER OF INDIA

Structural Imperatives and Aspects of Change

A.C. Sinha
Department of Sociology
North-Eastern Hill University
Shillong, Meghalaya

INDUS PUBLISHING COMPANY
NEW DELHI

First published in 1994 by
Indus Publishing Company
FS-5, Tagore Garden, New Delhi

ISBN 81-7387 009-8

Published by M.L. Gidwani, Indus Publishing Company
FS-5, Tagore Garden, New Delhi 110027, and printed at
Efficient Offset Printers, Shahzada Bagh, New Delhi 110035

To
Professor B. Pakem
The First Tribal from the North Eastern Region
To Become the Vice-Chancellor of a Central University

Preface

A series of titles on the aspects of land and people of the region appear regularly. At times one feels that there is too much rush for the print media to come out with publications on the region. To the extent that old ethnography, reports and monographs have been reprinted, rather shabbily, under different titles. Then a series of quickies, and mostly from the journalists on occasional assignments to the region, are in the publication market. We find the ex-soldiers penning down thier sojourns on the strategic issues of their charge. The various Christian churches have their theological, missionic and occasional academic exercises in publication. Lastly, the different academic institutions have their theses, anthologies, textbooks, research reports, seminar proceedings, etc, published on the region. In short, if it is not a spate, at least it is a good shower of publications on the region.

I gave a serious thought to this before I decided to go for this publication. I have done, a year before, two books on two important themes—urbanization and environment respectively—of the North East region, besides my books on Sikkim and Bhutan. They were well received by the critics as well as the readers.

I weighed my occasional writings on the region and found that most of them were either on the social structural aspects or on the social dynamism and rapid regional transformation. I felt the need to put some of them together. Some of them were updated, revised and edited for the purpose. I added the *Prologue* and the *Epilogue* for introducing the various themes and summing them up at the end. The volume is of a modest size on the regional aspects of continuity and change and I hope the readers will find it relevant for understanding the region in a better way.

As a tribute to the fast changing regional scenario, one of the senior academics of the North Eastern Hill University, Shillong.

with whom I have a privilege to work for years as a colleague, was elected as the first tribal from the region to be the Vice-Chancellor of a Central University in India. As a token to celebrate such a choice he gracefully accepted my dedication of this volume to him, for which I feel gratified. Before the raw idea of publication took a distinct shape, a number of my colleagues—Prof. Imdad Hussain, Dr. David R. Syiemlieh, Prof. P.K. Mishra, Prof. R. Gopal Krishnan, Dr. P.M. Chacko, Dr. I. Lanu Aier to mention just a few—helped me in various ways to clarify the issues through occasional discussions. And for that I am obliged to them and 'others' whose names do not appear in the print. The secretarial assistants of the Department of Sociology, M/s R. Dutta, A. Dkhar, N.P. Sharma and A. Rahman, did the typing and related rigmarole as usual, for which they deserve my special appreciation. Lastly, I am thankful to Mr. M.L. Gidwani, my publisher, not only for attractive and quick publication of the book, but also for his various professional advices.

A.C. SINHA

Acknowledgements

We thankfully acknowledge the kind permission for inclusion in the present anthology granted to us by the organizers of the 'International Conference on Environment and History in South and South East Asia' at the National Institute of Science, Technology and Developmental Studies, New Delhi for the paper on 'Forests of British Assam'; the Director, Indian Institute of Advanced Studies, Shimla for the paper on 'the American Baptist Mission Among the Nagas' presented in the Seminar on 'Continuity and Change'; and 'the Nepalese Immigration' from N.K. Rustomji and C. Ramble (eds) *Himalayan Environment and Culture*, published by Indian Institute of Advanced Studies, Shimla; the Member Secretary ICSSR for 'Inequality and Stratification in the Hill States' based on the 'Trend Report on Tribal Studies', Indian Council of Social Science Research, New Delhi.

B.L. Abbi (ed) *North East Region: Problem and Prospects of Development*, Centre for Research in Rural and Industrial Development, Chandigarh, for chapter five; M.N. Karna (ed) *Peasant and Peasant Protest*, Intellectual Publishing House, New Delhi, for 'Peasant and Peasant Conflict in Nagaland'; the Editor, *Journal of the Indian Anthropological Society*, Vol. 27(1), for 'Tipaimukh Hydel Electric Project and the Hmar Apprehensions'; the Director, ISRO, Ahmedabad, for chapter ten from the Research Project Reports on 'Video Penetration in North East India' and 'Rural Messaging Needs in Meghalaya', and NEHU publication for 'Structural Imperatives of the Indian Core and North East Region' from B. Pakem (ed) *Regionalism in India*, Har Anand Publishers, New Delhi.

Contents

Contents

Prologue

The North-Eastern Frontier Region of India, the ancient Pragjyotisa and historical Kamrupa and the British province of Assam, consisting of Arunachal Pradesh, Assam, Manipur, Meghalaya, Mizoram, Nagaland and Tripura, has a distinct identity. This land-locked territory representing as much as 7.97 per cent of the Indian geographical area has Bhutan, Bangladesh, Burma and Tibet region of China as her immediate neighbours and a tenuous link to India in the West. Topographically, the entire region as the encatchment area of the Brahmaputra river system is the part of the Eastern Himalayan Extension. Historically, it had strong links with the Gangetic plains, though its natural orientation was towards North to Tibet and East to the South East Asia. Ethnologically, though there have been distinct Caucasoid and Austroloid strains in its population, the main ethnic stream belongs to the larger Mangloid stock and their legends of ethnic migration link them to the North and the East. Same is the situation in terms of linguistic affiliation. The region has a variety of social formations from the highly complex state systems such as the Ahoms to the small, isolated, nomadic band organizations. As an Indian territory its destiny is intimately linked with the larger Indian Union. However, its regional characteristics are so pronounced that the scholars find it convenient to emphasize its closeness to the South East Asian Communities.

It goes without saying that animism was the most prevalent faith among the various communities before they came in contact with the great religions of the world such as Hinduism, Islam, Buddhism and Christianity. Meiteis, Ahoms, Kochs and Tripuris among others were the earliest communities to come within in the Hindu fold. However, under the influence of the Vaishnav movement and Swami Shanker Deb the Hinduism in the region has been free from the various caste disabilities prevalent elsewhere. Islam entered the region during the Mughal period of the Indian history and got assimilated within the regional dominant cultural contour. In this context, Azam Fakir's *Zakir* and *Zikir* are the precious ingredients of the regional folk cultural commonwealth. The Hinayan Buddhism of Chakma, Magh, Nocte and Singphos and the Mahayan faith of the Monpas and Sherdukpens add further to the religious mozaic of the region. By the middle of the 19th century A.D. a number of Christian missionaries came to the region with their evangelical, medical and educational expertise and they could establish various denominations among Ao, Angami, Garo, Lhotha, Mizo, Khasi, Tangkhul, Kuki and other communities. It is a fact that by the time the colonial rule came to an end in India, Christianity turned out to be the most dominant faith among the hill communities of the region south of river Brahmaputra and it could open a modern, westernized and technologically superior window for them. The various buffer and bridge communities of the past, adopted new names for themselves; collated to form larger identities such as the Adi, Naga, Chakhesang, Mizo, etc. and some of them fragmented to new formations such as Hmar from the earliest larger communities.

The historians inform us that there were various principalities before the Ahoms could establish themselves in the Brahmaputra valley. The way they organised their water managed economy through an intricate system of *pyke* on the basis of *Khel* and *Mel*, which was reminiscent of Witfoegel's *Oriental Dispotism* (Witfoegel, K.A., 1962). Though plains were ruled with a heavy hand, frontiers were secured through the payment of *posa* and institution of *Kakoti*. Many of these distant communities were loosely linked with the Ahom state and at times their services were requisitioned. There was a limited social intercourse and, at times, Ahom princes were married beyond their limits for the benefit of political alliance. Though there was an economic hierarchy, Ahom Hinduism was largely free from social disabilities experienced in other Hindu kingdoms in India. At the cultural level, early Assamese language was emerging as a lingua franca for the entire region.

At the formal political level, there were three dominant models available in the region: (i) Hindu and Hinduized kingdoms such as Meiteis, Ahoms, Jaintias, Kochs, Dimasas, Tripuris, etc.; (ii) Buddhists like Chakmas, Khamtis, Bhutanese etc, and (iii) tribal polities such as Khasi Syiemships (Sinha, S.C., 1987). Then there were a number of incipient state formations such as Mizos (Lushais), Angamis, Konyak and others. The basically subsistence hill economy generated an extremely limited surplus, which was too insufficient for maintenance of a state structure. On the other hand, the region was on a difficult and agriculturally unsuitable locale, where possession of a plot of land was not preferred to an extensive topographical niche for hunting, grazing or transhumance. The basic character of a hill man is that of defiance and struggle against the natural obstacles and human intrigues (Lattimore, O., 1982). Thus, if a surplus was not generated locally, it was considered imperative to acquire such articles of necessity and luxury by force leading to raid, feud, invasion and even war.

After 1824-26 Anglo-Burmese War, Lakhimpur district, which touched all the geographical sub-regional variations to a great extent, was considered an ideal location for colonization of the white settlers. As luck would have smiled on them, a stray and insignificant vegetation of the region—tea—caught the imagination of the then technologically advanced British entrepreneurs. This resulted in an organised expansion of the tea plantation economy on an entirely technologically primitive base. The natural resources—land, forest, minerals and wild life—were considered inexhaustible. The key word was expansion through adventure, intrigue, greed, treaty and treachery. Among the *posa* articles offered to the Adis and the Mons tribesman bottles of rum, opium, tobacco, were the items gifted to the hillmen (Sinha, A.C., 1986). Still the hillmen were referred as barbarians, savage, uncivilized, wildmen, headhunters and what not. In this way, while the valley land in the region was being transformed into one of the most progressive plantation economy in the world, the newly emerged formation was causing a havoc to already stagnant indigenous economy.

In case one may make very broad generalizations on the pre-British hill formations, the scenario presents relatively simpler contour. The hill communities possessed of extremely crude technology with their sparse population and abundance of natural vegetation, were engaged in hunting of the wild animals and collecting of the forest products for their subsistence. A second formation was taking shape in the form of family/community-based subsistence farming through slash-and-burn type of rotational cultivation (*jhumming*) often described as the 'Asiatic mode of production'. Ethnographers have described this economy in which there were no roles for the specialists. A few of them were engaged in barter trade in wild products for exchanging them with salt, dried fish, threads, iron and other necessities. As their legends of migration indicate, hill areas witnessed incessant human movements leading to feuds, raids, repraisals and even wars. It appears by the middle of 19th century the entire hill tract was closely identified with various ethnic groups. Thus, there was hardly a patch of land in the region, which was 'no man's land'. However, the hills with their almost impregnable forests were no 'isolates'; in fact, there were trails across all the significant ranges.

It is a fact that the British did not directly administer the hill districts as they did in the case of the Brahmaputra valley. But over-all British control on the regional economy and inter-tribal relations led to the freezing of the tribal situation as if their natural process of growth was clipped off. A far reaching process was introduced in terms of capital and house taxes. Slowly and slowly, the entire hill region barring the upper ridges of Arunachal Pradesh was brought within the British capitalist economy. This was secured through introduction of cash economy, petty blue coat jobs, elementary education through the Christian churches and creation of administrative market and urban centres (Aier, L. 1986). What resulted in the process was the scenario in which subsistence farming tribes were exploitatively linked to the world metropolitan market in which they were reduced to suppliers of the marginal raw materials and consumers of the industrial goods. To the extent that even *Jhumias* were induced to cultivate some minor crops for cash transaction which were channelled through markets to the urban industrial centres. However, with the carving out of the *scheduled districts* in the hills the British appeared to be reluctant rulers to some of the native tribesmen. Though even their paternalistic caring for the tribesmen did not stop enroad of the private commercial establishments such as Rajasthani wholesalers, timber merchants etc. to tribal areas.

The present book is divided into two parts: the structural imperatives of the region and the various aspects of change. While the first part with its six chapters provides the geographical, historical, ethnic, religious and societal background of the region on the larger context, the second part delineates specificity of the transformation in terms of agrarian, urban, environmental and technological situations in the next five chapters. The first chapter introduces the region, its various natural sub-divisions, vegetations and related economic activities and the broad contours of the pre-colonial regional economy. The second chapter on the Forests in British Assam informs the readers how did the British introduce the 'Forest Reserves' on community land, encourage the cattle grazing by the Nepalese on the wasteland for the sake of revenue, get the captive labour from the newly settled 'forest villages', provide tea chests to the tea plantations at the cost of the forests, tackle the Garo movement for de-reservation of the forests and divert the revenue earned by the Forest Department to elsewhere at the cost of the ill-paid forest personnel.

The third chapter on 'The American Baptist Mission Among the Nagas' introduces a new dimension to the regional scenario. The missionaries were introduced to the region with the open support from the administration, they received support from the colonial rulers for their educational and medical activities and occasionally were hand in glove with the colonial masters in their efforts 'to civilize the savages' on the frontiers. There were many reasons for tribals' conversion to Christianity and Christianity has led to some new problems for the tribesmen. However, the Christianity has provided the tribal Christians with a new sense of identity, a window to the modern world and an affiliation to the larger Christian World religion. Chapter four on the tribal social stratification introduces a rather little known social fact that the tribal societies have not been necessarily equalitarian. After providing the ethnographic details of the traditional tribal stratification, the author describes the various processes through which the inequality has further increased after the creation of the tribal states in the region. With the emergence of private landed property in place of a flexible communal control, phenomenon of absentee landlordism, wage labour, share cropping, landless labour, agrarian tension, neo-rich contractor-politician elite have turned out to be the significant fixture in the regional market oriented economy.

Chapter five reviews the basic character of the regional communities and the tribal states as necessarily that of 'small scale communities'. This chapter raises a number of issues than it answers them. The last chapter (six) of part one is on the Nepalese immigration to the region, which analyses its various aspects. This chapter may be seen in terms of the second chapter on the forest history, which reports the presence of herdsmen and graziers on the waste land and degraded forests. Broadly speaking among the Nepalese immigrants the chapter records the ex-soldiers resettled by the Government on certain strategic locations as 'soldiers' farm', the herdsmen and land hungry farmers and artisans and professionals. Many of the immigrants do not possess documents to establish their citizenship. However, the problems of the ethnic identity in the tribal states for the Indian Nepalese is very serious. The community has suffered hardships in the past and is presently confronted with making a hard choice in terms of reinforcing and re-evaluating the Nepalese identity in India rather than melting away among the various ethnic groups and sub-nationalities in India. In this way, part one identifies geography, history, religion, social structure, smallness of the communities and the immigration as unique structural imperatives, which demand proper understanding before a serious analysis of social transformation is undertaken.

Part two with its five chapters begins with emergence of the peasants on the substantive communal production systems, which was necessarily an aspect of subsistence economy of the past. With the land and economy intricately linked with the world-wide metropolitan marketing system, the past ethnic autonomy on their lands is replaced by co-existence of multi-ethnic communities, leading to occasional conflicts, as reported from the Medziphema Development Block in Nagaland. The chapter eight examines an entirely a new and different aspect of social scene in terms of the nature of urbanization in the tribal states in the region. After informing the readers that urbanization among the hill communities is hardly a hundred years old and a creation of the British 'administrative outposts' in the tribal heart-land, author examines the structure of hill cities, the nature of the urban political participation in the civic affairs and comes out with about half a dozen recommendations for a meaningful urban management.

Chapter nine on the Tipaimukh Hydel Electric Project examines the social and environmental consequences of a large scale, high technology and multi-purpose river-valley project on a small community such as the Hmars. This chapter reports confusion among the Hmars, callousness of the state authorities and non-concern and mechanical approach of the technocrats. It rightly warns the authorities to examine all the implications before undertaking a Rs. 1400 crore ambitious project in an insurgency-prone frontiers. The chapter ten explicates a different scenario in which the roles played by electronic communication medium has been examined. This chapter reports the social and economic consequences of the availability of the video parlours on the tribal heartland and way it had affected the regional social fabrics. Similarly, it highlights the ground realities of relatively isolated tribal rural set-up, where satellite based telephonic and telegraphic devices are being set up. The process of sending a message is yet to be developed as a mechanical facility; rather it is seen as an occasion to re-establish face to face interaction among the individuals in the region. The last chapter (eleven) examines the conflicting national and the regional perceptions on the character of the social realities and the nature and extent of participation in the public affairs. The epilogue at the end summarizes the structural compulsions and direction of change undergoing in the region.

References

Aier, L.I. 1986, 'Contemporary Social Formations and Ethnic Identity: A Case of Development or Decay' MSS Ph.D. thesis, NEHU, Shillong.

Lattimore, O. 1962, *Studies in Frontier History*, Mouton, Paris.

Sinha, A.C. 1986, 'Video Penetration in North East India' MSS, Deptt. of Sociology, NEHU, Shillong.

Sinha, S.C. 1987 (ed), *Tribal Polities and State Systems in Eastern and North Eastern India*, K.P. Bagchi, Calcutta.

Witfoegel, K.A. 1962, *Oriental Despotism*, Yale University Press, New Haven.

Part I
Structural Imperatives

1

Natural Resources and Pre-Colonial Economy

The Himalayas—the abode of the snow—is the rampart and fosses of the giant ranges which wall off the Indian sub-continent from snow bound Central Asia. Its massive ranges extend from Gwador (south-western Arabian coast in Pakistan) in the west to the Mizo-Arakan ranges (on the Bangladesh south-eastern border) in the east measuring more than 5,500 kilometres. Of this the Western wing Baluchistan and trans-Sindhu (Indus) upto the syntaxial bend at Nanga Parbat in Kashmir is 1,500 kilometres. The eastern wing from Namcha-Barwa (on Arunachal-Kham border) to the Mizo Hills is 1,000 kilometres and the Central Himalayan arc is 2,500 kilometres (Bose, S.C.: 1972: 11). Though the width of the Himalayas varies from area to area, the great Himalayan arc between Nanga Parbat to Namcha-Barwa or between the Indus and the Brahmaputra bends has an average width of about 200 kilometres. Normally the Himalayas is divided into three major regions: Western Hills and ranges in the Indus encatchment area (now in Pakistan and Pakistan occupied Kashmir), the Central Himalayan arc of the Ganges, and the Eastern Himalayas drained out by the Brahmaputra and her tributaries. The Central Himalayan arc or the Great Himalayas has further been divided into three: the western, the central and the eastern. The central zone of the Great Himalayas extends from the Yamuna-Satluj-divide to the Koshi-Tista watershed in the east forming the eastern limits of Nepal.

The Great Himalayan arc is further divided into three distinct parallel systems from north to south on the basis of physiography: the Great Himalayan ranges, the Inner Himalayas, and the Lesser Himalayas,—*bhabar, terai, duars* or the foothills. While the greater Himalayas is snow bound northern tundra type topography above the snow line, it covers all the world famous high Himalayan summits such as Nandadevi (26,645 ft.), Kemet (25,447 ft.), Everest (29,028 ft.), Kanchenjunga (28,146 ft.), Chomo Lhari (23,997 ft.), Namcha-Barwa (25,445 ft.) etc. There is little permanent human settlement in the virtual snow desert except occasional trans-humance herdsmanship. However, the region is the last haven for adventure seeking mountaineers. It also abounds in varieties of rhododendrons and alpine co-niferous forests. Most of the snow-fed rivers originate in the religion and there are passes to cross from north to south such as Niti, Chumbi etc.

The inner Himalayas is the real flat valley interposed between the mountain ranges and forested mountains. In between there are extensive valleys such as Kathmandu, Thimpu, Tongsa, etc. which are undulating pastureland thickly populated and known for ancient civilizations such as Newari in Kathmandu valley. There are rich alpine forests and all types of tropical and winter crops are grown in the valley and on the river banks. But the rivers are fast, meandering and unfordable. The bulk of the people are peasants but many of them subsist on grazing and trans-humance. The Garhwalis, Kumayunis, Gurkhas and the Bhotias have tradition of marshal race and are reputed soldiers. The topography of the region conditioned the residents in such a way that they developed fighters 'instinct' leading to establishment of numerous small principalities such as *Chaubis* (24 principalities) or *baisis* (22 principalities). Atleast three of them Nepal, Sikkim and Bhutan could survive till 1975 and first and third among them have become independent nations, the only Hindu and the only Lamaist monarchies in the world. As bulk of population belongs to marginal farmers, who are polygamous with numerous children, the forests are turned into agricultural field. However, agricultural technology is primitive, plots are uneconomic and agricultural investment is next to nothing leading to large scale erosion of the top soil because of repeated cultivation. Consequently, the inner Himalayan region is ranked among the least developed and the poorest countries of the world.

The foothills are low ranges running from east to west-south of the Inner Himalayas consisting of boulders, moraine and sandy soil, on which evergreen tropical forests abound. It was known as "negative zone", because of its unhealthy climate. Moreover, the evergreen forests abounded in ferocious wild animals, besides being hot, humid, and malarial (Sinha A.C.: 1987: 337; Karan, P.P.: 1963: 11). There was no permanent human settlement except some wild tribes such as Tharu, Koch, Mech, Toto etc. The hill principalities and tribes such as Gurkhas, Sikkimese, Durkpas, Nishing (Daflas), Adis (Abor) were in habit of raiding the settled Gangetic and Brahmaputra plains for capturing slaves to work in the inner Himalayan agricultural fields. All these came to an end with establishment of the British empire in India. It took the British roughly 75 years between Nepal war of 1813-14 to 1988, when Sikkim was finally turned into an Indian protectorate, to bring the Himalayan foothills from Murree (now in Pakistan) to Sadiya on Arunachal borders under an effective British control. The British did realise the economic significance of the regions. With the establishment of law and order, the jungles in the foothills were cleared first in Nepal terai by the land hungry agricultural communities from the Gangetic plains (Gaige, F.H.: 1975). There was a growing demand for *sal* timber for the railways. There were two significant developments effecting the Himalayan foothills. Firstly, the British felt the need of health resorts in the cool and rarified mountain air of the Himalayas. That is how Murree, Dolhousie, Dehradun, Simla, Mussoorie, Nainital, Ranikhet, Darjeeling, Kalimpong etc. were developed as summer hill stations on easy communication networks with plains for the British bureaucrats. Secondly, by the middle of the 19th century, it was realized that the Eastern Duars were ideal landscape for cultivation of tea plants. Thus, there was a mad rush from Lakhimpur, Darrang, Goalpara, Jalpaiguri, Darjeeling, Dehradun to Kangra for clearance of the forests, which were settled as wastelands to the planters. Incidentally, the third quarters of the last century saw the introduction of forest reservation in India with a view to ensuring timber supply for the urban industrial purposes. In the process, precious forests in the region were reserved as the Government property.

From another angle the Himalayas may be examined. There are four significant cultural processes operating in the Himalayas. Firstly, all along the northern Himalayas, Lamaist Buddhism developed in Tibet is prevalent from Arunachal Preadesh to Ladakh on the southern fringe of the Tibetan plateau. Secondly, Hindu ethos and social intercourse is evident from Kashmir valley to Bhutan Duars on the southern slope of the Himalayas inclusive of Himachal, Uttar Pradesh and Nepal in the Inner Himalayan zones. Thirdly, flow of culture from the west in the form of Muslim-Pertian character is dominant in the Kashmir valley. The Sindhu-Ganges watershed remains in a way its eastern limit. Fourthly, a basically animistic tribalism prevails predominantly in Arunachal Pradesh, which progressively decreases westward and is found mainly upto Limbuan i.e. eastern Nepal (Sinha, A.C.: 1983 A: XXIII). In a way, these four cultural processes broadly coincide with that of the northern, southern, western and eastern Himalayan zones respectively.

A. The Eastern Himalayas

Between 86°E and 88°E, the general character of the Himalayas changes so much that a new region of the Eastern Himalayas is warranted. Moreover, the Himalayan region just north of the Gangetic delta between the Rajmahal Hills and Shillong plateau is exposed to the direct impact of the monsoon causing high and dense rainfall and wet tropic evergreen jungle. The intensity of rainfall increases eastward upto the tri-junction of the eastern limit of the Himalayan arc, Patkai ranges and the Brahmaputra valley and so intense is the vegetation. Compared to its Western and Central counterparts, the Eastern Himalayas is less high. Similarly, because of high precipitation, the snow line is higher upto 14,000 in the Himalayas in the east. The region may be broadly divided into: (i) the eastern part of the Great Himalayan arc, (ii) the eastern hill ranges comprising Patkai-Manipur-Mizo-Arakan-Chittagong Hills, (iii) Shillong-Mikir plateau and (iv) the plains of the Brahmaputra and Barak valleys (see Map 1).

(1) The Eastern Himalayan Arc: This sub-region extends all along the Great Himalayan ranges in the north from Singalila ridge to Donkhya range (15,000-17,000 ft.), to Chumbi valley to Chomo-Lhari (23,930 ft.), to Kulakanari (24,749 ft.) to Kangto (23,255 ft.) to Gorichen (21,445 ft.) upto Namcha Barwa (25,450 ft.) in the farthest north-east bend and then to the Duars in the south from Darjeeling to Tirap-Lakhimpur. Again it may be divided into Tista

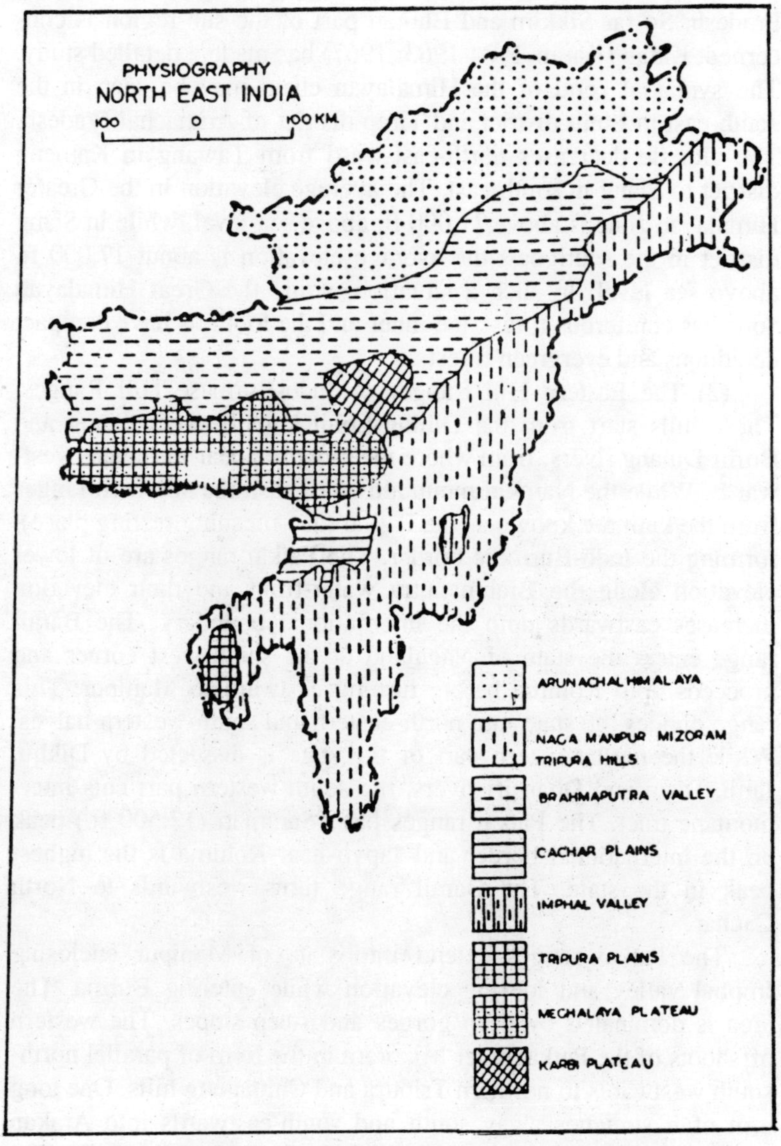
PHYSIOGRAPHY
NORTH EAST INDIA
100 0 100 KM.
ARUNACHAL HIMALAYA
NAGA MANIPUR MIZORAM TRIPURA HILLS
BRAHMAPUTRA VALLEY
CACHAR PLAINS
IMPHAL VALLEY
TRIPURA PLAINS
MEGHALAYA PLATEAU
KARBI PLATEAU

encatchment area (Sikkim and Darjeeling), Bhutan and Arunachal Pradesh. So far Sikkim and Bhutan part of the sub-region is concerned, Karan (Karan, P.P.: 1963: 1967) has made a detailed study. The syntaxial bend of the Himalayan chain may be seen in the south-east in Lohit district and Tirap district of Arunachal Pradesh. The altitude decreases north-east-ward from Tawang in Kameng district to Siang in south-east. The average elevation in the Greater Himalayan zone is above 21,000 ft. above sea-level, while in Siang district in the south-east the average elevation is about 17,000 ft. above sea level. In such a situation, while the Great Himalayan zone has coniferous forest, the inner and the foothills have compact deciduous and evergreen forests.

(2) The Eastern Hill Ranges or Indo-Burmese Hill Ranges: These hills start from the Dihing-Lohit knot between Siang and Burhi-Dihang rivers, from where the ranges appear to radiate westwards. While the Namkin mountains turn east, the southern ranges from the knot are known as the Patkai (ai—meaning resting place), forming the Indo-Burmese border. The Patkai ranges are of lower elevation along the Brahmaputra water-front and their elevation increases eastwards upto the international boundary. The Barail range enters the state of Nagaland at the south-west corner and proceeds upto Kohima before turning eastward to Manipur. This range divides the state into north-eastern and south-western halves. While the north-western part of the state is dissected by Dikhu, Janji, Disoi and Dhansiri rivers, the south-western part cuts intermontane tract. The Patkai ranges have Saramati (12,500 ft.) peak on the international border and Japvo near Kohima is the highest peak in the state. The Barail range turns westwards to North Cachar.

The Patkai ranges extend into state of Manipur enclosing Imphal valley and loosing elevation while entering Burma. The area is dominated by deep gorges and steep slopes. The western offshoots of the Patkai enter Mizoram in the form of parallel north-south westwards to northern Tripura and Chittagong hills. One long arm of it stretches away south and south-eastwards into Arakan ranges, whose extreme northern hills are lost into Mizo hills. The western spurs of these hills are covered with forests of fine timber, but on the east, the bamboo is the principal growth. With a monsoon rainfall upto 100 inches, the hills have a heavy cover of forests, ranging from tropical evergreen which giant dipterocarps in the wetter and lower south, through monsoon deciduous forests, to some pine and even grass on the highest ridges. But these forests have been much affected by jhum cultivation resulting in very dense secondary scrub-jungle and vast stretches of bamboo (Spate, et al: 1972: 606-607).

(3) Shillong plateau or Meghalaya-Karbi plateau: It is the North-easternly extension of the Deccan peninsula separated by the Gangetic delta between the Rajmahal and Garo Hills and extended upto the Naga hills within an area of 10,590 square miles or 12% of the region. The Meghalaya—the abode of clouds—is normally divided into Garo, Khasi and Jaintia hills—the tribal divisions—is in fact one compact geographical unit. It is almost a rectangular block of 150 by 60 miles with highest elevation at Shillong (6,432 ft.) and Nokrek (4,631 ft.) peaks in the Garo hills. The plateau rises abruptly to above 3,000 ft. from the delta plains in Bangladesh, loses its elevation to the Brahmaputra plains through a series of isolated hills and it is deeply dissected because of high precipitation. Its eastern extension is separated by Kopli gorge in the west and Dhansiri river system in Nagaland in the east turning it into a circular shape. Meghalayan plateau with its appropriate Sanskrit name (Chatterjee, S.P.: 1936) is reputed to be under heavy forest with pines on the higher sides but elsewhere it is covered with a mixture of woodland and secondary bushes because of repeated *jhumming*. It is reputed for its rhododendrons, orchids, a variety of flowering plants and bamboos, potato, chillies, orange and ginger are the chief cash crops, cultivation of which is leading to erosion of thin top soil.

(4) The plains of the Brahmaputra and the Barak valleys: The river Brahmaputra—the mythological son of the creator-Brahma—the master-stream is claimed to be one of the most astonishing rivers in the world. It originates near Mansarowar lake in Tibet, flows as Tsangpo almost parallel to the eastward Himalayan arc upto Namcha-Barwa, turns south-west and then moves westerly almost parallel to its northern Tsangpo branch for better than 500 miles upto Dhubri and finally takes a southern bend to meet Ganges near Goalando in Bangladesh. At the higher altitude it receives

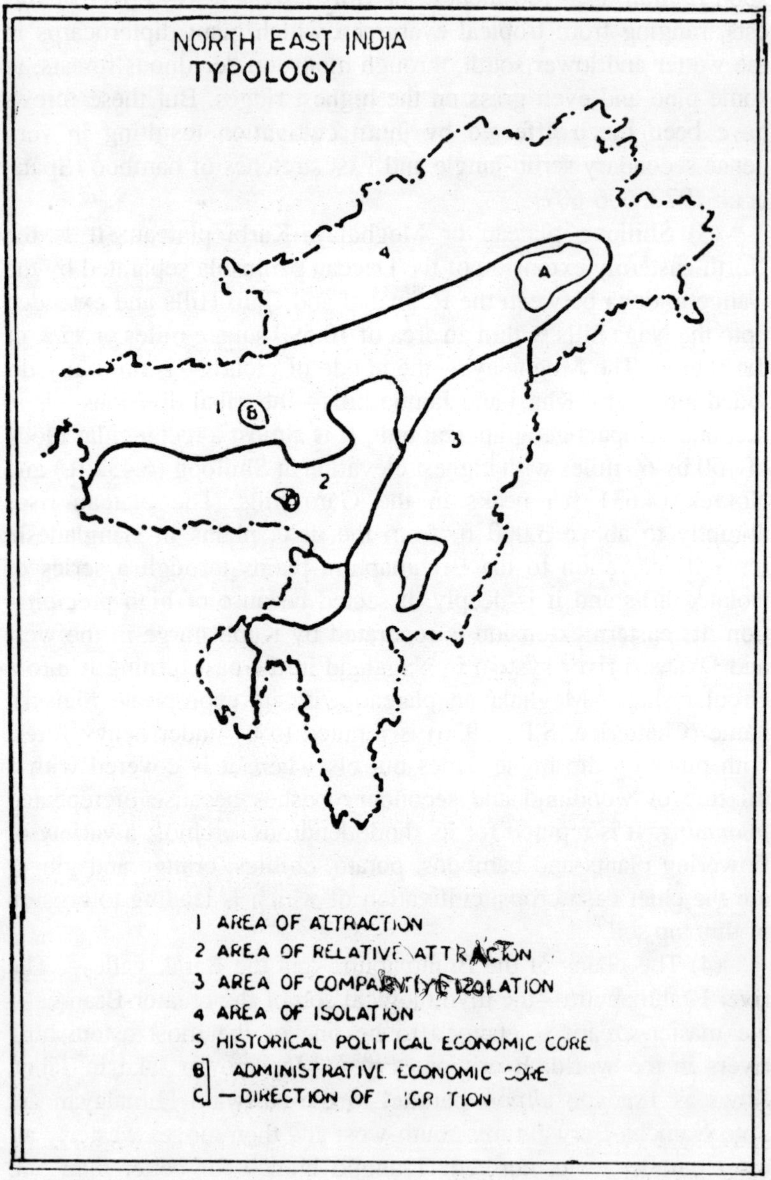
NORTH EAST INDIA
TYPOLOGY
A
4
1
B
3
2
B
1 AREA OF ATTRACTION
2 AREA OF RELATIVE ATTRACTON
3 AREA OF COMPARATIVE ISOLATION
4 AREA OF ISOLATION
5 HISTORICAL POLITICAL ECONOMIC CORE
B] ADMINISTRATIVE ECONOMIC CORE
C] —DIRECTION OF IGR TION

massive doze of snow melt water after its Dilhang-Dibang-Lohit confluence some 900 miles from the sea, it enters the land which receives the highest rainfall in the world. The valley named after it or Assam proper extends some 600 miles east to west and 60 miles north to south is, in fact, a gift of the river, as it is formed out of the alluvial soil. The river has as many as 125 tributaries. "Due to conditions of slopes, the north bank tributaries are very active and carry usually heavy load of boulders, pebbles and silt. This is added by heavy precipitation in the entire catchment area. Besides this, as the area lies within the seismic belt and with large scale deforestation, the erosion activity of these rivers has been further intensified. As a result, the alluvial fans are a common feature" (Gopal Krishna, R: 1991: 65-66). The extensive parts of such river banks are covered with sal forest and toll reed jungle in the swamps, which is inhabited by a rare animal species of one-horned rhinoceros.

The Barak or Surma valley covering 16 per cent of the region in its south-eastern portion is, in fact, an extension of the Gangetic delta. The river Barak itself rises in Senapati district of Manipur in the Barail ranges, takes a western course and then a big U-turn before entering Cachar plains on way to Sylhet in Bangladesh. The Barak has a sluggish meandering course with a number of ox-bow lakes and *bhils-swamps*. The vegetation is similar to the Brahmaputra valley, but on the thinner side with preponderance of bamboo and cane-brakes. The Imphal valley or the Manipur plains is a lacustrine area like Kashmir valley with numerous depressions, marshes and lakes. One of the unique features of the physiography of the Brahmaputra and the Barak valleys is the development of the plantation industry within last 150 years. The tea bushes are spread over 400,000 acres or 162,000 hectares in about 800 tea estates on the higher terraces of plains hills producing over half of the Indian tea produce and employing more than 1,500,000 persons. The development of tea plantation in the region has a bearing on the environment in general and forests in particular.

Some broad generalisations may be made on the basis of above presentation. Firstly, a distinct North-Eastern Frontier Region of North East India excluding Sikkim, Darjeeling and Bhutan has emerged as significant geo-political entity in the Indian context.

Secondly, North-East India consisting of the Seven Sisters (Arunachal Pradesh, Assam, Meghalaya, Manipur, Mizoram, Nagaland and Tripura) has evolved its strategy of development in terms of its physical features and natural resources. With that the region has the following sub-divisions: (i) the area of attraction—the Brahmaputra and the Imphal valleys; (ii) the area of comparative isolation—Meghalaya-Mikir plateau; (iii) the area of comparative isolation—the Patkai and Barail ranges; (iv) the areas of isolation—Arunachal Pradesh and (v) the areas as the gateways—Goalpara, Cachar and Lakhimpur districts (see Map 2). Thirdly, the region as such has a strong cultural, linguistic, ethnic and vegetation links with both south-east Asia (Burlings, R.: 1965) and India (Chatterjee, S.K.: 1951) from the very beginning of the human history. And lastly, the region, as it remains today, has variously been organised and reorganised since 1826 to 1947, when it was better known as Assam plus princely states of Manipur and Tripura.

B. The Natural Vegetation

The forests, the green gold of the nature and largely dependent on the physiography of the land, may be classified in a number of ways such as by composition, legal status, ownership, exploitation and functions. Among them, the first two, the classification by composition and legal status are the most significant and we shall examine the forests of the region from these two points of view.

Forest Composition in the Region

Dietrich Brandis, the Inspector General of Forests in the British India, paid a visit to Assam in 1879 and wrote his famous "Suggestions regarding Forest Administration in Assam." He described seven types of forests in the Privince: Savannahs, sal, sissu and Khair, mixed deciduous, evergreen, bamboo and cane-brakes. This was followed by his successor, B. Ribbentrop, in 1889, who filed a "Note on an Inspection of the Forests of Assam" (Ribbentrop, B.: 1889). In terms of classification of the forests, he retained the seven-fold divisions of the Province proposed by his predecessor and added an eighth one, the pine forests. Some five decades after Ribbentrop, M.C. Jacob, Deputy Conservator of Forests, Assam prepared a report in 1940 (Jacob, M.M.C.: 1940) and revised the above typology in the following manner: Sal, evergreen, mixed deciduous, pine, riverine, highland savannah and lowland savannah.

(1) *Sal Forests:* Sal forests are found in the areas where the annual rainfall is below 80 inches, or if more and the sub-soil drainage is excellent. Such a situation is found in the Himalayan foothills of Goalpara and Kamrup districts and Shillong plateau extending from Mikir Hills to the western edge of Meghalaya. Sal forests have suffered greatly because of the practice of *jhumming* found among the hill tribes as an agricultural pattern. The areas, which were declared as the forests and the story of sal-reservation in the Garo hills and consequent agitation to declare them dereserved will be unfolded in the next chapter. A tram service was introduced after the first World War with a view to extracting sal timber in the Goalpara district for supplying them as the railway sleepers. Just before the second World War, about two million four thousand, c.f.t. of sal timber was exploited in Assam in 1937-38. At that time the province had 177,000 acres of sal reserves, distributed in seven forest divisions of lower Assam.

(2) *Evergreen Forests:* They are found in the hills where rainfall is upward of 80 inches and in the plains, where subsoil permits of the retention of water near the surface. The whole of Upper Assam with the exception of savannah and bamboo forests are covered with evergreen forests. Similarly such forests skirt the Himalayan ranges. These forests exhibit a great variety of character in vegetation. However, certain trees such as *Nahor* (Mesua Ferrea) are found in all evergreen forests. A large amount of *jhumming* takes place within these forests and fire does not spread because of the wet-evergreen vegetation. Jacob divides them into two: (a) highland evergreen and (b) lowland evergreen. The former are spread in Sadiya, Lakhimpur, Darrang, Sibsagar, Nowgong and Cachar divisions and abound in Hollock, Hollong, Cham, Amari, Gonseroi, Naher, Surjan, Spoas, and Sundim species of trees.

The lowland evergreen is found on the fringes of smaller streams, ravines, *bhils* and swamps. With the exception of Ajhar (Jarul), very few important timber trees are found among them. Unlike the sal forests, there are rarely 10 to 15 trees per acre of the same species in these forests. However, certain significant timber trees such as Hollock, Hellong, Nahor, Bonsum etc., have been identified lying at the foothills in the Arunachal Pradesh and efforts have been made for their extraction for the saw mills. The eastern-most tip of India in Arunachal Pradesh abutting China and Burma, known as Namdhapa Wildlife National Park, is spread in Lohit and Changland districts. The Zoological Survey of India found in 1982 60 per cent of its birds and animals belonging to the most endangered species and proposed to the Government to declare it a biosphere reserve for the rare flora and fauna.

Indiscriminate felling of the trees and large-scale soil erosion because of heavy precipitation leading to water-scarcity at Cherrapunji have attracted worldwide attention. Cherrapunji highland evergreen forests have come to be known as the 'wet desert' because of the fact that the bare hillocks have already been washed away the limestone rich top soil at the rate of 300 tonnes per year. Alarmed with the barrenness of the world's wettest place, the local Government has proposed a project to 'regreen' Cherrapunji. The forest department of the State Government had identified eight species of trees including the Khasi pine planting in the bleached soil as part of the restoration of ecological balance to Cherrapunji.

(3) *Mixed Deciduous Forests:* These are found all over the region on the outer fringe of the evergreen forests on the drier ridges. Constant *jhumming* has transformed an extensive part of such forests into inferior bamboo and savannah grassland. The most common species in lower Assam are Makria (*Sachima wallichi*), Siola (*Lagerstroemia parviflora*), Akshi (*Dillenia perrtagyna*), Satian (*Alstonia scholaris*), Paroli (*Stereopermus chelonoides*), Simul (*Bombax mallabarium*), Bhelu (*Tetrameles nudiflora*), Haldu (*Adina cordifolia*). The timber from many of these trees are strong enough but they have not been tried as a substitute of the commercial timber such as sal. However, Simul and Bhelu are used for manufacture of tea chests.

(4) *Pine Forests:* Such forests are found above an elevation of 2,500 feet above the sea level in Meghalaya, Naga, Mikir, Mizo hills and Arunachal Pradesh. Constant *jhumming* and firing have destroyed good patch of some of these forests, where hill savannah bushes have grown. There has been limited reservation of the Kha-

sia pine forests around Shillong with a view to supply the local demands in timber and firewood. Though transportation of such timber to the plains was considered inexpensive at one time, tapping of resin was recommended, but it was soon realized that the pine forests were neither extensive nor old enough to make such an enterprise viable (Jacob M.C.: 1940: 4).

(5) *Alpine Forests:* Alpine forests are found in the high altitude in Arunachal Pradeshspecially in the upper reaches of Kameng and Subansiri districts. Normally at such elevations, the vegetation is stunted gnarled and dwarf shrubs with roots (Gopal Krishnan, R.: 1971: 74)

Legal Status of the Forests in the Region

With the introduction of the Forest Act, 1878 in Assam, the forests were examined from legal points of view. Before we analyse the legal status of the Assam forests, certain popular views pertaining to the forests need to be recorded. Firstly, there was a popular opinion that the vegetation grows very fast in the region because of heavy rain and humidity. It was figuratively said: "If you leave your walking stick after your evening walk outside your house in the open, it will turn into a plant next morning." Secondly, it was universally said in an industrially under-developed region such a Assam, there was no market for the timber. Moreover, the forests were located on the geographically inaccessible difficult terrain. On the other hand, the tea plantation in its early years tried to import tea chests from Britain, Norway and China. Thirdly, it was believed that there was an acute shortage of labour for timber extraction. Not for nothing that the forest administration in Assam began from north-western corner e.g. Goalpara sal forests which were closest to the industrial market of Calcutta, with labour supply and located on ideal waterways.

The forests in Assam came under effective administration from 1878 and within a few years sal forests were declared as *reserves*. By 1889, 2,333 square miles of forests came under Reserves and another 323 square miles were declared as the protected one (Ribbentrop, B.: 1889: 15). After five decades, 6,514 square miles came under the reserve in the province, which included 77,650 acres of Protected Forests in Sadiya. As against 20 per cent stipulated forest

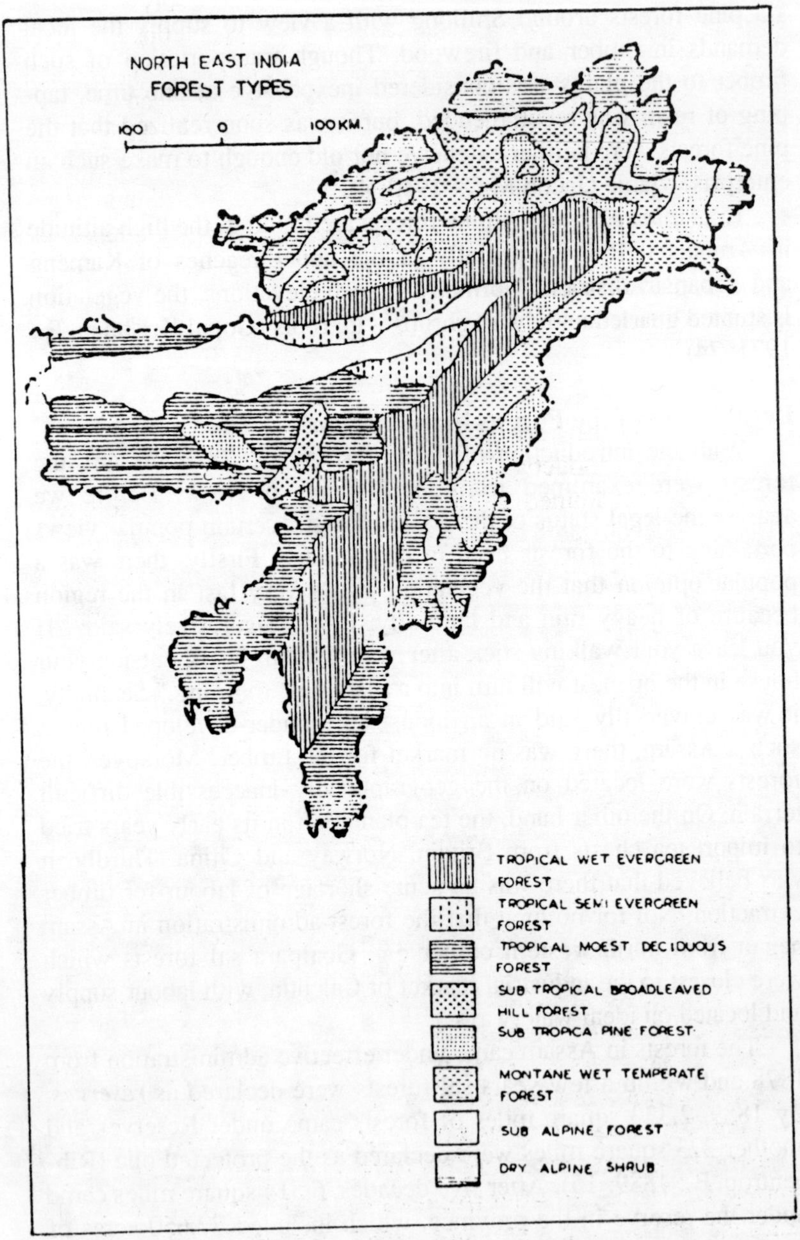
NORTH EAST INDIA
FOREST TYPES
100
0
100 KM.
TROPICAL WET EVERGREEN FOREST
TROPICAL SEMI EVERGREEN FOREST
TROPICAL MOEST DECIDUOUS FOREST
SUB TROPICAL BROADLEAVED HILL FOREST
SUB TROPICA PINE FOREST
MONTANE WET TEMPERATE FOREST
SUB ALPINE FOREST
DRY ALPINE SHRUB

Table 1. Classification of N.E. region forests 1984-85

State	Year	Geographical area in sq km	Total forest area in sq km	Area by legal status (in '000 hec.)				Ownership			
				Reserved	Protected	Unclassified	Other forest	Forest Deptt.	Civil authority	Corporate bodies	Private individuals
Arunachal Pradesh	1984-85	83,740	5154.0	1337.0	0.8	3790.9	25.3	1323.1	3790.0	25.3	14.7
Assam	1984-85	78,523	3070.8	1727.7	337.3	1005.8	-	1745.9	138.9	1186.0	-
Manipur	1984-85	22,356	1515.4	137.7	417.7	960.6	-	1515.4	-	-	-
Meghalaya	1984-85	22,429	851.4	70.6	1.2	779.2	-	72.2	-	-	779.2
Mizoram	1984-85	21,087	1593.5	804.8	164.7	524.0	-	712.7	178.6	702.2	-
Nagaland	1984-85	16,531	862.5	100.4	-	7762.1	-	100.4	-	-	762.1
Tripura	1984-85	10,478	630.9	386.3	386.3	244.6	-	630.9	-	-	-

Source: Ministry of Forests and Environment, Govt. of India.

cover of a region at that time Assam had got only 9.7 per cent of its total area constituted as Reserve Forests (Jacob, M.C.: 1940: 1). There are three main categories of forests in Assam:

(1) *Reserved Forests:* These forests are managed by the trained staff of the Forest Department and scientific silvicultural working plans provisions are implemented under the guidance of the experts, who are the Government employees. Besides industrial, commercial and construction commitment for supplying of timber, they are maintained as protective forests to prevent soil erosion and regulate flood control. Before independence of the country, the Assam Reserved Forests were divided into 11 divisions: Sadiya, Lakhimpur, Sibsagar, Nowgong, Kamrup, Darrang, Cachar, Sylhet, Haltuagaon, Kochugaong and Garo Hills.

(2) *Unclass State Forests:* These are theoretically under the control of the State Forest Department, but they are governed by the customary laws prevalent in an unregulated state of Assam. In fact, these forests come under heavy *jhumming* inclusive of even those, which came into the District Councils after independence as they are governed under Sixth Schedule of the Indian Constitution. In March 1939, such forests were spread in an area of 14,557 square miles in Assam, but they were under heavy threat of deforestation. Even at that time the main factors responsible for continuous deforestation were identified as: (a) indiscriminate *jhumming*, (b) uncontrolled grazing, (c) indiscriminate felling of the trees by the settlers for household requirements and (d) unauthorised squatting.

(3) *Protected Forests:* Such forests are very limited and trees are granted limited protection. Even the forest officials have restricted authority to operate among them. Table 1 provides the present statistical status of the forests in the region. (see Map 3).

Two points need to be noted at the end of above presentation. Firstly, the forests are located on the geographically difficult terrain such as mountain crests or low-lying marshes. The technologically simple tribal communities have made such forests as their abode. In this way forests are located on the inter-state boundaries inhabited by the tribes men leading to inter-state conflicts and boundary disputes. Examples from the region are in plenty. The disputes between Manipur and Burma, Manipur and Assam on Cachar forests,

Meghalaya and Assam, Nagaland and Assam, Assam with Arunachal Pradesh and Assam with Mizoram may be cited. The worst example of such a dispute leading to armed clashes between Nagaland on one side and Assam on the other occurred in the Marapani forests on the Dhansiri river requiring the Central Government to station its own armed forces to defuse the situation. However, the inter-state boundary is yet to be settled. Meanwhile, both the states are reported to be hacking the *Reserved Forests* stealthily to settle their citizens with a view to buttressing their claims.

Secondly, armed insurgents chose forested and mountainous terrain as the areas of their operation from strategic point of view. As most of these insurgent and extreme political groups were recruited from the tribal/local communities, they were better acquainted with topography, vegetation, and overall logistics. The state armed forces, on the other hand, were relatively less sure of local logistics and topographical details. As a part of their counter insurgency operations, invariably they have caused destruction to forest cover. Examples of such actions may be cited from Nagaland and Mizoram in the past and of late Lakhimpur-Sadiya forests, where ULFA insurgents were reported to be running their regular camps. The issue from our point of view, in either of the cases—insurgency or counter-insurgency—is the forests, which suffer leading to ecological problems.

C. The Pre-Colonial Economy of the North East Region

Broadly speaking from the economic consideration the region may be divided into two: (i) The Brahmaputra, Barak and Imphal valleys—relatively of intensive agricultural, settled and areas of water managed wet plantation economy and (ii) the hill communities resorting to dry slash-and-burn type of rotational cultivation regionally known as *jhumming* resorted to with an extremely simple technology. From ethnic, linguistic, cultural and technological points of view the two broad areas were not walled off from each other in the precolonial period. Human movements across the valleys and hills were normal activities inspite of serious communicational limitations. The navigable rivers and certain road ways

(*Alis*) in the plains were the highways extending even across the hills and mountains on certain trade routes. Even the most simple tribesmen resorted to some sort of trading in relatively lighter articles of significant domestic use or of status symbol. The British Governor General of India, Warren Hastings sent George Boggle in 1773 to Bhutan and Tibet with a view to having friendly relations after the Bhutanese Koch conflict of 1772 in which the British had intervened against the Bhutanese (Markham, C.: 1973). Within next 50 years, Sikkim, Jaintia, Cachar, Tripura and Manipur came in effective contact with the British. The Burmese invasion of Assam in 1817 culminated in the British declaration of war against the Burmese on March 5, 1824. Within less than two decades Jaintia, Khasi chiefs, Cachar, Manipur, besides entire Brahmaputra valley came under the British control. Within another fifty years, Garo hills, Naga hills, Mizo hills and parts of Arunachal Pradesh were brought within the British subjugation. Once the British got a foothold in an area they tried to introduce cash economy in place of the traditional subsistence. The entire revenue system was reorganised, land relations reoriented and all markable surplus was channelled to the British industrial estates. In fact, the subjugated areas were turned into suppliers of cheap raw materials for the British industries and the captive markets for the factory produced industrial goods. In the process, the local economy lost its autonomy and was tagged to the apron string of the British metropolitan economy resulting in deflation of regional resources such as forest and minerals. We propose to throw light on such processes in the next chapters. But it will be illuminating to identify the major contours of the pre-British economy of the region.

The Pre-British Economy of the Brahmaputra Valley: The Ahom rule in Assam was based on management of agricultural activities based on a type of serfdom, in which the occupational guilds (*khels*) of the individuals (*pykes*) played significant roles. It is claimed that the *khel* system was introduced by an Ahom officer, namely Momai Tamuli Borbarua in 1607 during the reign of king Pratap Singha (1603-41). The *khel* system envisaged that the entire male population of the country with the exception of men of rank, priests and their slaves to be divided into guilds according to the occupations such as *Khargharia* (gun powder makers), *Sonowals* (the gold washers), *Kaathkatias* (the wood cutters), fishermen, etc. (Barpujari, H.K.: 1980: 24-25). Such guilds or *khels* were further divided into *gots*—units—of three individuals (the *pykes*) such as *mul* (first), the *dewal* (second), and the *tewal* (third). Every *pyke* was bound to serve the King either as a private or a public servant for one-third of the year or to supply certain quantity of his produce in lieu of his services. He was entitled to two *puras* (equivalent to 5877 square yards or $3^2/_3$ Bengal *Beegha*) of *ropit* (wet paddy land) as body-land (*gamati*). During his period of service to the King, the *Dewal* and *Tewal* continued to cultivate their respective *ropit* land provided by the King. They believed each other at the regular intervals so as to ensure that the King had uninterrupted service. The *pykes* were supervised by the *Boras*, *Saikias* and *Hazarikas*, who again commanded by *Baruas, Rajkhowas* and *Phukans*, the higher civil and military functionaries.

The state officials were renumerated with a number of *pykes* to work on their rent-free grants. These officials had two types of land grants: *Nankars*—hereditary—and *manmati*—the one to be used only during the tenure of office. They could occupy free of cost tracts (*khats*) of waste land, where their own *pykes,* slave or attendants would work on. The state granted a number of rent-free tracts known as *Lakhiraj*. Of these the *debottar* was assigned to the maintenance of the temple and worship of deities; *brahmottar* was allotted to the Brahmins for religious services and in recognition of meritorious deeds; while *dharamottar* was set apart for the support of the *satras* (religious and charitable institutions) and persons attached thereto (Borpujari, H.K.: 1980: 26). Besides the personal services and articles of produce as the state collected revenue in terms of cash from surplus land rented out to the pykes, special professionals such as goldwashers, fishermen etc., markets (*haats*), customs duties (*chokis*), annual tributes from the vassals and defaulting *pykes*.

Apparently, the state and the ruler required limited amount of money to run the administration as payments to the functionaries was made in kind and services. When special occasions arose, the Kings raised cash taxation by imposing house tax and extra cess (*barangarni*) from the *shatras,* Hindu shrines, in upper Assam. Robinson wrote in 1841 that the Assamese cultivators, with their imperfect agricultural instruments such as plough, either from insecurity through an imperfect police or from mere customs lived in large villages. They never thought of expanding their capital base because of uncertain land tenure. They were for the most part poor and oppressed people paying as much as one-fourth of their produce in rent besides other forms of extractions from the state officials (Robinson, W.: 1975: 217). It was a thinly populated, oppressed, demoralised and extremely poor country in terms of material resources.

The Pre-British Economy of North Eastern Hill Region: We have limited data from the hill communities in terms of economy as they were little exposed to the people in habit of writing on the social institutions and they themselves were in the pre-literate stage of their evolution. However, some broad contours of hill economy may be identified on the basis of the ethnographers' description, as the economy of the hill communities was not drastically altered by the British till 1910's. As a whole all the tribal communities may conveniently be divided into pastoralists, hunter-cum-collectors, *jhumias* and settled peasantry. In many cases, than one type of the above four were in practice in most the tribes. However, these were dominant economic activities. For example, there were only first three categories prevalent in Arunachal Pradesh, Monpa and Sherdukpens were the Buddhist pastoralists with limited *jhumming* and still less wet paddy cultivation on the river banks. The highlander Nishing, Paurik (Sulung), Hills Miris, Boris were excellent hunters, and Mishmis were root collectors. Apatanis and Khamtis were intensive paddy cultivators. Various Adi tribals were *Jhumias.* Singphos used to farm their fields with the help of slaves.

On the eastern hills we had all powerful Konyak, Sema and Lushai (Mizo) chiefs, who owned everything within their territories. There were clan based village economic communities among the Aos in the middle and terraced rice cultivation among the Angamis. Khasis, Tripuris, Dimasa-Kacharis and Jaintia had graduated to a level of economic surplus, which could support various forms of principalities. But in most of the cases, the land was communally owned and the individual enterprise was recognised at a dormant level. The Kings or chiefs were paid in kind and services. Though there were status differentials, there was little of economic differentiation in the hills. Most of the hill men were Jhumias. As population was sparse and land in plentiful with vigorous growth of vegetation, the *jhum* cycle was extended upto 20 years. Mountain peaks, hill ranges, rivers and streams, dense forests were identified as the frontiers between the village or tribal territorial limits. Many of the communities such as the Khasis had a tradition of preserving certain patch of trees as sacred groves. The Singphos were known to possess tea bushes and had a limited use for consumption. Mishmis, Khasis, Mizos, Hmars used to tap rubber juice. Garos supplied *sal* timber to their southern neighbours for cane building and Khasis and Jaintias traded lime, coal, iron, timber, betelnuts and leaves against clothes, dry fish, ornaments, etc.

To sum up, the pre-British hili economy was village based, informal, entirely dependent on the immediate environment such as land, forests, water bodies and animal lives. It was technologically a simple society with little surplus and specialization of duties. The main story of their life was on the *jhumming* in which they used to raise the crops for their consumption. Their needs appeared to be extremely limited, which were satisfied with the produce of their *jhum* fields. The forests played a very significant role in their lives because the forests provided a universe to them in which they resorted to *jhumming*, hunted their games; collected fruits, roots, herbs, tapped rubber juice; and caught wild animals for games, trade and exchange. The dominant mode of exchange in their economy was barter of the goods. Of course, coins were known to them, but not as common mode of exchange, but as ornaments and curios. As their economic needs were extremely limited, they were economically autonomous in their relative isolation.

In this chapter we have taken up three issues. Firstly, we have analysed the various aspects of physical features of the Eastern Himalayan regionas part of the Himalayan physiography and as a unique entity in itself. Secondly, we have described the four physical sub-divisions of the region in terms of (i) The Eastern Himlayan arc, (ii) the eastern hill ranges, (iii) the Meghalaya plateau and (iv) the plains of the Brahmaputra and the Barak valleys. Thirdly, we have endeavoured to report on the natural vegetation of the region on the basis of the physical features for common readers and not the specialists in sericulture and botany. Fourthly, we felt the need to examine briefly the pre-colonial economic scene of the region, as the British metropolitan economy introduced certain distortion in the regional economy not only through revenue administration and altered land tenure, but it also introduced tea plantation economy and forest farming for timber export at the cost of the local dominant resources of forests. How was the forest policy evolved? How was the forest administration organised? What were the considerations in declaring the forest reserve in the region? What type of relations forest managers and tea planters had? Answers to some of the above questions will be provided in the next chapter on the British forest policy and forest administration.

References

1. Barpujari, H.K.: 1980, *Assam in the Days of the Company,* Spectrum Publications, Guwahati.
2. Bose, S.C.: 1972, *The Geography of Himalayas*, The National Book Trust, New Delhi
3. Chatterjee, S.K.: 1951, *Kirata Jana Kriti*, Asiatic Society of Bengal, Calcutta.
4. Chatterjee, S.P.: 1936, *Le Platea de Meghalaya*, Les Presses Modernes, Paris.
5. Gaige, F.H.: 1975, *Regionalism and National Unity in Nepal* ,Vikas Publishing House, New Delhi.
6. Gopal Krishna, R: 1991, *North East India: Land, Economy and People*; Har Anand Publications, New Delhi.
7. Jacob, M.M.C.: 1940, *Forest Resources of Assam*, Assam Secretariat Press, Shillong.
8. Karan, P.P.: 1963, *The Himalayan Kingdoms*, Nostrand Torchlight Book, Princeton, New Jersey.
9. Markham, C.: 1971, *Mission of George Bogle to Tibet and the Journey of Thomas Manning to Lhasa*, Bibliothaca Himalayica, Vol. 6, New Delhi, Reprint.
10. Ribbentrop, B: 1889, *Note on an Inspection of the Forests of Assam*, the Govt. Central Press, Shimla.
11. Robinson, W. 1975, *A Descriptive Account of Assam*, Shanker Prakashan, New Delhi, Reprint.
12. Sinha, A.C.: 1987, 'Frontier Feudalism and State Formation in Sikkim' in *Tribal Polities and State Systems in Pre-Colonial Eastern and North Eastern India* (ed) S.C. Sinha, K.P. Bagchi & Co., Calcutta.

13. Sinha, A.C.: 1983, *Studies in the Himalaya Communities*, Books Today and Tomarrow, New Delhi.
14. Spate, O.H.K. et al: 1972, *India, Pakistan and Ceylon*, B.I. Publications, New Delhi.

2

Forests in British Assam

Assam was separated from Bengal and instituted into a separate province in 1912. By then certain aspects of its future ethnic complexity began to emerge. The Assamese in the plains maligned as the opium eating indolent community by the British were proud of their wet paddy cultivation, history, culture, language and destiny. The Hill Districts with their variety of ethnic groups were exposed to the Christian missionaries for their evangelical activities. The hill tribes were mainly subsistence farmers and marginally hunters of the wild games. The tea plantations were spread on the low-lying forested land between the plains and the hill districts with their endentured labour imported from the Central tribal belt of India. Besides these three ethnic groups (the Assamese, the hill tribes and the plantation labourers), two other ethnic groups began to appear on two distinct ecological settings of the province. They were the *Mymsinghia* immigrants (Bengal) in the riverline plains and the Nepalese pastoralists on the degraded forests and wasteland in the hills.

By the turn of the 20th century forestry in Assam was placed in a paradoxical situation. It was presumed that because of high precipitation and limited agriculture, there would be extensive forests. But reality presented a different picture. An extensive forest was axed for tea plantation in the Brahmaputra valley and because of strategic considerations, extension of forest reservation in the hill districts was considered inadvisable. The Forest Department of the Province had a relatively small and ill-paid personnel. Not infrequently, there were cases of desertion, dismissal and corruption at the lower level. Quite a number of employees died in harness of malaria and other diseases prevalent in the province. However, there was an unseen pressure on the Department to exhibit a continuous increase in the forest revenue. The forest revenue was divided into two: major and minor sources. The major sources were timber supply to the railways, tea industry and match factories. Here they were faced with the shortage of labour for timber extraction and a dependable transport system. For transportation the Department did construct its own small railway tram line, but at no stage mechanized felling of the trees was considered as a possibility.

Consequently upon reorganization of Eastern Bengal and Assam in April, 1912, the forests of Assam were organized into *Eastern* and *Western Circles.* While the former consisted of the forests in Lakhimpur, Sibsagar, Lushai Hills, Cachar, Sylhet and North East Frontier Tracts (Arunachal Pradesh) and it also dealt with the forestry issues of the Naga Hills District and the princely state of Manipur. The latter circle consisted of Nowgong, Kamrup, Darrang, Goalpara, Khasi and Jaintia Hills and Garo Hills District. The *report* on the forest administration, filed annually, has a set pattern. The reports are divided into six chapters: constitution of state forests, management of state forests, financial results, research and experiments, administration, and 'general'. We propose to discuss the nature of the forests in terms of reservation, *jhumming*, and timber-wise and area-wise extension on the basis of the annual reports. Secondly, the issue of forest villages, grazing rights and over-all labour problems will be examined under management of the forests. Thirdly, annual financial results will be viewed in terms of revenue generation from major and minor forest products, timber extraction for the railway sleepers and tea boxes. Lastly, issues pertaining to personnel and policy will be analysed on the basis of last three chapters of the various annual reports.

Constitution of State Forests

The year 1911-12 saw dereservation of some 15,364 acres of reserved forests in the Garo Hills due to a popular agitation leaving behind 4,321 square miles of reserve forests. There was a considerable area known as *unclassed state forests,* which was to be brought under cattle grazing and cultivation. Out of them, 15,000 square miles was expected to be brought under reserve leaving behind another 12,000 square miles as *unclassed state forests.*[1] Two Forest officers, W.R.L. Jacob and A.J.W. Malroy, were deputed to prepare reports on the forests of southern Bhutan and coniferous forests of Dihang encatchment areas on the occasion of Abor Expedition respectively. In the following years, the Department estimated existence of 18,290 square miles of *unclassed* forests in Assam.[2] An area of 26 square miles of *Nongkhyllem Reserve* was added to the reserve forests in the Khasi and Jaintia Hills District. In the *Frontier Tract* action was taken by an Executive Order to declare reservation near Sadiya and Pasighat with a view to supplying timber to the 'stations' and 'cantonments'. Forty square miles of *unclassed state forests* in Sibsagar district near Dimapur was transferred to Naga Hills district in 1913.[3] Because of the paucity of the gazetted officers, no body was posted to the Lushai and North Eastern Tracts to administer the extensive forests, which were left in the charge of District *Superintendent* and the *Political Officers* respectively.[4] Malroy, the Divisional Forest Officer of Kamrup, submitted a report on the forest management of Manipur state. Again the annual report for the year 1918-19 informs us that owing to the paucity of forest officers, Darrang, Nowgong and Sadiya forest divisions were left under the respective Political Officers and Deputy Commissioners.[5]

About 422 acres of Shillong pine forests were burnt on 7 occasions in the Khasi and Jaintia Hills district in 1918-19. These incidences of the fire were attributed to malice, but no sufficient proofs were found to apprehend the culprits. The expenditure on fire protection was Rs. 575. It was surmised that the fires generally originated towards the end of the dry season on days of *barra-bazaar* in Shillong. It was proposed to introduce an active patrol of the paths and roads through forests by which the surrounding population pass to attend the bazaar and enforcement of the prohibition against smoking and carrying fire.[6] Lantana grass was removed from Short Round Forests, Riatkhawn Reserve, Laikor and Upper Shillong at the cost of about Rs. 43.7.[7]

In the year 1923-24 Daldali (37 square miles) in Nowgong, Idangi (70 square miles) in Naga Hills, Morapagladia (5 square miles) in Kamrup Division, Dhansiri reserve (100 square miles) in

Nowgong, and Desai Valley (4 square miles) and Rangapahar (5 square miles) to the Sibsagar Division were added to make it 5814 square miles of reserve forests.[8] After three years another 57 square miles in the Dahalia (13 square miles) in the Sylhet and Gorghanga (44 square miles) in the Kamrup Division were extended to make the total reserve forests 6,011 square miles[9] in the state. Previous year's annual report estimated the *unclassed state forests* to be 20,086 square miles, In the year 1930 the *reserve forests* were increased to 6,147 square miles, while the *unclassed state forests* were decreased to 14,693 square miles.[10] By 1933 the areas of reserved forests rose to 6,146 square miles[11] and that of the *unclassed state forests* to 14,882 square miles.

The growth of the reserve forest within the decades between 1911-12 and 1932-33 increased by 50 per cent, which may be shown in the following table.

Table 2.1. Growth of reserve forests in Assam

Year	Area in sq miles
1911-12	4,344
1912-13	4,321
1913-14	4,381
1922-23	5,601
1923-24	5,814
1925-26	5,937
1926-27	6,011
1928-29	6,105
1929-30	6,147
1931-32	6,145
1932-33	6,186

Management of State Forests

Under the chapter on management of the State Forests the annual reports dealt with (i) regulation of management, (ii) communication and building, (iii) protection of forests, (iv) silviculture and (v) explorations. However, there are two aspects, which need to be described, the forest villages and grazing of cattle in the reserve and *unclassed state forests.*

The Cattle Grazing on the Wasteland and Unclassed State

Forests: The increase of buffaloes in the province was remarkable. In 1893-94 there were 12,915 grazing buffaloes at full rate in the *unclassed state forests.* After 11 years the figure rose to 26,257 in 1904-05 and 45,893 buffaloes were grazing officially in the forests in 1911-12. In Garo hills their number trebled within 20 years. The total number of buffaloes in Assam was reported to be 73,902 in 1911-12. Many of them were swept away in the floods and died out of rinderpest. The establishment of grazing reserve for the location of professional Nepalese graziers was under consideration in 1911-1912.[12] The next year some 86,389 buffaloes, mostly belonging to the Nepalese, who habitually evaded payment of grazing fees by moving their cattle away, were grazing on the *unclassed* forests. Similarly, there were 3,36,323 cows and bullocks on the forests, but only 5,079 were charged for the grazing fees. In October 1912, a conference was held at Shillong between the civil and forest authorities to discuss the regulation of grazing.[13] It was unanimously decided to provide grazing grounds to the hardsmen, to levy grazing fees at lower rates to prohibit the removal of cattle from one place to another grazing ground without special permission and to prevent grazing grounds to be used for cultivation.

In the *Eastern Circle* of the *Reserve Forests,* 1976 square miles of the reserves were closed to all grazing[14] and only 470 square miles in Sibsagar Division was open to the grazing. The whole of the Government Wasteland, 7700 square miles in all, was open to free grazing by settlement holders. In a portion of the forests to the North Cachar Hills, the professional graziers were to pay Re. 1 per buffalo and *anna* four per cow per annum. In the *unclassed state forests* 25,706 fee paying (Rs. 20,031) and 27,543 free of payment animals were permitted to graze. The rapid increase in the number of cattle and immigration of Nepalese cattle owners into the Assam valley had been significant. As pressure on grazing ground increased, damage to crop was a frequent complaint against Nepalese herdsmen. In the year 1913-14 fees were realised from professional graziers on 25,409 buffaloes, 15,898 cows and 632 other animals and 22,178 buffaloes, 65,265 cows, 100 other animals grazed in the government wasteland free of payment under the privileges granted to settlement holders.[15] B.C. Allen records on the issue ". . . not nearly enough suitable grazing grounds will be available, and since the number of cattle continue steadily to increase and with this increase greater damage to thatching grass and other areas occur, it has been decided to increase the fee in respect of buffaloes during the current year from Re. one to Rs. two and those for other horned animals from four to six annas. Further, a detailed investigation will now be made district by district by an officer of the Indian Civil Service in order to endeavour to arrive at a satisfactory policy for future."[16]

82,205 buffaloes, 2,25,603 cows and more than 18,028 other animals grazed on the forests of the western circle and a revenue of Rs. 3,11,055 was secured from them. From the Eastern Circle a sum of Rs. 2,11,274 was received as grazing fees. As much as about Rs. 29,649 remained arear on this account[17] in the year, 1918-19. The revenue from the grazing fee for the year 1920-21 was Rs. 3,41,499, which was reduced to Rs. 14,304, a bare 4.2 per cent in the next year.[18] This was because of the Government decision to credit receipts from the grazing fees to land revenue instead of forests. But this decision could not remove the irritant from the forest department. Deforestation, poaching, squatting, land alienation and other forest related crimes continued to be reported from the marginal barrenland areas of the region.

The Forest Villages: The establishment of forest villages in suitable situations and of the right class was of great importance in Assam, where labour was not easily available. Till the end of the first decade of the present century, most of the Forest Divisions had some villages, but none existed in Nowgong and Lakhimpur Divisions. Some desertion was reported from Sibsagar Division, because of the migratory nature of the Mikirs.[19] While Goalpara was reported to have 37 such forest villages, four additional of them were sanctioned in 1912-13 for the Garo hills,[20] and the villagers were provided with muzzle loading guns for crop protection. One new forest village was established in Kamrup, another composed of Daflas was settled near Charduar plantation in Darrang Division.[21] Simon, the Divisional Forest Officer in the Garo Hills, tried to induce the Garos for terrace cultivation. Many Garo forest villages were abondoned due to outbreak of Kala-azar. Some of the villages in the Songsak Reserve had to be abandoned on account of the menace of the man-eating tiger[22] in early 1920's. In the first four years of the decade beginning 1920, 31 new forest villages were sanctioned.

At times considerable conflicts between the forest staff and forest villages were reported. For example during 1921-22 non-cooperation movement, the Assam Rifles had to be called for ejection of old established villages at Kachugaon in the Goalpara district because the forest villagers had refused to work for the Forest Department. Same was the case with the forest villages in Boko Range in the Kamrup district. As the Forest Department required that such villagers should work for about 3 per cent of the time if required on clearing boundaries, etc., the forest work was never popular among the villagers. For example in Kachugaon in Goalpara Division there was so much paddy land around the forest villages that many of the villagers had little inclination to work for the Department. In such situations, "the more *jungli* and inarticulate the cultivator, the more conscientious he is in carrying his part of the bargain."[23] Two new forest villages—one each in Cachar and Lakhimpur—were started in 1924. The forest village labour in the Goalpara Division was fully engaged in new tramway extension work. The Manipur villagers at Jarul Tola in the Cachar Division were to be evicted from the site with the help of the armed forces.[24] Three new forest villages, one each in Goalpara, Garo Hills and Nowgong Divisions, were started in the year, 1926-27.[25]

The *annual report* for the following year, 1927-28 noted[26] that the number of forest villages came down to 4 from 12 in the Darrang Division. Six new forest villages were added in Cachar Division during the period. The villagers work in the Garo hills was reported to be most unsatisfactory and it was felt that the village Forest Rules in Goalpara required revision urgently. In the following year (1928-29)[27] two new villages in Cachar and one in Lumding Range of Nowgang Division were started. Four new forest villages were established in the year 1929-30 in Cachar Division. A Census of the *forest villages* in Goalpara revealed that over 1,000 unauthorised persons were in residence. A *Forest Enquiry Committee* consisting of the forest and civil authorities was set up previous year to examine the issues associated with forest villages.[28] In spite of the above Enquiry Committee providing its report, 16 forest villages were sanctioned to be established during 1931-32 and some of them were actually established. Some new settlers were also permitted to fill in the occasional vacancies in the existing forest villages. The question of fixing rates of land revenue to be realized from these villages in different Forest Divisions was taken up during the year in light of the revised rules sanctioned previous year.[29] Side by side, the Government decided to abandon the policy of village forests under the Regulation. Those, which were already created, were cancelled.[30]

The minority Muslim League provincial government in Assam (1937-46) launched a programme known as "*Grow more food*", which came to be euphemistically termed as "*Grow more Muslims*". It is alleged that taking advantage of the Indian Forest Act, 1927, thousands of *Mymsinghia* Muslims were settled on the swamp and reserve forests. The provision of the above Act allowed for a limited number of forest villages to be located inside reserved forests. Each family was entitled to eight hectares of land to clear and cultivate and also to keep five heads of cattle. While the provision was selectively used, it created no problem. But after the Independence of India, the scenario changed for the worst. *The First Citizens' Report* records: "After independence, however, the forest villages began springing up at a rapid rate. Those living in them worked outside the forest, but used provisions, such as tax exemption to their advantage. The size of the original clearing would grow unchecked and eat into the forest. In just one Division of Cachar district, Silchar, there are 116 forest villages today. The creation of more forest villages was stopped with the promulgation of the Forest Conservation Ordinance on October 6, 1980, which was later converted into an Act. This law restrains State Governments from using any forest land for a "non-forest" purpose without prior approval of the Central Government" (Agrawal, A. et al. 1982: 45).

Communications—Roads, Bridges and Tramways: The most of the timber forests were located on the topography away from the communication network. Originally, the timber was cut near the river side so that they could be floated manually or dragged to bank with the help of elephants and buffaloes. Then certain forest roads with wooden scantilever bridges across the streams were constructed for transporting forest products. But in the areas such as

Goalpara, Sibsagar and Lakhimpur, where precious timber extraction was to be conducted for longer period, it was considered advisable to develop its own reliable means of communication. Tram lines for short distance linking railway station sidings and river ghats were considered essential. The most significant such a device in the province of Assam was the Goalpara tramway project. The project dated back to the year 1900-1901, when a tram line was made to bring water upto the forests for the labourers working in the waterless forest tracts and to bring timber to the nearest point (Kachugaon) from where it could be floated. The trucks were first pushed by hand, but the steam engine was introduced in 1912. By then the total expenditure on 20 miles long tram ways amounted to Rs. 1,03,069.[31] In the rainy season of 1921 the tract was damaged requiring new alignment of 17 miles known as Kachugong-Pakiragram alignment at the cost of Rs. 2,90,850. By January 1924, most of the line and almost all the 42 bridges across the streams were ready.[32] F.H. Cavendish, the Conservator of Forest, Eastern Circle, Assam informed that by 1929, the cost of the tramways had risen to Rs. 4,58,849. During the previous five years, it carried 14,00,790 cft timber, 75 per cent of which could not have been transported in the absence of the tramways system. Another significant role it played of supplying water to the waterless tracts in the *sal* forests, where labourers were located for timber extraction.[33] For the first time we learn in the year 1927-28 that the Forest Department bought 56 iron trucks from Messrs Martin & Co. at the cost of Rs. 17,468 for replacing the old style wooden trucks.[34]

Forest Revenue

We have seen above in the previous chapter the dual motives behind creation of forest reserves as timber supply to the urban industrial sectors and raising revenue for the state. The forests were organised scientifically as a profit making enterprise. To begin with it had a small staff, and poorly paid *forest watchers* and *guards* at the bottom. As the Forest Department was a part of the Government establishment, its expenditure had to be sanctioned at the highest level subject to financial rules. Success of the Department and efficiency in its management were measured in terms of increase in revenue and consequent surplus over expenditure. It was obligatory on the part of the Conservators of Forests to draw progress report on their charge annually, which was sent to the Government for its perusal and approval. The Governor of the Province in Council would review the *Report* and the *Proceedings* would be sent to the Conservator of the Forests by the Chief Secretary of Assam.

We have drawn a table of the financial results of the forest administration for the years, 1910-11 to 1932-33 with the break-up in terms of expenditure, revenue received, surplus over the expenditure and the percentage of the surplus of the gross revenue (Table 2.2). An analysis of the table shows that the Department spent the lowest of money (Rs. 6,46,877) in the year 1917-18 and the maximum (Rs. 22,21,304) in the year 1929-30. The annual maximum revenue (Rs. 37,67,873) was received in the previous year (1928-

Table 2.2. Annual financial result 1910-1911 to 1932-1933

Year	Revenue (in Rupees)	Expenditure (in Rupees)	Surplus (in Rupees)	Per cent of surplus of the gross revenue
1910-11	13,01,640	8,02,514	4,99,126	38.3
1911-12	11,17,569	8,32,158	2,85,411	23.5
1912-13	11,33,228	8,15,671	3,17,557	28.6
1913-14	10,89,878	9,16,657	1,73,221	15.9
1917-18	14,63,297	6,44,877	8,16,420	55.8
1918-19	15,11,823	7,49,951	7,63,872	50.5
1922-23	17,18,853	11,14,635	5,99,218	42.1
1923-24	19,79,709	11,48,062	8,31,647	42.1
1925-26	30,35,762	15,67,980	14,67,782	48.0
1926-27	31,23,473	14,43,619	16,89,854	53.9
1927-28	36,13,460	14,32,200	21,81,260	60.04
1928-29	37,67,873	21,32,472	16,35,401	42.4
1929-30	35,20,007	22,21,304	12,98,703	36.9
1930-31	22,62,793	21,16,657	1,46,136	6.5
1931-32	19,27,078	16,11,208	3,15,870	16.4
1932-33	16,16,405	14,10,217	2,06,188	12.8

Source: Progress Reports of Forest Administration in the province of Assam, 1910-11 to 1932-33.

29), but the maximum expenditure appears to have resulted in a poor result, the lowest surplus (Rs. 1,46,136) recorded during the period resulting in the lowest percentage of surplus over the gross revenue (6.5 per cent). The surplus ranged between Rs. 21,81,260 and Rs. 1,46,136, which were 60.0 per cent and 6.5 per cent of the respective gross revenues. We see the continuous rise of the gross revenue upto the year 1928-29 to the maximum and then it is on the decline. Similarly, with the exception of 1917-18, the expenditure kept on rising from 1911 to 1930 before it starts declining. There was a sharp drop in the revenue from Rs. 35,20,007 in 1929-30 to Rs. 16,16,405 in 1932-33, which turned out to be about 46 per cent in less than three years. The little surplus was shown by reducing expenditure by 36.52 per cent between 1930 and 1933. This slump was caused by the pre-Second World War economic depression in the market.

The Conservator of the Forests of Assam also drew quinquennial reviews of the financial statements for the internal consumption. We have the data for the years 1905-06-1909-10 to 1926-27-1930-31 (Table 2.3), with us. The lowest average expenditure (Rs. 6,01,879) and revenue (Rs. 9,30,300) was recorded in the first

Table 2.3. Quinquennial financial results 1905-06–1908-10 to 1926-27–1930-31

Year (average of)	Revenue (in rupees)	Expenditure (in rupees)	Surplus (in rupees)	% of surplus on gross revenue
1905-06–1909-10	9,30,300	6,01,879	3,28,421	35.3
1907-08–1911-12	10,64,196	7,31,627	3,32,569	31.3
1912-13–1916-17	10,61,623	8,15,303	2,46,328	23.2
1918-19–1922-23	14,98,566	9,17,084	3,31,462	38.0
1921-22–1925-26	21,01,021	12,30,603	8,70,413	41.4
1922-23–1926-27	24,86,310	13,21,030	11,47,280	46.5
1923-24–1927-28	28,55,055	13,84,543	14,70,512	51.5
1924-25–1928-29	32,05,866	15,81,425	10,24,440	50.6
1926-27–1930-31	32,66,344	18,70,027	13,96,317	42.7

Source: Progress Reports and Quinquennial Review of Forest Administration in the Province of Assam.

quinquennial year. The average surplus revenue was lowest for the period 1912-13 to 1916-1917. Rs. 2,46,328, which was the lowest percentage of the gross revenue for the year (23.2%). With that exception, the average percentage of surplus on gross revenue fluctuated between 31.3 per cent and 51.5 per cent. The forest revenue was divided into major and minor sources. Again, the major sources of revenue were the timber for the railway sleepers and tea boxes. The minor sources of revenue consisted of a variety of forest products besides timber, fuel wood, wax, ivory, elephants, grazing fees etc. Among them, issues of the tea boxes associated with saw mills and the railway sleepers require detailed discussion.

Saw Mills and Tea Box: Improvements in tea box royalty was secured when the Department controlled to felling of the required timber. It was felt necessary for saw mills working on tea boxes to secure additional *simul* areas so that they could keep up with the present level of supply of timber. The question of allotting a definite area to each saw mill was considered in 1912. A temporary remission of royalty on timber used for tea boxes was sanctioned from 22nd August, 1912. 323,290 cft timber was sold to saw mills in the Assam valley on the box royalty system.[35] The tea box industry continued to enjoy the use of timber free of payment, a concession granted to them upto September, 1914, and again extended, upto January 1, 1915 to enable the mills to complete the whole season's demand.[36]

It was noted that the concession remitting the royalty on timber for tea boxes had not assisted Tezpur Saw Mills, as it turned out 15,588 tea boxes against 29,582, the average of the three preceding years. Elsewhere there was abnormal extraction of box timber in view of this. A total of 495,544 cft free timber of tea box mills at concessional rate was extracted for Rs. 30,059.[37] The saw mills in Lakhimpur, Sadiya and Darrang divisions continued to obtain timber for the manufacture of tea boxes under the box royalty system. The system by which royalty was assessed on the manufactured tea box was unsatisfactory as it was wasteful; it was proposed to be substituted with royalty on the logs. While 3,13,686 boxes with Rs. 45,076 as royalty in 1917-18 were produced in Darrang, Lakhimpur and Sadiya Divisions, only 6,88,260 boxes with Rs. 38,685 as royalty were produced in the following year.[38]

The quinquennial period—1920-24 had been a distinctly unfavourable to the various saw mills in the Assam Valley. Furkating, Tezpur, Sissi, Hopewell and Saikwa saw mills had ceased to work. They had to compete with tea shooks, venesta etc. imported from Japan and Europe for supplying boxes to the tea industry. Machinery at large capital investment for the manufacture of three plywood had been set up at Bhanga (Sylhet), Margherita (south Lakhimpur) and Murkong Setlek (Sadiya). Tea industry favoured boxes of one kind of wood only. An interesting point was noted that the royalty paid on the timber used in each box was less than one anna, whereas the cost of the glue worked out to upwards of nine annas and as the box sold for Rs. 2.5 the sum received for the timber by the Forest Department was practically nominal.[39]

The next quinquennial review recorded[40] that an Indian company, connected with the Swedish Match Company, had commenced the manufacture of matches at Dubri. A saw mill had been erected at Sorbhong to convert *simul* into packing cases for the Calcutta market. In view of that it was felt that there would be a good market for *simul* timber for the coming five years. The most important saw mills in Upper Assam were (i) the Assam Saw Mills Timber Co. at Murkong Sellek and Laimakuri, the former manufactured plywood tea boxes and the latter using bandsaws for turning out packing cases, etc. and (ii) the Assam Railways & Trading Company's bandsaw and plywood mill at Margherita. In addition to them, there were small privately owned saw mills at Calcutta, Churunia and Bordesbam. The timber industry was facing a lean period requiring protection. However, there was an increasing demand for match wood and packing case timber requiring soft wood. The terms of the lease granted to the Assam Saw Mills and Timber Co. in Sadiya Frontier Tract for extracting timber for tea boxes was reviewed in 1927.[41] The royalty on timber used for plywood tea boxes was retained at old rate of six pie per cft, unless and until the protection recommended by the Tariff Board was granted. In that case rate would be raised to one anna six pie per cft. Since then the next five annual reports on forest administration in Assam continuously showed decline in operation of the saw mills.

Railway Sleepers: Railway emerged as substitute to the old boat making industry in terms of timber utilization. As its network increased in operation, requirements for sleepers increased. It contributed something like 60 per cent revenue in the year, 1912 to the total forest income. Its main operation was in the western Circle—specially Kachugaon, Goalpara, Garo Hills and Kamrup divisions—which produced *sal* timber. The price offered by the railways was so unrenumerative compared to the private traders, that a representation was made to the Railways (Eastern Bengal State Railways) by the authorities of the Goalpara Forest Division in 1912. Consequently, it was agreed to accept the tender for sleepers from Goalpara division at a price 23 per cent above that of formerly paid.[42] Even that was hardly to compensate for the labour involved in extensive departmental sawing operations, but that might enable the Department to assist the Railway Company without an actual loss of potential revenue.

The description of the railway sleepers is fraught with ambiguity: The sleepers are categorised as broad gauge (B.G.), metre gauge (M.G.): special and tram sleepers in number; they are also shown occasionally in cft; they are described as per the clients—Assam Bengal Railways, Eastern Bengal Railways; they are displayed as per the timber *sal*, or others; they are shown against sources of production, Departmental, sold locally or supplied through timber agents; then there are problems of sleeper produced, remained at the sidings, or delivered; then they are reported circlewise and divisionwise; the figures of the timber produced is mixed with sleepers, scantilever, logs and other types. And in terms of revenue received, there are problems of the advance payment, failure of supply, sleepers ordered but not lifted from the sidings, etc. In such a situation, working out a comparative development of the railway sleeper supply is not an easy task.

It looks the railways had problems in accepting sleeper supplied from the Upper Assam Divisions. There is a reference in the Annual Report of a joint inspection of the timber treatment plant at Mariani junction on the Assam Bengal Railways.[43] The results were found satisfactory and possibly the railways would be "prepared to take all the sleepers they required from the reserves of the Lakhimpur and Sibsagar Divisions." The following table shows the production of railway sleepers[44] during early 1920's.

The above report also notes that there had been a gradual increase in price for sleepers. In the Kamrup Division, sleeper operations were done departmentally and no particular pains were taken to get the figures so arranged as to show the profit on the transaction. The trees were cut into M.G. and special sleepers and tops were sold at varying prices. The net result was: sale of sleepers, etc. Rs. 1,01,353 + sale proceeds of stock in hand Rs. 2,165 + Rs. 1,04,18, deduction on expenditure Rs. 55,396 left a balance of Rs. 48,622.[45]

Table 2.4. Production of railway sleepers in 1920s

Year	No. of B.G. sleepers	No. of M.G. sleepers	Special sleepers (cft)	Total (cft)
1919-20	-	13,658	21,725	42,213
1920-21	-	14,532	20,839	42,667
1921-22	-	17,062	12,456	38,049
1922-23	3,250	7,179	55,057	90,576
1923-24	27,243	18,839	26,567	134,555

The next quinquennial review reports an overall production of various types of 8,50,282 railway sleepers. It also informs that a contract for supplying 10 lakh sleepers of miscellaneous species had been entered into which would ensure a sustained demand of 2 to 3 lakhs of sleepers annually.[46] The annual report for the year 1926-27 recorded production of 102,095 B.G. sleepers, 50,203 M.G. sleepers and 21,756 special sleepers worth Rs. 9,53,400.[47] The following year 3,05,457 sleepers were supplied to the Eastern Bengal and Assam-Bengal Railways.[48] In the year, 1928-29[49] some 1,75,607 railway sleepers of various specifications were supplied to the railways.

The Goalpara Division stopped sleeper operation in the year, 1920-30. The Eastern Circle comprising Lakhimpur, Darrang and Sibsagar, supplied 3,49,804 railway sleepers in the year.[50] Except Darrang Division, there was no departmental sleeper operation in Upper Assam. Two hundred and twenty thousand sleepers of miscellaneous species were treated by Naharkatia Treating Plant (Assam-Bengal Railway) during the year. Though the full capacity of the plant averaged about 24,000 sleepers a month, but because of the restriction imposed by the Railway Board for treating not more than two lakhs of sleepers during the financial year, the progress was slow. In the following year,[51] railway sleepers of various species numbering 211,359 were purchased from the contractors in the Lakhimpur and Sibsagar divisions and were supplied to the Bengal Assam Railway for its treatment plant at Naharkatia.

Jhumming with Special Reference to the Garo Hills: We have referred to the movement of the Garos for dereservation of the forests above. The Arbuthnott Commission found enough grounds to restrict the spread of forest reserve and, in fact, recommended certain portions of the reserves to be opened for the *jhumming*. The 1912-13 annual report found the position of forest in the district "pitiable" and "utterly unsatisfactory" and the majority of the forests were being ruined owing to inability on political grounds to introduce in the local Forest Regulations.[52] The Conservator of Forests, Western Circle, A.V. Monro sounded a warning:[53] ". . . I saw no evidence of jhumed land turning into anything but grass or more rarely bamboo. Indeed between Fulbari and Tura there are large stretches of grass covered slopes with a few dry burnt stems among them . . . . One sees virgin forest, the recent jhums and the fallow, jhums, chiefly coming up in grass, occasionally bamboo, with no sign of turning into anything better and no *sal* at all. Hence, it is probable that the original custom was not to jhum in *sal* areas. Any way the oldest and densest jhumed areas are not in *sal* areas."

The forest officials were reluctant to let go the reserved forests as they saw in the decision their three decades old efforts wasted. But it was not to be; the political consideration weighed heavy on civil administration. The forest officials took the second best option[54] to clear the reserve of the *sal* timber before it was dereserved. The Government decision to dereserve certain forest reserves led to thinking in two directions. Firstly, the Chief Commissioner of the Province, prohibited felling of *sal* trees by *jhumias* on February 1914. Secondly, a suggestion was made that the Garos be encouraged for terrace cultivation as in the case of the Angamis of Naga Hills District.[55] The Secretary to the Government of India, Department of Revenue and Agriculture did not appear to be convinced by the above steps[56] proposed by the Chief Commissioner: The Government of India "concur with the opinion expressed by you on the difficult subject of shifting cultivation in the Garo Hills; but although they consider the prohibition of the cutting of *sal* in *jhum* is a good beginning, experience in other provinces lead them to doubt whether this will be sufficient to preserve *sal* bearing areas in this tract."

The issue of timber extraction from the *jhum* areas and *unclassed forest* did not die. F.H. Cavendish, the Consevator of Forests, Eastern Circle, Assam, found out that the out-turn of timber and fuel removed from the Garo Hills Division decreased considerably in 1920-29.[57] The cause of the decrease was attributed to the interference by the *Nokmas*, who demanded excessive commissions from the permit holders. The government had decided that the State was the owner of the *unclassed state forests*, but the conservator pleaded whether state's interests were being served in such a situation. The Chief Secretary to the Province reacted to the above plea.[58] "The conservator suggests that the claims of the Nokmas to compensation for the removal of timber from the areas of *unclassed state forest* over which their families have hereditary rights of *jhumming* was partly responsible for the decrease in forest revenue in the Garo Hills. The Officers responsible for the general administration of these hills do not always see eye to eye with the forest officers and as stated in the report some friction has occurred. The Divisional Commissioner has been asked to visit the district along with the conservator and advise government what working arrangements will be most suitable in view of the peculiar circumstances of the *unclassed state forest* of the Garo Hills."

The Forest Department of Assam used to manage the Manipur State forests on 25 per cent to 75 per cent share of the revenue. For example, the Department earned Rs. 12,256 as one-fourth share from the revenue of Rs. 49,024 from the Manipur forests.[59] Similarly the Assam forest Department used to derive revenue from Lashai Hills, Naga Hills, Khasi Syiemships and North East Frontier Agency. Among the minor sources of revenue elephants played a curcial role as source of income as well as beast of burden. Departmental in *kheda* was organised in Nambor, Sibsagar, Khasi, Garo, Lakhimpur and Manas forests to catch elephants, Khamtis and Singphos were reported poaching for elephant tusk-ivory and rhinoceros' horns.

Personnel and Policy

With the organisation of the Province in 1912, personnel in the joint Forest Department got divided. Many of them opted for Bengal, Bihar and Orissa and it looks Assam got a poor share in the deal. Moreover, that was the time forest reserves were being expanded in the province. Consequently, in most of the Hill Districts such as Lushai Hills, Naga Hills, North East Frontier Agency, the civil authorities were incharge of the Forest Department besides their normal administrative and political duties. At the top of it, the subordinate staff was ill-paid. Thus, there was corruption, inefficiency, desertion at the lower level. W.F. Parrece, the officiating Conservator of Forests, Eastern Circle recorded in 1912-13:[60] "During the period one Ranger retired, one Ranger died, one Forester and five guards were removed from the service, eight guards and one office peon were dismissed, one clerk, one moharir and three guards resigned and the services of the one clerk, one moharir and two guards were dispensed with. The above proves that the Department does not attract a class of Government servants suitable for the work, or who will serve in order to profit by the attraction of the upper grades. The general conditions of service among subordinate and clerical establishment were under consideration and proposals for their improvement were submitted to Government after the close of the year. The controlling staff has proved wholly inadequate to deal with the work now before the Department . . . Apart from the routine work connected with existing charges, which increases daily with expansion of the demand, there are important questions to be dealt with connected with the reservation of sufficient forests for the future, the provision of village forests and grazing grounds, the control of professional graziers and reservation of thatch producing lands, while applications for concessions for pulp manufacture from reeds have been received, and enquiries have been instituted regarding suitability and quantity of Assam timber available for railway sleepers, etc. . . . all the point to the work being quite beyond the capacity of the present establishment."

The same source records R.M. Williamson from the Western Circle of Assam Forests:[61] "The large population of forest guards, whose services had to be dispensed with, in many cases for failure to return from leave, or who formally resigned, is a clear indication of the inadequacy of the pay offered to retain men in these posts. Though the pay scale is higher than that given in other provinces, it is yet below the earnings of unskilled labour, and in view of the very keen competition among employers in Assam for labour, it is hardly surprising that this Department finds the greatest difficulty in maintaining a parmanent staff of subordinates. The same may be said of all classes of the subordinate service."

The *Western Circle* reported in 1913-14 that many of the members of the subordinate establishments had chiefly been employed on revenue collection and were unable to assimilate new ideas. While the starting pay offered was not sufficient to attract probationers of required stamp, during the year five guards and one peon died; three guards were dismissed; services of one clerk, 17 guards and four peons were dispensed with; one clerk, one forester, 20 guards and 4 peons resigned; one guard was convicted and sentenced to two months' imprisonment; 2 guards retired and one clerk was transferred to another department. Among guards and peons out of a total of 299 posts, there were, thus no less than 57 (nearly 20 per cent) casualty indicating the fact that the conditions of service were not sufficiently attractive. Out of 15 Garos appointed in 2 years, 9 had already resigned. They appeared to have little or no idea of order and discipline and resented interference with their inclinations.[62] It was not possible to post a gazetted officer to the Mizo Hills, though the Superintendent of the District drew attention to the desirability of taking up the question of forest management. It was equally important to station an Officer in the North East Frontier Tract, but that huge region was constituted as a Forest Range under D.F.O., Lakhimpur.[63] Because of the paucity of Forest Officers, Darrang, Nowgong and Sadiya Divisions were put under the charge of the civil administrators in 1918-19. It was also observed that the lower paid men could not live on their salaries and the temptations to supplement their exiguous pay must be nearly overwhelming.[64] Again, shortage of staff was so acute that silviculturist was not provided with an assistant in 1928-29 affecting the collection of data for analysis.[65] On the issue of staffing pattern vis-a-vis surplus revenue earned by the Department an interesting controversy was raised between the Forest Department, and the civil administration of the Province in 1926-28. W.R.L. Jacob, the Conservator of Forests, Assam, noted that the resignations of foresters and guards had not decreased and the number of yearly resignations showed that the forest service in lowest grades was not sufficiently attractive to hold them back to their posts.[66] Further he (Mr. Jacob, the Conservator of Forests) observed that the surplus revenue for the year (Rs. 16,89,854, i.e. 53.9 per cent of the expenditure) was far too large compared with the expenditure (Rs. 14,43,819). He pleaded for more money to put back into the forests in order to increase the value of the forest estate of the province for the future.[67]

In the following year the surplus was further increased to Rs. 21,81,260 (60.04 per cent of the expenditure of Rs. 14,32,200) and expenditure went down (see Table 2.2). In view of the Conservator of the Forests, Assam,[68] this position was entirely false. Every division in the Eastern Circle was under-manned and the newly created working plan branch was carrying on with a totally inadequate staff. Improved housing of subordinate staff and provision of suitable camping grounds in the forests with good water supply, opening up of communications in the forests were among some of the most urgent undertakings. Without additional staff and funds the existing position would steadily grow worse. The Governor in Council[69] recognized the justice of the above views of the Conservator and acknowledged the need for revamping the forest administration. However, the Governor asserted that the large surplus which the Department had yielded, had been of inestimable value in restoring the financial stability of the province and providing funds for many important schemes of provincial development in other fields.

Our review of the forestry in Assam ends in 1933. We have examined the constitution of State forests, management of the State forests, financial aspects of the forests and the problems of personnel faced by the Department. By the end of our presentation, the international and Indian economic depression was already calling on the forest revenue (Table 2.2). Within next five years another disaster knocked on its door in the form of the Second World War. North East Region in general and eastern forests in particular were turned into a limited theatre of war causing havoc to the forest resources. A number of forest officers were drafted for the war duties. There was heavy demand on timber of all types resulting in unplanned felling. By the time the World War ended, the British were ready to leave the Province as rulers (Rawntree, J., 1981: pp. 86-110). Organisationally, it was in an enviable position, but it had potentiality. In the words of the last British Conservator of Forests, forest revenue had increased over 600 per cent of the pre-war figures. It may be befitting to quote W.R. Leg Jacob, the indomitable Conservator of Forests of Assam,[70] two decades before independence: "the prospects for the future of forests of Assam are very promising; but it will take years of strenuous appli-cation before the efficiency of the management equals that of the majority of Indian Provinces; this is not intended as a reflection on the present forest staff; they are badly handicapped by having area too large for proper control, by poor communications, and by unhealthy climate."

References

1. Progress Report of Forest Administration in the Province of Assam, (PRFAA) for the year, 1911-12, dated Shillong, Sept. 1912, pp. 1-2.
2. PRFAA, 1912-13, dated October 1, 1913, p. 2.
3. PRFAA, 1913-14, dated Sept. 23, 1914, pp. 1-2.
4. Ibid, p. 27.
5. PRFAA, 1918-19, dated Sept. 25, 1919, p. 270.
6. Ibid, p. 7.
7. Ibid, p. 8.
8. PRFAA, 1923-24, dated Shillong, August 15, 1924, p. 1.
9. PRFAA, 1926-27, dated Shillong, August, 17, 1927, p. 3.
10. PRFAA, 1929-30, dated Shillong, Nov. 1, 1930, p. 1.
11. PRFAA, 1932-33, dated Shillong, August, 1933, p. 1.
12. PRFAA, 1911-12, dated Shillong, Sept. 6, 1912, p. 6.
13. PRFAA, 1911-12, dated Shillong, Sept. 6, 1912, p. 6.
14. Ibid, p. 10.
15. PRFAA, 1913-14, dated Shillong, Sept. 23, 1914, p. 9.
16. Proceedings of the Chief Commissioner of Assam in the Revenue Department, No. 5109R, dated the 21st December, 1914.
17 PRFAA, 1918-19, dated Shillong, Sept. 26, 1919, pp. 7-8.
18. Quinquennial Review of Forest Administration in the Province of Assam

(Q.R.F.A.A.) for the years, 1919-20 to 1923-24, p. 8.
19. PRFAA, 1911-12, dated Shillong, Sept. 1912, p.18.
20. PRFAA, 1912-13, dated Shillong, Oct. 1913, p. 31.
21. PRFAA, 1913-14, dated Shillong, Sept. 23, 1914, p. 28.
22. QRFAA, 1919-20—1923-24, p. 11.
23. Ibid, p. 10.
24. PRFAA, 1923-24, dated Shillong, August 15, 1924, p. 23.
25. PRFAA, 1926-27, dated Shillong, August 17, 1927, p. 20.
26. PRFAA, 1927-28, dated Shillong, August 23, 1928, p. 19.
27. PRFAA, 1928-29, dated Shillong, August 20, 1929, p. 19.
28. PRFAA, 1929-30, dated Shillong, August 21, 1930, p. 18.
29. PRFAA, 1931-32, dated Shillong, August 24, 1932, p. 20.
30. PRFAA, 1932-33, dated Shillong, August 16, 1933, p. 1.
31. PRFAA, 1911-12, dated Shillong, Sept. 6, 1912, p. 4.
32. QRFAA, 1919-20 - 1923-24, p. 2.
33. PRFAA, 1924-25 - 1928-29, p. 2.
34. PRFAA, 1927-28, dated Shillong, August 23, 1928, p. 4.
35. PRFAA, 1911-12, dated Shillong, September, 1912, pp. 9, 12.
36. PRFAA, 1913-14, dated Shillong, September, 23, 1914, p. 13.
37. Ibid, pp. 17, 21.
38. PRFAA, 1918-19, dated Shillong, Sept. 1919, pp. 13-21.
39. QRFAA, 1919-1920 to 1923-24, p. 6.
40. QRFAA, 1924-25 to 1928-29, p. 3.
41. PRFAA, 1927-28, dated Shillong, August 23, 1928.
42. PRFAA, 1912-13, dated Shillong, October 1, 1913.
43. PRFAA, 1918-19, dated Shillong, Sept. 1919, p. 26.
44. QRFAA, 1919-20, 1923-24, p. 7.
45. Ibid, p. 7.
46. QRFAA, 1924-25 - 1928-29, p. 5.
47. PRFAA, 1926-27, dated Shillong, August 23, 1928, p. 12.
48. PRFAA, 1927-28, dated Shillong, August 23, 1928, p. 12.
49. PRFAA, 1928-29, dated Shillong, August 20, 1929, p. 12.
50. PRFAA, 1929-30, dated Shillong, August 21, 1930, pp. 10-11.
51. PRFAA, 1931-32, dated Shillong, August 24, 1932, p. 12.
52. PRFAA, 1912-13, dated Shillong, Oct. 1, 1913.
53. Ibid, p. 12.
54. QRFAA, 1919-20 to 1923-24, p. 1.
55. Proceedings of the Chief Commissioner of Assam in the Revenue Department No. 5109R, dated the December 21, 1914.
56. From L.J. Kershaw, Secretary to the Government of India, Deptt. of Revenue and Agiculture to the Chief Commissioner of Assam, File No. 450, 1915, Serial No. 2, No. 449, dated Shimla, April 1, 1915.
57. PRFAA, 1928-29, dated Shillong, August 20, 1929, p. 13.
58. Proceedings of the Governor in Council in the Revenue Department, No.

4225R, dated Shillong, the 3rd November, 1930.

59. PRFAA, 1926-27, dated Shillong, August 27, 1928, p. 16.
60. PRFAA, 1912-13, dated Shillong, October 1, 1913, p. 30.
61. Ibid, p. 29.
62. PRFAA, 1913-14, dated Shillong, Sept. 23, 1914, pp. 25-26.
63. Ibid, p. 27.
64. PRFAA, 1918-19, dated Shillong, Sept. 26, 1919, p. 27.
65. PRFAA, 1926-29, dated Shillong, August 20, 1929, p. 10.
66. PRFAA, 1926-27, dated Shillong, August 17, 1928, p. 19.
67. Ibid, p. 17.
68. Ibid, p. 18.
69. Proceedings of Governor in Council in the Revenue Department, No. 3559R, dated Shillong, the 20th Oct. 1928.
70. PRFAA, 1926-27, dated Shillong, August 17, 1928, p. 2.

3

The American Baptist Mission Among the Nagas

There is a deeply rooted western view that the history of the Third World countries is still new compared with that of Europe, the cradle of modern metropolitan industrial civilization. Their history only really begins from the time when they were 'discovered' and integrated into the history of western expansion and progress. It all began in 1493, hardly a year after Christopher Columbus' discovery of America, when Pope Alexander VI divided the New World between Spain and Portugal and termed the conquest of foreign territories as the sacred extension of 'God's kingdom on earth'. Thus, from the very beginning the conquest of distant lands had been associated with a strongly developed sense of Christian mission. Since then colonial authorities and missionaries have worked in more or less overlapping areas. Both were conscious of representing and disseminating Christian culture: mission and civilization went hand in hand (Witvliet, T: 1985).

The interests of church and state were tightly inter-woven in the period of Iberian colonization, as both were equally concerned to transplant the hierarchical and feudal structures of church and society to American soil as faithfully as possible. The *Papal Bull* of 1493 not only authorized mission by the sword, but also made it virtually impossible to criticize in principle the robbery and exploitation practised by the conquistodors. As a result the colonists and the missionaries alike did not consider the Red Indians as human being till 1536, when Pope Paul III proclaimed them as 'true human beings'. If the Catholic mission in the period of Iberian colonialism is set against the background of a feudal society of an agrarian kind, the background to missionary activities from Protestant countries was the rise of bourgeoise capitalist society with the industrial revolution. The growth of an industrial capitalistic society went hand in hand with the rise of an aggressively nationalistic sense of mission. When the period of imperialism began, round about 1870 (Hobsawn E.: 1989), both the expansion of the world market through colonial wars and increasing conflicts between nations bolstered by a nationlistic sense of mission, conveniently called cultural messianism.

The missionaries were commanded to bring the colonized people into contact with the achievements of European culture. However, many of them were not unaware of the devastating effect of economic and political self interest of colonized people and cultures. In the words of the German missionologist, Gustaw Warneck: ''In making the pagans Christians, mission also makes them real human beings, and in implanting the Kingdom of God among them it also implants true culture. Culture is not the main aim of mission, but its necessary consequence, a free gift, a by-product, a blessing which falls to the earth from the rich table of the gospel''. Ernst Troeltsch, German theologian, philosopher and sociologist, believed that despite all the faults, conflicts and impurities, the Christian religion is the supreme form and power of spiritual life. Therefore, in his views, the Christians feel obliged and justified in intervening with their higher possession whereover higher and better things seek to be formed. Such a point of view finds unanimity over the conception of a world culture along the lines of Western social structures. Similarly, development and progress were thought to be products of European culture and history and the world was considered to be Europocentric. The American Baptist missionaries, as the representatives of the above ideology, came to Nagaland in 1876 and established a mission station with a view to converting the indigenous communities to Christianity.

The chapter reviews some of the events, ideas, antecedents and personnel involved in the introduction of the Christianity of the American Baptist denomination among the Ao Nagas and its subsequent spread to others. It examines some of the salient trends of events on the basis of the reports filed by the missionaries from Impur station, Nagaland. It is commonly believed that conversion to Christianity brought various Nagas on a common platform leading to a shared ethnic identity, which found its echo in political aspirations of the Nagas. On the other hand, with attainment of almost hundred p^r cent Christianity, the Naga Baptist Church Council (NBCC) has reached a plateau and its various functions are subjected to severe scrutiny. The chapter based on the church documents, refers to the Ao Nagas mainly and extrapolates to the Nagas at large. It has a limited purpose to examine the texture of the Naga Christianity in the light of their indigenous cultural traditions and emergent Naga identity as a bonus in the changed geopolitical context of mid-twentieth century.

The Ao Traditional Belief and Social Context

The religion of the traditional Ao is not a moral code. It is a system of ceremonies and an Ao will not prosper, if he omits the sacrifices due to the deities around him, who, if unappeased, are ever ready to blight his crops and bring illness upon him (Mills, J.P.: 1973). The Ao universe is filled with multitudes of spirits with whom they must deal. From them come disease, madness, death of cattle and famine. The propitiation of the evil and capricious spirit is practically the sum and substance of their religion. They believe in benevolent spirits, who are not propitiated, as such spirits do not interfere in their daily lives (Smith, W.C.: 1925). It is the ambition of every Ao to proceed as far as he can in the series of feast of merit. By doing so he gains for himself honour both in this life and after death, and for his clan and village the favour of spirits and the prosperity of great men of the past.

The present Mokokchung district of Nagaland is located east of Dikku river on four parallel ranges running south to north towards the Brahmaputra plains. This undulating and evergreen forested land is the traditional home of the Ao (or *Aor*: those who came across the Dikku), known to their Assamese neighbours as *Hathiguria* (the elephant catchers). They were settled on strategically located hill top villages which were governed by 'elders' council'; were engaged in subsistence slash-and-burn type of rotational cultivation (*jhumming*) with their simple technology; and were in habit of seeking slaves across the land through occasional raids. Though hunting of the wild animals was an inseparable part of the traditional economic activities, it was resorted more as a sign of bravery, achievement and leadership. The practice of catching a slave and hunting a wild game perhaps got combined into the practice of head-chopping, for which occasional sorties were conducted to the Brahmaputra plains in the north. Though they could meet most of their needs locally in their hills, at times they took their limited produce to the plains for exchanging them against salt, betel nuts and leaves, iron, dry fish and threads. These scantily clad and athletic warriors were feared for their ferocity and admired for their bravery. With a view to securing a more settled relationship with the Aos the Ahom *Kakotis* (the officials responsible for maintaining a working relationship between Ahoms and hill tribes) negotiated disputes after gifting of certain articles for the *Poss,* which were regularly paid to the hillmen. The scenario continued till the Burmese invasion of the Brahmaputra valley in the first quarter of the 19th century, as a result of which the British descended on the North Eastern Indian horizon as a significant political force.

The American Baptist Mission and Its Entry into North Eastern India

Some of the early British administrators believed that the conversion to Christianity and spread of education through the missionaries might lead to 'civilizing' the 'heathen' and 'pacification' of certain tribes. Captain Francis Jenkins, the Governor General's Agent and Commissioner of Assam, was one such person, who was persuaded by Charles Bruce, a pioneer tea planter, to invite the Baptist mission in Burma to Sadiya (Barpujari, H.K.: 1985: 2). He wrote to the missionaries: "No attention of mine should of course be wanting to make the place (Sadiya) comfortable to any missionaries, and I will be willing to contribute my mite to their establishment. You may mention that I will subscribe, 1000 rupees, if a family is settled as a mission at Sadiya, and who have had a (printing) press at work for six months I will be happy to double that sum if I remain incharge of the Province" (Baptist Missionary Magazine: 1837). He was also willing to grant a plot of waste land free of rent for 15 to 20 years for the sake of establishing a Christian colony. The *Board* accepted Jenkins' proposal and sent about half a dozen missionaries between 1836 to 1840 on what came to be known as the Shan Mission (named after Shan tribes of upper Burma closer to China) at Sadiya. Anglo-Singpho skirmishes led to the mission moving from Sadiya to Jaipur. Miles Bronson's evangelical and educational efforts among the Namsangea Nagas came to a sudden halt because of personal tragedies. For coming next three decades the Baptist mission concentrated in the Brahmaputra valley. But the success in conversion to Christianity was extremely unsatisfactory. To the extent that Rev. C.E. Patrick reported only of few over 100 Assamese Christians after 60 years of untiring efforts and they too were mostly orphans, diseased, social drop-outs and out-castes. The only redeeming features of the evangelical efforts were the optimism generated in 1860's among the Garos at the behest of the Garo evangelists themselves.

Rev. Bro. Edward Winter Clark, born at North-East New York and a graduate of the Brown University, was trained in missionology at Newton and Rochester Theological Seminaries. He along with his wife, Mary reached Sibsagar, Assam in June, 1969 to take the charge of the church and the printing press after departure of William Ward. Lack of success in proselytizing plantation labourers around the mission head-quarters, unpleasant working relations with Mrs. Ward, ill health and unhealthy climatic conditions and a better prospect of conversion among the Nagas, encouraged Rev. Clark to look for better pasture among the Aos. He assessed them positively even before he could initiate evangelical work: "These Nagas have a good name for truthfulness and for general purity of life, except that they are dirty and blood thirsty. They are probably as faithful friends and as they are implacable enemies" (Barpujari, H.K.: 1986: 267). He encouraged a willing and adventurous Assamese evangelist and school teacher, Godhula alias Rutus Brown, to undertake an exploratory visit to Ao village of Haimong in October, 1871. Godhula's visit to Haimong was so encouraging that he returned to Ao hills in April, 1872 along with his wife and remained there for about six months. By the end of 1872 as many as two dozen Aos were converted to Christianity as part of Sibsagar Church (Downs, F.S.: 1971: 65).

Clark was so optimistic about the prospect of evangelical success among the Aos that he wrote to the *Home Board*: "We are willing to give our whole strength to labour along, if needs be, but we cannot distribute ourselves to many places beyond, where we believe the standard of Immanuel should be planted and sustained. We want a man for these Nagas, upon whose mountain homes our eyes daily rest. They have some crude and indefinite conceptions of a great spirit and evil and, further than this, they have no religion. Our hearts go after whom, our prayers ascent for them and a petition comes to you in their behalf." (Clark, E.W.: 1872: 50). The period between the discovery of the Naga field and Clark's actual residence in the Naga Hills was marked by internal resolve against an initial cold response from the *Home Board.* We wrote to John N. Murdock on April 10, 1873 and August 4, 1873 expressing his determination to take up the evangelical work among the Nagas at any cost: "After weeks of consultation with my wife, I have come about to the conclusion that if the Mission Union persists in thus hampering the preaching of gospel, I had better resign and preach in the region beyond without the aid of the Union." Again "if to save this Naga work it shall become necessary for me to resign my connection with the Union, I shall not hesitate. I have given you notice. I cannot see such a great opening as that badly damaged" (Puthenpurakal, J.: 1984: 54).

Rev. Clark came to be known as inventor of the Naga field among the Baptists. He along with his wife, Mary, the celebrated author of an autobiographical little book, *A Corner in India*, got settled in Naga hills for almost four decades. Dr. Clark was extremely dedicated to the envangelical cause to the extent that he spent his personal money to move Rev. and Mrs. Witter from Sibsagar to Wokha among the Lotha Nagas. He produced text books on theological and biblical themes for the Aos. His most monumental work will remain the *Ao Naga Dictionary.* According to B.I. Anderson, Clark refused to move to Impur because he objected to the construction of *Pukka* bungalows for the missionaries. He argued that the Nagas would not feel at home visiting the missionaries in the bungalows. When he finally moved to Impur, an Ao style house was constructed for him in which he lived until he retired in 1911 (Downs, F.S.: 1971: 116). It goes without saying that Clark seems to have adopted the cultural style of life of the Aos as closely and sincerely as he could within the limitations of his Christian commitment and his American heritage (Pruett, G.E.: 1974: 53).

Ever ready, hard working, adventurous and impetuous Godhula was encouraged by Rev. Clark to move to the Hills in 1873 for evangelical work and remained effective in-charge of the mission till Clark himself moved to Deka Haimong in March 1876. Godhula, besides his unstable character, was not a great organizer. His own performance inspired a mixed following at times detrimental to his main evangelical work. It appears that he avoided closer scrutiny and took undue advantage of Clark's liking for his positive works. To the extent that the Sub-Divisional Officer of Mokokchung had issued an order forbidding his entry to the Naga Hills on the complaints that he had been extracting money from the simple Nagas, on the plea of divine intervention in their favour (Longkumer, N.: 1988: 71-72). He turned out to be a drunkard as well as an opium addict. However, it was more of Godhula's policies and methods which shaped the beginning of the Naga evanglical work especially from 1871 to 1876 than that of Rev. Clark's. And when the latter came to the Naga Hills in 1876 to live among the Nagas, he found it hard to undo what Godhula had done (Puthenpurakal, J.: 1984: 68).

The Ao Baptist Association and Growth of the Church

The first Ao Baptist Association, the precursor of the present Ao Baptist Arogo Mungdong (ABAM), was held at Molung in 1897. The first subject on the programme of the association meeting was the prayer. "Other topics were evangelization, the Holy spirit, Christian benevolence, shall the Nagas burry their dead? Should all Christians learn to read? By what changes in food, houses, sanitation, and clothing shall Christians better their mode of living?" (Clark, M.M.: 1978: 143). Immediately after those meetings a Teachers' and Preachers' institute was conducted by Rev. Perrine. It was decided to hold associational meetings annually.

Besides establishment of various services and institutions the graph of the Baptist membership among the Aos indicates that within a century (1871 to 1972) almost entire Ao community has turned out to be Christian. From 24 in 1872 to 368 in 1900, to 8,973 in 1926, to 16,680 in 1950, and there were 58,757 Christians out of 59,859 in 1971 (Philip, P.T.: 1983: 78; Longkumer, N.: 1988 Chap. II). Fredrick Downs identifies three revival movements among the Aos between 1895 to 1915 (Downs F.S.: 1971: 116-120) in 1895, 1910 and 1914-1915 respectively. Phillip reviews the growth of the Ao Church in two periods: (i) the period of slow growth 1897-1920 and (ii) the period of spectacular growth 1921 to 1971 (Philip, P.T.: 1983: 67-68) with a possible formative phase between 1871 and 1896. Longkumer slightly differs from Phillip and suggests his different periods with different dates (Longkumer, N.: 1988: 15-25). For him the hundred years long history of Ao Baptist Church may be divided into (i) The planting of the first church in Nagaland, (ii) Expansion of church, 1897 to 1926 and (iii) Expansion of the churches, 1927 to 1972. Various authors, such as Downs, Puthanpurakal, Phillip, Longkumer, identified various reasons for the spectacular success of the Baptist missionaries among the Aos. However, it will be instructive to follow the broad trends through their annual reports and periodic correspondence.

The *Baptist Missionary Magazine*, the house journal of the American Baptists, recorded in its 55th annual report filed by Haggard and Parrine: "The (Ao) Christians now have an increasing ambition to dress better, to live better in better houses, and to be cleaner. They have more desire to learn how to read and write, and to use that knowledge and powers they have for God's glory. For the past two years the village schools have been self supporting in the sense that they receive nothing from the mission. They are supported in part by the Government and partly by themselves . . . The village schools are also becoming self managing and directing so that we feel that a good start is being made towards their self support . . . A sort of Naga Renaissance was brought about, and that too by a very humble agency, namely, the mere matter of a considerable number of Naga boys and girls learning to write. It would seem as if this alone would do more to show the Naga people the value of education than all our talk and religious instruction combined . . . We still insist that each pupil shall support himself or work for at least a part of his support" (B.M.M.: Vol. 79. 1895: 75-77).

The Eighty Seventh Annual Report of the *American Baptist Foreign Mission* from Impur records in 1900: "No evangelists have been employed but each church has reported a certain amount of evangelistic work in the neighbouring villages. At the (Ao) Association (meeting) there were 190 delegates and the meeting was regarded as the best so far held. The whole business including programme was attended by the Nagas themselves, the missionaries were merely "visiting brethren" . . . The station training school numbered only 35 as against 60 last year . . . Twelve of the scholars were baptized during the year, and we believe all four of the remaining unbaptized pupils are Christians." (B.M.M., Vol. 81: 1901-99).

Rev. Dawn records in 1902 from Impur for Eighty-ninth Annual report of the *Board* . . . "Many children and adults got their first knowledge of the gospel from the village teachers and the results to the religious work are considerable. The churches have to look after themselves for the most part of this year. Five are self supporting, one receives a small grant from the mission and others avail themselves of the village school teachers for their pastors. Much good work has been done, and in three villages notable results in the way of baptisms have appeared. In two of these villages, Asongma and Mapongzukat, the converts were practically the first fruits after many years of seed sowing in these villages. Another most encouraging event was the starting by the churches, at the recent association, a fund for home mission work (B.M.M., Vol. 83: 1903 July: 110).

The Assam Baptist Mission Conference (*ABMC*) proceedings in its eighth session in 1907 records Rev. S.A. Perrine's Report on Impur: "I believe our chief efforts should be to reach those people which by virtue of their position from the human heart of Asia . . . The Naga Mission must not, then, be looked at as simply of and for the Nagas, but rather as a part of a great system to reach the Mongolian people of Asia . . . The Naga Mission is chiefly valuable because of its position and what is it is potentially in relation to the whole Mongolian race . . . At Longkum, the most important village among the Aos, the prospect is also as helpful as can be desired. In spite of severe persecution the church and school are growing nicely. The results at Longkum are having a decided influence on the whole tribe" (*ABMC*: 8th session, 1907: 56).

Further "through schools the Gospel is made to reach the mountaineers more rapidly and permanently than by any other means. The importance of the school work, among the Hill tribes, cannot be over-estimated. We have, therefore, made the school work a speciality, we have depended upon our Training School in a peculiar way and have not found it wanting . . . Naga school books were aspecially desired by the Government . . . It fell to my let to do this, and I have prepared, by means of *Pundits* (knowledgeables), Primers and Arithmetics in Ao, Lotha, Sema and Mozunger Naga, also an English-Lotha Vocabulary and the Gospel of Matthew in Lotha. The manuscripts of all these have gone to Shillong; the (British) Government (of Assam) has passed part of them and part of them are now in press. We have been assured of our Naga officials that they will all be approved though, of course, that remains to be seen. Mr. Reid, our D.C., was kind enough to write some very strong recommendations of this work" (*ABMC*: ibid: 58).

Rev. R.G. Longwell reported in 1911 the arrival of Dr. and Mrs. Bailey to and departure of Dr. Clark from Impur. In his opinion: "(day) schools, like the evangelistic work receive very little attention from the missionaries. The teachers bring their monthly report, have a little talk about their work, get their money and go back. Their work is rarely inspected and their school seldom examined. The fourteen village schools which the Mission turned over to Government some six or eight years ago have nearly all been closed. A few of those have been reopened by the Mission. Others doubtless will be. At present eleven villages are asking for teachers. Some of those are new villages and some are old. Many of Nagas want education. The Christians everywhere want it . . . While the Christians have felt that the local Government official (S.D.O., Mokokchung) was their worst enemy; and his antipathy to them and a set of laying *dobhashis* have deprived Court proceedings with the Christians of every vestige of fairness."

"The unsatisfactory state of things at the Impur station is fully explained by just the facts:

(a) For exactly twenty years, 1892-93 to 1912-13 the work has been utterly without continuity of efforts . . . a station is better off with one missionary crank, who is given a life time work out his cranky schemes than with twenty years long procession of missionaries.

(b) . . . The spirit of revival was among us as never before nor since . . . Evangelical bands were touring in all the adjacent hills. Converts were coming from every directions. New Churches were springing up in villages. The blessing was indeed poured out and there was no capacity to take care of it. The one missionary who was supposed to be giving his time to actual missionary work was writing letter after letter on behalf of the Christians in the hope of securing justice and true liberty; was trying to conduct training school of 80 or 90 pupils with an inefficient staff of native teachers, and with a literature neither sufficient in quantity nor fit in character for school purposes; and was trying to do an extensive field work by proxy" (*ABMC*: 12th session: 1911: 50-51).

Rev. J.R. Bailey's report on Impur informs us: "I am glad to see the Churches and individual Christians doing evangelistic work. They go in bands of two or more and visit distant villages. I met one band of seven women in a village *thirty* miles from their homes. They were on tour in the interest of women's work. Those Christians arouse interest and break down oppositions and make way for a permanent workers" (*ABMC* 13th session: 1912: 23). Next year W.F. Down reports of the religious revival: "A good religious spirit has prevailed. The Christian Endeavour Society was reorganised by the boys and their meetings did much to help in their spiritual life" (*ABMC*: 14th session: 19).

The Impur Report for the 24th session of the Assam Baptist Mission Conference was filed by Rev. R.B. Longwell: "In the Ao Naga Tribe there are fifty eight villages varying in size from twenty houses up to six and seven hundred. Among these fifty eight, there are fifty four with churches, by far the majority of which are self supporting. We could probably have churches in all but one or two of the remaining villages if we had funds with which to start them. Our policy from the beginning has been to establish churches with financial help from the Mission, and then withdraw mission support the churches become able to carry their own burden . . . In the month of April the Ao Naga Christians in number of 3,000 or more celebrated the fiftieth anniversary of Dr. Clark's arrival in Naga

Hills. It was a worthy time of reminiscing and of scanning the future of plea to complete the work in their own tribe and to carry the message, to another tribes" (*ABMC*: 24th session 1926: 63-64). Longwell's next Report on Impur in 1927 informs the readers how Aos have been over-reaching Sema and Lhota villages for evangelical work.

In February, 1941 Edna and B.I. Andersons reported from Impur 56 Churches, 657 Baptist and 16,150 members to the Church among the Aos. They reported on the various Ao evangelist-cum-teachers, whose services were requisitioned by the Government. They mentioned two typical cases of conversion to Christianity from the Chang tribe, which influenced positively the spread of Christianity among the Nagas. A powerful Chang village chief was a head Interpretor (*Dobhasi*) at the Mokokchung court who had been opponent of the British power among the tribes over 30 years. But his health was ruined by drink and this year (1940) he became seriously ill. At the end he sought conversion to Christianity and his example would be followed in future. Similarly, another Chang, who had saved the British officials from an attack from ambush and was subsequently decortated by the King-Emperor, was converted to Christianity along with members of his family. He was an affective voice among the Chang, whose opinion was honoured by the Government officials. He had taken to his heart the conversion of his people to Christianity (Assam correspondence: *American Baptist Foreign Mission Society* 1941 type script).

In August 1942, B.I. Anderson reported to the *ABFMS*, Valley Forge on the evangelistic activities among the Aos: "Evangelistic Work in the Ao field has now passed at most entirely into the hands of the Ao Naga pastors and evangelists. They are showing both ability and zeal in doing their work. Only half of our churches have thus far licensed their pastors but a special examination in this, other young men will be set aside for full time Christian service. The missionary has visited 25 Ao villages this year and assisted in dedication of two new permanent church buildings. One of these is in the largest Ao village where a feud between two rich men had defied all attempts at settlement . . . As a happy solution the village authorities decided to give the land to the Church and in a very short time a beautiful and expansive church was built to the glory of God . . ." (Assam Corres-pondence: *ABFMS*: 1942: 24). Furthermore Anderson reported that two compaigns were put on by Ao students for their less fortunate and illiterate brethren. Some of the boys even composed poems to commemorate the drive. The Government (of Assam) had sponsored evening schools for the illiterate and with the means at their disposal the students were making a real contribution towards enlightenment of the Aos. The Missionaries felt their responsibility in producing books for the students as the heaviest among all their works. In the previous year they had produced a new edition of the Ao hymn book and first edition of *Pilgrim's Progress* besides a reprint of the *First Reader*, all printed at the cost of Rs. 3,000 and were paid out of the earnings of the Book Room.

Rev. C.E. Hunter filed the annual report for the 1940 "During the year the Aos have supported an evangelist, whose salary they voted to increase; they have given partial support to the Impur School which is under the control of the association, they have given support for a full time Old Testament translator, supported an evangelist for the Konyaks (tribe), and eight pastors for the border tribes churches. At the annual association meeting the Aos took the following steps: gifted Rs. 1000 from the Clark Memorial Fund for aid to Chang Churches, voted to raise the scale of pay for the Impur School staff to the Govt. Middle English standard, but to discontinue this school from 1950 and to open a Teachers' Training School. Also, it was decided to open a Bible School in Impur in 1949 to provide scripture teachers for pupils in the various M.E. Schools and the Mokokchung High School . . . to recommend to the churches that pastors should be paid a minimum salary of Rs. 20 per month, and for each church to set aside Rs. 10 annually to be given to the pastor upon retirement. Much consideration was given to the proposal that all churches give a little of their income to the association, but action was postponed; for the present the expenses of the associational budget will be prorated among the churches on the basis of membership. The churches reported over Rs. 1,00,000 spent in 1948. A proposal to open a mission station among the Konyaks (tribe) and to support workers there was considered, but action was deferred" (Assam Correspondence: *ABFMS*: 1940: 3).

The Baptist Church, British Administration and Ao Social Structure

The attitude of the British administration to the Baptist Mission has been ambivalent. The British Government informed Rev. Clark that he could enter the Naga Hills at his own risk and no protection could be provided to him (Clark, M.M.: 1970: 18). On the other hand, the Missionary schools were run on the Government financial support. On occasions, the Government provided certain medicines to the missionary medical unit. The Government 'pacification forces' did not hesitate to take help from missionaries in their efforts. In fact, the missionaries pleaded for the extension of the British rule to the Naga Hills in the interests of their evangelical activities, as they considered the British empire to be a Christian Government favourable to them (Clark, M.M.: 1970: 126-127). Rev. Longwell expressed his concern in 1913 on the local officials at Mokokchung siding with the indigenous faith again the Baptist Missionaries. J.H. Hutton and J.P. Mills, the I.C.S. Officers posted at Mokokchung, by far were serious scholars and committed colonial administrators. Hutton had been of the view that role of the Baptist mission among the tribals in general and Nagas in particular had been injurious and disruptive to their culture. Mills added an appendix on "The Effects of Mission Work Upon the Aos" in his celebrated monograph on the Aos (Mills, J.P.: 1973: 410-424). He found the Baptists demanding actions against the animist believers imposing their practices and customs on their newly converted brethren but they themselves dishonoured and desecrated the indigenous practices (Clark, M.M.: 1979: 59) leading to a phenomenon of social maladjustment. For instance, the controversy about the role of the younger folk with the mission. Mrs. Clark found them: "Instead of congregating promiscuously at different houses to sleep at night, singing objectionable songs, telling doubtful stories and engaging in lewd conversation these young reformers separated themselves and built a dormitory in which purity and holiness should reign. Here at morning and evening time the voice of prayer and songs of praise are heard" (Clark, M.M.: 1978: 139).

In contrast to the above scenario with the following, written some two decades after: "The American Baptist Mission is carrying on certain amount of education among the girls. This does not meet with the approval of conservative Aos, who regard it as useless, and leading to idleness and immorality. There is something in what they say. The circumstances under which the matter came to my notice were as follows: Some girls returned to a certain village after spending some time at the Impur Mission School. They refused to demean themselves by working in the field like their uneducated sisters, and preferred to sit in the village during the day doing nothing. In the village there also remained, as it is the Ao custom, a few young men whose duty it was to give the alarm in the case of an outbreak of fire and carry on any urgent message coming through from village to village. If idle girls and idle young men spend long days together in a deserted village trouble may be anticipated. It was when a baby or two arrived that I heard some forcible opinion on female education" (Mills, J.P.: 1973: 213-214). Incidentally, William C. Smith, another Missionary from the same field, commented on the controversy in his monograph on the Aos (Smith, W.C.: 1925: 198) and tends to agree with Mills. Similarly he found the Ao students from the Mission Schools above manual labour.

Like Mills, Smith devotes a chapter on "Changes through Contacts with More Advanced People" in his book on the Aos (Chap: VII: 179-200). At the end, he raised a number of questions: "what light may an analysis of the process of social and personal disorganization and reorganization in a primitive group through contact with group on a higher cultural level throw upon our policy of educational and missionary activities among the backward peoples in general? Will it be possible in the future to avoid many mistakes of the past? Have the ethnologist and sociologists sufficient data upon which to base the formulation of mechanism for controlling the process of social change so that in the experience itself the backward group may not be made to deteriorate during a period of transition, if not indeed be made utterly degenerate, as has often been true in the past?" To the above list, another one from J.P. Mills may be added: Why does an Ao give up his old religion and become a Christian? (Mills, J.P.: 1973: 411).

The Baptist Mission in Nagaland played a salutary role among the Aos. Indirectly it made a common cause with the British rulers to end the practices of head-chopping and slavery. It introduced a strict moral code of conduct, marital fidelity and prohibition against drinking of intoxicant beverages among the believers. A number of fruits, vegetables, edibles, dresses were made in vogue. Construction of living houses, segregation of animals from the living quarters, personal hygeine and physical cleanliness, disposal of dead through burial in a community cemetetry were some of social practices, which were initiated by the church. Mission literacy programmes resulted in a number of positive reactions such as spread of education, women employment through the church and production of literature in Ao languages. Again it was the Baptist church, which made certain occupations such as teaching, nursing, evangelical etc. as honourable ones. The Baptist always emphasized the socio-economic upliftment of the new converts leading to the emergence of a new urge among the Aos for economic prosperity.

Ao Association was instrumental in spread of Christianity among other hill tribes, raising the slogan: "Nagaland for the Christ". The Church did play a positive role in the emergence of a common Naga identity through Christianity, education and literature. It was a fact that the Nagas remained divided denominationally, but it goes without saying that in place of conventional intertribal warfare and conflict, the Baptist Mission played a pivotal role as an apex body of the Christian Nagas. The most salutary role of the Mission in the shape of *Nagaland Bapitst Church Council* (*NBCC*) was its efforts to bring peace and reconciliation in 1950's and 1960's and its work in the *Peace Mission*. It provided a reliable neutral forum between the Naga dessenters fighting for independence and the Indian Union (Rao, D.M.: 1986; Ao, W.N.: 1989).

The Baptist Church, Ethnicity and Naga Acculturation

The Ao Baptist Arogo Mungdan (*ABAM*), the Ao Baptist Church conference was organized at Molungyinsen in 1885 and since then it has been holding its conference at various Ao villages. It is claimed to be the 'mother' organization among the Nagas as it spends a huge amount of its budget for the benefit of the border tribes and it trains Aos and other evangelists for missionary activities across their boundaries. In fact, this association functioned as the foster mother to a number of tribal associations like Lotha,

Sangtam, Chang, etc. In Fredrick Downs' opinion the authority and influence of the missionaries held these associations together in the past. However, "An association became a means of asserting tribal identity and independence. Minority groups wanted to get out from domination by the majority tribe . . . It (co-existence of various tribes) introduced a principle of division within the church. Whenever a minority was not satisfied with the actions of the majority, it has sought separation as the appropriate response" (Downs, F.S.: 1971: 125). However, the Naga Baptist church has been aware of the problem and thus they organised the *Naga Baptist Church Council* (*NBCC*) in 1963 with a view to co-ordinating the inter-tribal evangelical interests.

In case one looks for the reasons for the success of the Baptist missionaries among the Aos or for that matter among the Garos, credit does not necessarily go to the missionaries insight and the vigour. It so happens that the Baptist polity enmeshes happily with the Naga tribal polity. Both polities are 'congressional' and solidly committed to the concept of local autonomy. Thus, the local or village Church receives the maximum of support, financial or others. The level of support increases in reverse proportion to the diversity of community (Pruett, G.E.: 1974: 60). There has been a general impression that the ethos of the Naga culture has conflict and violence at all levels: inter-clan, inter-village, inter-tribal. Location of their settlements, lay out of construction, fortification of villages, etc. are loud testimony to their utmost concern for defence and offence in the pre-Christian period of their history. But as a whole there has been a sea-change in the administrative and political climate of the Nagaland since then. In spite of the insurgency in certain pockets of the state, it is the Nagas, who manage their affairs and control their destiny in the regional geo-political context. It is not the will of the distant British rulers or New Delhi bureaucrats, who decide for the Nagas, but they themselves come forward in a big way. The Nagas have no choice to go back in terms of their integration to the world market economy, a process affected by the British and accelerate by New Delhi. In such a dynamic situation, it appears logical that the traditional Naga aggressive instinct and defence mechanism are directed vigorously to the evangelical work among the out-reach tribes with a view to winning more souls and defeating the satan. Thus, there appears to be a happy co-ordination between the two apparently opposite impressions of violent Naga culture and docile Christianity. The best illustration of such impression may be drawn from the lives of the pioneering Ao missionaries: Kijungluba, Langri, Nokden to mention a few. They had been aggressive missionaries all their lives, but were equally steadfast in their resolve for peace and reconciliation among the communities.

Against the puritanical approach of some of the missionaries regarding use of youth dermitories (*morangs*) and rice bear Rev. Langri Ao made use of the *morang* as his halting camps and preaching grounds in the villages and considered the rice bear as part of his food, and not an intoxicant beverage. His innovative and pragmatic approach to the Naga style of life endeared him to his brethren and far beyond. Similar views echoed in the expression as Dr. Renthy Keizer, Professor of Old Testament at the Eastern Theological College, Jorhat: "I am an Ao, I eat as an Ao; I dress as an Ao; I live in an Ao manner; I am also a baptized, so the culture is baptised" (Pruett, G.E.: 1874: 64). As against the above there is a common refrain among the scholars such as John H. Hutton, J.P. Mills, Verrier Elwin, Furer Haimendorf and a host of others that Christianity will eclipse the distinct diacritical marks of the Nagas. In their views Christianity poses a threat to the tribal identity. In light of the views of the tribal Christian intellectuals and elite of the region the above apprehensions appear to be notional. Can one ignore the resurgence of ethnicity and ethnic movement prevalent among the highly Christianized tribes of the region? If Christianity is not synonymous to the Western culture how can it be equivalent to a distinct ethnic identity, specially when the ethnic elites are conscious to maintain their identity?

Undoubtedly there is a strong process of acculturation sweeping Nagaland and far beyond the tribal areas of the Indian eastern frontier region under the Christian churches. This process signals to the quest of a new integrated form of society which will overcome to deep split introduced into their lives by colonialism and imperialism. This quest may have many forms and names: 'Nagaland for the Christ'; 'Naga nationalism'; 'Naga insurgency'; 'Naga statehood'. It has undergone a tremendous process of fission and fussion, which is yet incomplete. "The forming of the ties with new communities is a typical African (Naga?) reaction in times of crisis and change: When Africans (Nagas) take the step of being baptized and thus initiated into the life of Jesus Christ, they do so in the expectation of finding a way towards solving everyday problems like sickness, lack of food, homelessness and so on. What the African (Naga?) has been and is concerned with is life here and now. A life that depends on God and ancestors, but which is also dependent on those who are still to be born. And it was only when it was understood that the old organisation of life was endangered by all kinds of modern contracts and developments, that people began to look around for a new organisation to belong to" (Witvliet, T.: 1985: 102). It is a sad commentary that the evangelist failed to create a unified Naga Baptist Church on Christian principles, yet he succeeded where his actions were least tangible. In restructuring the native conceptual universe in important respect, he laid the foundation for its integration into the industrial capitalist world (Comaroff and Comaroff: 1986: 2).

Religion helps create systems of social values, which are integrated and coherent and it also provides the constraining power that underwrites and reinforces customs (Nottingham, E.K.: 1964: 14). Construction of the subject in the evangelical mould requires the internalization of a set of values, an ineffable manner of seeing and being. While the colonial process often entitled material disposition, critical part of the subjection of native peoples lay in the subtle colonization by the missionary of indigenous modes of perception and practices. What happened in the case of Africa is equally relevant for the Nagas: "From the beginning, the impact of the colonial power and the pressures of their missionary activities on traditional African cultural patterns has a strongly racist impact; the inferiority of the African 'natural man' to the civilized European was an established fact which was taken for granted; the African was regarded as a creature without culture and history." (Witvliet, T: 1985: 09). However, in spite of the large scale conversion to Christianity one of the problems continues to revolve around the question how African creation myths, rites of initiation, ancestor worship, clan solidarity and so on can be adopted or integrated into the Christian doctrinal tradition.

The above scenario naturally led to some of the African thinkers to speak in terms of 'African experience', 'African view of life', view of man, 'African philosophy' and the African 'Life-force' consistent with the basic view of humanity. The African sense of community is contrasted with Western individualism. This sense of community is based on a holistic vision of life which African theologians contrast sharply with the Western dualism of body and soul, matter and spirit, secular and sacred. Elizabeth Colson reports from Tonga Valley, Zambia on the impact of Christianity on the indigenous faith. The hymns, prayers and order of service were treated almost as though they were magical formulae, which would bring about the desired result, the control of the European knowledge. By equating the Bible with the source of truth, was the source of the European power and wealth. This belief convinced the new Christians that those who learned to read, could acquire the knowledge and power of the European! The power and the position of the European was for taking; the Bible was a means to an end (Colson, E.: 1970: 149-151). The Naga scenario consisting of Naga acculturation, Naga life force, Naga sense of community and Naga quest of meaning goes closer to the above African experience and demands dispassionate analysis.

References

A. *Journals and Reports*

1. *Ao Baptist Aroga Mungdang* (*ABAM*) Constitution, Mokokchung.
2. *American Baptist Foreign Mission* (*ABFM*) Report, Valley Forge, USA.
3. *Assam Mission Conference Proceedings* (*AMCP*) Guwahati.
4. *Constitution of the Nagaland Baptist Church Council* (*NBCC*) and Nagaland Missionary Movement.

B. *Books and Articles*

1. Albagh, D.M. 1935, *Between Two Centuries*, ABFMFS, Valley Forge.
2. Ao, W. Nokden, 1989, *Kept by the Power of God; The Story of My Life*, Published by the Author, Duncan Basty, Dimapur.
3. Barpujari H.K. 1986, *The American Missionaries and North East India*: 1836-1900 AD, Spectrum Publications, Guwahati.
4. Bowden, Henry, W. 1991, *American Indians and Christians Mission*: *Studies in Cultural Conflict*, Chicago History of American Religion Series (Ed) Martin E. Marty, University of Chicago Press.

5. Clark, M.M. 1978, *A Corner in India*, C.L.C. Guwahati (Reprint).
6. Colson, Elizabeth, 1970, 'Converts and Tradition: The Impact of Christianity on Valley Tonga Religion': *Southern Journal of Anthropology*.
7. Comaroff, Jean and John Comaroff, 1986, 'Christianity and Colonism in South Africa, '*American Ethnologist*, Vol. 13 (1).
8. Downs, Frederick, S. 1971, *The Mighty Works of God*: A Brief History of the Council of Baptist Churches in North East India: The Mission Period 1836-1950, Christian Literature Centre, Guwahati.
9. Downs, Frederick, S. 1973, *Christianity in North East India*, Christian Literature Centre, Guwahati.
10. Dozo, P. 1978, *The Growth of the Baptist Churches in Chakhesang Naga Tribe*, Nagaland Missionary Movement, Kohima.
11. Durkheim, Emile, 1969, *The Elementary Forms of Religious Life*, A Free Press Paperback, 1915, Sixth Printing.
12. Hicks, David, 1976, *Totum, Ghosts and Kin*: *Fieldwork in an Indonesian Community*, Explorations in World Ethnology, Series, Mayfield Publishing Co., Polo Alto, California.
13. Hobsbawm, E. 1989, *The Age of Empire*: *1875-1914*, Vintage Book, New York.
14. Lewis, I.M. 1986, *Religion in Context*: *Cult and Charisma*, Cambridge University Press.
15. Longkumer, N, 1988, *The Growth of Baptist Churches among the Aos of Nagaland*, Changtongya Baptist Church, Changtongya.
16. Mills, J.P. 1973, *The Ao Nagas*, Oxford University Press, Bombay (Reprint).
17. Nottingham, E.K. 1964, *Religion and Society*: *Studies in Sociology*, Randem House, New York.
18. Paden, William, E. 1988, *Religious World*: *A Comparative Study of Religions*, Beacan Press, Beston.
19. Pruett, Gordon, E. 1974, 'Christianity, History and Culture in Nagaland', *Contributions to Indian Sociology*, Nov. 1974.
20. Philip, P.T. 1983, *The Growth of Baptist Churches in Nagaland*, C.L.C. Guwahati (2nd Edition).
21. Puthanpurakal, J. 1984, *Baptist Missions in Nagaland*, Vondrome Missionological Institute, Shillong.
22. Rao, D.M. 1986, *Longri Ao*: *A Biography*, C.L.C. Guwahati.
23. Sangma, M.S. 1987, *History of American Mission in North East India*, Mittal Publications, Delhi.
24. Smith, W.C. 1925, *The Ao Naga Tribe of Assam*, Macmillan and Co., London.
25. Turner, Harold, 1977, *Living Tribal Religions*, World Lock Educational Ltd., London, 1971, Reprint.
26. Witvliet, Theo, 1985, '*A Place in the Sun*': *An Introduction to Liberation Theology in the Third World*, Orbis Books, New York.

4

Inequality and Stratification in the Hill States

It is a common knowledge that in the aftermath of 1857 Sepoy Revolt, the British evolved a strategy to look more closely at the structure of Indian society. In this endeavour, social evolution and racial distinction prevalent in the Victorian ethnography were liberally used to maintain difference rather than to attempt to create uniformity (Owen, R.: 1973: 236) in India. E.T. Dalton informs us how an ethnographic fair was organised in 1860s at Jubbalpore in the Central Provinces with specimen drawn from every caste and tribe of British India, who were to be measured and photographed for a 'scientific study'. And that's how the 'Descriptive Ethnography of Bengal' was published followed by series of publications on the castes and tribes of other provinces. The British Assam, stuck in the Eastern Himalayan backyard between the Patkai and the Arakan ranges, established some four decades later the 'Ethnography of Assam' series of monographs on individual tribes under the supervision of ethnographer-administrators. These ethnographically excellent monographs provided the rounded picture of the communities under study as if they were suspended in time and air. Among the many myths they helped to perpetuate is the claim that there was no inequality and social stratification among the tribes of the British Assam.

North East India as a region is well identified from geographical, historical and ethnic points of view. It is an extensive area with all possible ecological, economic and social formations. In spite of its relative isolation, centuries and decades have been encapsulated into years in terms of social change during the last fifty years for the region. The nature of state intervention in the region has induced a plethora of changes so silent and sudden that social scientists have not been able to document, not to talk of analysing them, adequately. Thus, considering the complexity of social situation, there is a lack of sophisticated and analytical literature on the region. Even the present paper does not propose to provide an exhaustive analysis of emerging social stratification in the region, as it is impossible to do so in the space allotted to. However, our endeavour is to examine the nature of regional social stratification in terms of inequality and class formation among the hill tribes of Arunachal, Nagaland, Mizoram and Meghalaya.

I

The North Eastern Region is well defined, spread in seven states of Arunachal Pradesh, Assam, Manipur, Meghalaya, Mizoram, Nagaland and Tripura forming 7.7 per cent of total Indian land space and 3.88 per cent of people within an area of 2.55 lakh square kilometres spread in 38,000 villages. About 90 per cent population lives in the rural areas and as much as 22.19 per cent of the total belong to the ethnic groups legally known as the scheduled tribes. While Assam has only 10.99 per cent tribals, Mizoram has 94.26 per cent, Nagaland 88.61 per cent, Meghalaya 80.84 per cent and Arunachal Pradesh 79.02 per cent and the total number of recognized tribes is 196. Among them only three—Garo, Khasi and Naga—have been studied in depth and there are monographs and books on another 22 tribes (Mann, R.S.: 1984: 32). There are various papers on different aspects of the tribal societies, but there is paucity of thematic and in-depth studies.

There had been internal ethnic push and pull within the region, but with emergence of British rule, by the end of 19th century, the territorial limits of various ethnic groups existing at the time were as if frozen. There have been studies which report that even the traditional slash-and-burn type of communal cultivation was not free from market forces. The British administration brought in a number of innovations for the near isolated tribal groups. Firstly, it was extension of a pattern of administration in which tribal systems were linked formally within an elaborate colonial rule resulting in the presence of armed forces even in the farthest corner. Secondly, Christian missionaries, with their Western medical knowledge and educational institutions, were allowed to introduce their evangelical activities. Thirdly, a number of administrative outposts were established first on the tribal fringes and then in the tribal heartlands and they were connected with a functional communication network linked to London, Calcutta and Shillong (Sinha, A.C. et. al.: 1993). Fourthly, market economy, with payments in cash, introduction of factory made cheap consumer goods and cash crops such as potato and fruits, purchase of raw materials, imposition of *house tax* and extension of regular markets and shops, effectively linked even the farthest tribal corners to the world-wide metropolitan economy. Moreover, the British did create a class of tribal 'notables' in the form of '*dobhashis*', '*Gaon buras*', *political interpreters* and *political jamadars* with formal recognitions. All these resulted in status differential even at the grass root level.

With emergence of independent India, two new aspects have been added to the above. Firstly, a conscious extension of state sponsored welfare and developmental activities as part of planned development of the backward and tribal regions was made as constitutional obligation. Secondly, politicization of the ethnic groups as part of participative democratic process led to emergence of ethnic consciousness ranging from insurgency to autonomy movements, to the carving out of the states on the ethnic criteria. All these resulted in the emergence of a new elite among the tribals first in the form of a little educated, Christian blue-coat wage earners and then an educated, accomplished and ambitious contractor-politician as political operators.

The areas of tribal concentration were enclaved during the British rule 'to reclaim to civilization' the tribes which had often rebelled or were difficult to pacify. It was in these enclaves that the concept of protection of the tribes as an ethnic community developed in stages. Its main features were: (a) the paternalistic rule of the district officers—the tribes needed a government by men and not by a system; (b) keeping tribal areas out of the regulations, laws, etc. which were alien to tribal ethos and undermined it; (c) laying down a set of simple rules to settle disputes, restriction of the jurisdiction of the courts which enforced normal laws, exclusion of the lawyers from courts; (d) special agrarian laws; (e) regulation of the entry of the aliens into tribal areas; and (f) strengthening tribal institutions and traditional leadership (Singh, K.S.: 1985: 9). Besides the above, the British, used to a hierarchical and a cephalous system, liberally labelled the unique ethnic institutions on the European pattern. Two instances may be cited from the North East Region: terming some of the village elders as the chiefs or headmen, even when the local communities did have such prescriptions; and terming some socio-economic institutions as slavery, even when the said ethnic groups were far removed from the classical feudal structure. Not for nothing some of the scholars rightly consider slavery in Arunachal as an inappropriate term to explain the social formation in question (Mishra, S.N.: 1983).

With the dawn of the British rule on the region, agricultural, horticultural and commercial innovations were made among the Khasis. It is claimed that David Scott (1786-1831) the agent of the Governor General in the North East Region, introduced cultivation of potato, tomato, maize, millet, wheat and fruits such as plum, peach and pear at Nongkhlaw and Mairang in 1820's. Henry Inglish's trading interests in the Khasi cinnamon, coal and lime mines further gave impetus to commercial transaction and introduction of cash crops among the Khasis. In this context contributions of two Khasi individuals active in the last quarter of the 19th century and the beginning of the 20th century must be acknowledged. Babu Jibon Roy (1838-1903), the Khasi pioneer of dynamism, was not only the first Khasi Extra Assistant Commissioner, but he also turned into a model of successful entrepreneur after his retirement from the Government service. As an author, editor, printer, businessman and a coal mine lease holder, he reminds one of the typical Bengali middle class aspirations, for a 'suitable and respectable' means of living. Many of these activities were further extended by an highly westernized, Rev. J.J.M. Nichols Roy (1884-1959), the doyen of emerging middle class and the father of the cooperative movement and fruit orchards in the Khasi Hills. However, "whatever the innovation was attempted in the form of terracing and introduction of potato cultivation, was on such a limited scale that it could hardly commercialize the hill economies" (Chaube, S.K.: 1983: 45).

But the above innovations and individual efforts did create, however, a feeble climate of restructuring of the Khasi society. The private proprietorship in land (*ri kynti*) was though not completely unknown in the past, but now the control of the land was oriented to take note of introduction of cash crops and opportunities of free trade, land was no more cultivated only for subsistence, but also for profit that could be earned by trading in cash and horticultural crops. The value of land had gone up and there was a tendency for individuals to occupy more and more and claim as much *raid* land as possible (Dutta, P.N.: 1983: 126). Moreover, in the wake of Christianity, traditional elders were losing much of their influence and hold on their kith and kin. Thus, it was convenient for the *bakhraws*—the patrician to turn into landlords after alienating and leasing out communal ownership to individual proprietorship on capitalist model.

The same symptom was noted from Nagaland. With the conversion to Christianity, "the tendency was to abolish abruptly the old thing and substitute individualism for strong community feeling which had enabled tribes to survive for so long. Not only was the individualism wrapped up with strong emphasis on personal salvation, it induced a direct and natural reaction against all things that mattered in village life and the social genius of the tribes. The result was a conflict between the interests of the community and the individual, which caused cultural tension in society" (Alemchiba, 1972: 479-480). What resulted in was an arrested break-up of tribal society and a tendency of a near feudal relationship of production. Hence, the middle class that finally emerged among the Nagas and its roots neither in the landed aristocracy nor did it evolve through a commercial development. The growth of this class in Nagaland was inextricably linked with the spread of Western education, primarily at the initiative of the Christian Missionaries and rise of professions ranging from teaching to law, to medicine. And, not surprisingly, it was from this very Khonoma (Angami) village (where tendency for the growth of private property in land was the strongest) that a number of middle class leaders ranging from Z.A. Phizo (1903-1989) to Vizol emerged. Yet it was not Angamis, but the Aos, who as a tribe came to exercise a greater influence in the first decade of this century. This can be linked with the fact that it was the Aos, who were the first among the tribes to be exposed to Christianity and Western education of which they made the most (Mishra, U.: 1983: 126).

Normally, age, sex and kinship have been the criteria of social differentiation among the tribals and they have been projected as a rounded, homogenous and economically simple and politically stable communities as per culturological approach. Their origin, migration, kinship affiliation, animism, youth dormitories, social order and other exotic aspects are emphasized. Invariably, there relations with the neighbouring communities, political formations, administrative arrangements and political suppression and economic differentiation and exploitation have been ignored. Meiteis, Ahoms, Dimansa, Koch, Jaintias and Tripuris have been significant communities of the region, which do not fit in the above moulds. They evolved their state systems and elaborate social stratification and a level of economic specialization leading to enough surplus to support their state structures (Sinha, S.C.: 1987). Khasis and Jaintias developed their own ranking and political order based on their production system and trading ties across their boundaries. Mizos, Semas, Konyaks, Wanchus, Noctes had their chieftainships, which did not transfer themselves into state systems. Garos, Karbis, Angamis, Aos, Apa Tanis possessed a type of social differentiation, which was not strong enough institution to pave the way for emergence of chieftainship or state systems. North-western corner of the region had communities such as Monpa and Sherdukpens, whose social order is based on Lamaist theocracy in which significance of monasteries is all pervasive.

Roy Burman felt that the inter-tribal relationship could be explained in terms of some communities functioning as buffer or the bridge across the ethnic divides in the region (Roy Burman: 1972). While discussing the issues of stratification among the various tribes of the region, some points need to be kept in mind. Firstly, there have been relatively autonomous tribal communities in relation to domination and subordination in terms of power, control of resources and marital alliances. For example, small tribes such as Khoa (Bugun) and Sulung (Pui) were claimed to be Akas' and Daflas' (Nishis) slaves (Mishra, B.P.: 1982: 44). Angamis claimed to have a number of satellite Angami and non-Angami villages. Part of the Garos were integrated into the feudal system prevalent in the adjoining Mymensingh and Goalpara districts. Secondly, against the prevailing notion of tribal egalitarianism, there had been incipient class formation associated with free and un-paid labour, claim over resources and marital preferences. Such social formations range from near feudal structure such as Ahoms, Tripuris, Jaintias, etc. to chieftainship of Konyaks to division of society into patrician and plebeian as among the Apa Tanis and Khasis. It may be instructive to present the regional ethnic scenario in terms of status inequality:

Communities	Social Differentiation	
1. Akas	i. Khulo—slaves identified with Khoa (Buguns) and Sulung (Pui)	
	ii. Commoners—free tribesmen	
2. Angami	i. Slaves	
Ao and Rongma	ii. Free tribesmen	
3. Apa Tanis	i. *Mate, Mite—Guth*—patricians	
	ii. *Mura, Guchi*—slave—commoners	
4. Daflas (Nishis)	i. *Nera*—male slaves	Identified with Sulung
	ii. *Pane*—female slaves	
	iii. *Atto*—masters	
5. Gallongs	i. *Mipak*—slaves	
	ii. Free tribesmen	
6. Garos	i. *Nokoba*—free tribesmen	
	ii. Nokol—slaves	
7. Jaintias	i. *Raja-Syiem* (King)	
	ii. *Pators/Dolois*—Syiem's Governors(?)	
	iii. *Wahen Chnong*—village headmen	
	iv. *Langdoh*—priests	
	v. *Myntires*	categories of officials
	vi. *Laskars*	
	vii. *Sangtot*	
	viii. *Maji*	
	ix. Commoners or free tribesmen	
8. Khasis	i. *Bakhraw-batri*—Nobility (Patricians ?)	
	ii. *Paidbah-Paidkar*—plebeians or laity	
9. Khamtis	i. Chiefs	Feudal—incipient elements
	ii. Priests	
	iii. Commoners	
	iv. Slaves	

10. Miji-Dammais	i.	*Nyubhu*—free tribesmen
	ii.	*Nyullu*—inferior or carriers of loads
	iii.	Sulungs—as their alleged slaves
11. Mishmi	i.	Chiefs—wealthy and influential
	ii.	Commoners—Indebted, wage earners
12. Monpa	i.	*Ki*—highest class—aristocracy around sacred priests and chiefs
	ii.	*Muimo*—commoners
	iii.	*Kharmu*—the lowest class—slaves—butchers etc.
13. Mizos	i.	*Lals*—Chiefs
	ii.	*Uppas*—Chief's councillors
	iii.	*Bawi—Chungte*—Semi serfs
14. Nocte	i.	*Kepi* or *Lowang Jat*—Chiefs and chiefs kinsmen
	ii.	Commoners
15. Sema	i.	*Kekami*—Chiefs
	ii.	*Chockomi*—Chief's associates
	iii.	*Mughamis*—Orphans or commoners
	iv	*Akakhemi*—Chief's dependents
	v.	*Anukeshimi*—Chief's field cultivators
16. Sherdukpens	i.	*Thongs*—Aristocrats
	ii.	*Chhaos*—slaves and poters
17. Singhphos	i.	*Ddufan*—royalty or aristocracy
	ii.	*Chingmung*—*Mreng-dong*—commoners
	iii.	*Mayem*—Descendants of non-Singhpho progenitors
18. Tagin	i.	*Nibu*—Priests
	ii.	*Nite*—Richmen
	iii.	*Open*—Poor
	iv.	*Nyara*—slave
19. Tangkhuls	i.	*Aungma*—Chiefs
	ii.	Commoners
20. Tangsa	i.	*Regalantumo*—Chiefs
	ii.	*Binasa*—Servants—slaves—commoners
21. Wangcho	i.	*Wangham*—Chiefs
	ii.	*Wangpan*—commoners
	iii.	*Wangsha*—Progeny of Wansha father and Wangpan mother.

II

In the traditional Garo society land utilization for shifting cultivation and for homestead plots was considered to be the property of the 17 lineages (*mahary*). This territorial possession of the mahari was and is still known as the *a'king* and area is demarcated by natural boundaries. The right of management of the *a'king* is vested on a particular family, of which the principal female belongs to the owner-lineage. This family is known as *nokma* (the principal household). However, the term *nokma* is commonly used to indicate the principal male of the *nokma* household, whose position in the village polity is just like the position of a constitutional head of a state. G.D. Walker, the Deputy Commissioner of Garo Hills, granted documents of possession to all the *nokmas* of Garo Hills alongwith some Koch *nokmas*. The husband acquires the right of management of the *a'king* by virtue of the marriage to the female representing the *a'king* owning lineage. His lineage acquires a right to send a male member of his clan to the *nokma* household from generation to generation. In this way, they select one of the sisters' sons of the principal male of the household in the following generation. The man of the principal male's lineage zealously guard the right to send a representative to the *nokma* household and any contravention of this rule is liable to break or atleast cause some disorder in the *nokma* household. "Of late the principal of land ownership at the lineage level has changed to a great extent as a result of the following factors: (i) introduction of garden crops like pineapples, oranges, etc., (ii) occupation of land by Nepali graziers, (iii) adoption of permanent cultivation and (iv) expansion of urban areas". (Majumdar, D.N.: 1986: 125-127).

The customary law of the Khasis empower every member of the village or *raid* or *elaka* to claim his right of use and occupancy of the *ri raid* land without payment of land revenue for the land itself. Such claims are limited to actual use and occupancy; the land cannot be left uncared for more than three consecutive years after which it is to revert to the *raid*. In this way, the occupancy of the *raid* land is purely temporary for seasonal cultivation devoid of proprietary, heritable or trasferable rights. On the other hand, *ri kynti* or lands "set apart from the founding of the *elaka* for certain clans upon whom were bestowed the proprietary, heritable or transferable rights over such lands. They also include any part of *ri raid* lands which at later times were bestowed upon a person or a family or a clan for certain yeoman's service rendered to the *elaka*" (*Report of the Land Reforms Commission* (L.R.C.): 1974: 18). *Ri kynti* land is broadly divided into two: ancestral and self-acquired. However, the L.R.C. identified over a dozen varieties of *ri kynti* lands.

A critical view of the above traditional provisions indicates that "the roots of a stratified society with all its socio-economic and socio-political potentialities were present. This provided the real force behind the transformation of a latent differentiation into a manifest one within a decade after the coming of the British." Because "(a) the ruler of a Khasi state must belong to the *Jait Syiem* and the electoral college to elect the ruler consist of the *bakhraw batri* (the founders of the village/the noble men), (b) the whole Khasi society may be classified in broad terms into two categories: (i) the *bakhraw batri* or the noble men on one side (who paid no land revenue or any other type of tax and were generally the co-partners of the *syiem* in matters of administration) and (ii) the *paidbah-paidkar* or the masses (who were to pay entry and protection fee to the state). In the eyes of the people, *ri-kynti* rights were available to only those that were connected with the *jait syiem* and were prepetuated with the aid of state power and the *jait bakhraws* were the first to create a *ri kynti* for themselves" (Dutta, P.S.: 1989: 65).

What resulted from the incipient inequality gets reflected through the control of the most vital economic resources, the land. A study conducted in 1972 in a wet paddy cultivating village found 22 per cent households controlling 70 per cent of the village land, 54 per cent households controlled only 30 per cent of the land as much as 24 per cent households had no land to cultivate, turning them into landless labourers (Vincent, K.: 1978: 185). The above picture gets further clarified after Mathew and Nair's more elaborate and systematic study of the changing mode of production in Meghalaya (Mathew, T. and Nair, S.: 1983). The study covered 20 Khasi-Jaintia villages, besides another 31 Meghalayan villages, led to some significant conclusions: (i) As much as 61.89 per cent cultivators practised settled cultivation, 21.05 per cent were engaged in shifting cultivation and 17.05 per cent had a mixed types of above two cultivations, (ii) Signs of land lease market in its rudimentary form were discernible. Two factors responsible for that were identified. Firstly, the areas where population pressure had reduced the land man ratio, tribals with small plots of land or no land, lease in additional land for cultivation. Secondly, non-tribal immigrants, who have neither customary nor legal rights in land, lease in land as a desperate survival strategy, very often at an exorbitant rent. (iii) Though the bulk of the "hired labour" in Meghalayan agriculture was found to be a modified form of exchange, a certain number of landless agricultural labourers were found as rural proletariat. They basically consisted of immigrants from other regions such as Bihar, Nepal and Bangladesh and were denied of access of land by customary law as well as legislation. (iv) The production relations of a feudal type was emerging in certain areas of the state. The landless non-tribal immigrants are forced to enter the land-lease market, accepting very often highly unfavourable terms which gave rise to various kinds of extra-economic extractions. Such practices act as a fore-runner to the emergence of a land market and diffentiation of the peasantry in future.

Binay Lahiri, an activist of the peasant mobilization for decades and a keen observer of the rural scene in Meghalaya, concludes his study: (i) Though different classes in tribal society have emerged, the process of class polarization has not yet started and class consciousness is at the lowest level. That is why in Khasi villages even though there are instances of several class struggles, but ultimately such agrarian conflicts are resolved in favour of elite by intervention of *bakhraws*. (ii) Different strata of peasantry—rich, middle, poor and landless labour—have sprung up and feudal land relations with absolute landlordism has developed. Share cropping is rampant. In spite of the recommendations of the L.R.C., no cadestral survey of land and land records have been undertaken. There are no statutory provisions for protecting the rights of share-croppers and no clear stipulation regarding the mode of share-cropping leading to eviction from the land. (iii) New class of rich consisting of politicians, higher bureaucrats, contractors and lease holders have emerged as new bourgeoise, who invest their money in land (Lahiri, B.: 1986).

A characteristic feature of the customary tenure system is the absence of the concept of land as a marketable commodity and any distinction between community ownership of land and the rights of an individual or group to occupy and use a piece of land at any given point within the framework of the rights of the community as a whole. Taking land based social differentiation as a reality, Dutta pleads: "In other states where tribals are in a minority and live in a non-tribal milieu, land reform measures have long been initiated. But the paradox here is that the state with a tribal majority and tribals having monopoly political rights in the state, there is no initiative worth mentioning, in matters concerning abolition of intermediary rights security to tenants or fixation of land ceiling or restrictions on money-lending. Even while the different state governments enacted laws restricting the operations of the greedy and crafty private money-lenders, in Meghalaya there is neither any overt protest against it nor any initiative taken by the government on its own to tackle this" (Dutta, P.S.: 1992: 76).

III

During the Sailo chieftainship among the Mizos elementary principle of heirarchy was introduced. The line of social demarcation between chief, *Zalan, Bawi* (slaves) and the commoners was thin and often the kin relationship filtered to the commoners. Yet a notion of purity of blood of a chief by tracing descent from another significant chief was considered a strategy for establishing superiority. At the time of the British occupation of Mizoram in the last decade of the 19th century, the realms of the Mizo chiefs (fluid authority over an extensive area) were distributed into western Sailo, eastern Sailo. Towlongs and Kairuma chiefs. Superiority of the Sailo chiefs was because of political power attained over a period of time and their insistence in making the chieftainship hereditary. A chief's power for raids and warfare depended upon grain storage, kin relation and strong and brave followings. At last the whole concept of chief's realm got concretized by the British land settlement in 1898-99 and a rigid territorial administrative concept was introduced. J. Shakespear, the Deputy Commissioner of the Lushai Hills District, strongly advocated to administer the district through the chiefs, rather then to govern without them. He recommended educating the sons of the chiefs, but was opposed to the chiefs' power in forming new villages. In spite of the British ambivalence, the chiefs helped the British to raise 'Labour Corps' and signed a 'Voluntary Bond' for resistance to the Japanese forces during the World War II. However, it were the Mizos themselves who finally removed chiefs from seats of power by paying monetary compensation under the Lushai Hills District Acquisition of Chiefs' Rights Act, 1954. Chiefs' last role was to help in the growth of unrest in Mizoram (Goswami, B.B.: 1987: 321).

Chiefs appointed *Upa* (their assistants) from among their clansmen to assist them in matters of administration and justice and who were exempted from cooly duty. *Ramhual* (agricultural experts), *Zalen* (the customary reserver of the chiefs in distress), *Tlangua* (village crier) and the *Thirdeng* (blacksmiths) were appointed by the chiefs for specific functions and were exempted from cooly duty. The commoners (*Hnamchawn*) received land from the chiefs in return of *fathang* (paddy tax), *sachwiah* (a share of every animal killed or trapped to the chief), *chichhia* (chiefs' due on salt collected from the wells), *salam* (fines imposed on villagers as part of judicial proceedings) and could migrate to another village, if dissatisfied with the chief (Goswmi, B.B.: 1977). Orphans and widows in distress, criminals and war deserters taking shelter with the chiefs were the slaves (*bawi*) for the chiefs only. The Mizo Union, the first political party in Mizoram, came to existence on April 9, 1946, launched anti-chief civil disobedience movement against the privileges of chiefs, *ramhuals* and *zalens* and abolition of *sachhia* and *fathang*. The anti-chief movement succeeded after about a decade with the abolition of the chieftainship, but within another decade armed insurgency ensued, which ended in 1986 with signing of an accord between the insurgents and the government. In the process two decades between 1966 and 1986 cannot be considered as a normal period of social development.

The Council of Ministers, the Government of Mizoram, decided on November 24, 1984, a significant policy for rural development in Mizoram. Its salient features were the following: (i) That the Government of Mizoram shall take measures so that area under *jhum* shall be brought down progressively and it should be reduced to atleast 25 per cent of the present level at the end of the 7th Five Year Plan period. *Jhumming* in the traditional system in the form of distribution of *jhum* land by village council shall be completely abolished by 1994. (ii) Land areas other than the village lands and the lands allotted to individual families for permanent development of cultivation will remain natural, preserved and protected forests. The villagers will not be deprived of the right to use forest produce from such forests for their personal requirements, but not for commercial purpose. (iii) On the basis of the capacity of individual family to utilise land with available assistance by the Government and survey being made, suitable land will be allotted to individual rural families for permanent cultivation and utilization. (iv) A written understanding will be obtained from the head of every family to whom land is allotted on permanent basis that he and his family will not take up any other land for *jhumming*.

In pursuance with the above "Land-use Policy" the government propose to take measures and adopt operational procedures: (i) All existing land under Wet Rice Cultivation (WRC) shall be identified and surveyed. (ii) Land suitable for conversion to WRC will be identified and surveyed which will include land under individual ownership, but not utilised for WRC. (iii) The present owners of lands suitable for WRC, who failed to make use of such lands will be given one year time to develop and make use of the lands failing which either their passes will be cancelled or the land may be acquired by the government to be allotted to deserving families. (iv) The area of land to be allotted to individual rural families will depend on the capacity of such family to make use of the land and also the availability of assistance from government and financial institutions. (v) Land will be allotted to individual families at first instance on lease basis for a period of ten years and during this period no transfer or sale of the land will be permitted by the government. Permanent allotment will be given only after the land is utilised by the family for the purpose of which it was allotted (*Rural Development in Mizoram*, 1985: 33-37).

Only 3.1 per cent of the total land is under cultivation in Mizoram of which only 0.47 per cent is under permanent cultivation. Santals were brought in for teaching plough cultivation and Angamis to educate the Mizos terracing in the early years of the

British administration. In this way, terracing of the undulating *jhum* sites has been one of the attractive propositions of agricultural development in Mizoram. It is apparent from the above document that the decision makers have singularly opted for privatisation of land. After the statehood, the government is making available opportunities through the planning process to earn a huge amount of money for a select group of people engaged in contract works for different public constructions as well as lucrative border trading. This huge amount of "money will be left with no alternative but to enter into the agrarian sector where it will face no challenge from others (as land can be owned only by the Mizos). This will encourage and enhance the process of concentration of land in fewer hands either openly or in disguise. This will in return give rise to new economics classes of owners (and tenants) and agricultural labourers (Dutta, P.S.: 1986). In this way, in place of an incipient tribal stratification, abolished some four decades back, a new stratification based on landed gentry, professionals and neo-rich contractor-politicians is on way among the Mizos.

IV

The Angami agriculture was based on intricate and dexterous terracing of the hill slopes and indigenous water management devices. Even in 1874 they were found to till their terrace fields unlike their neighbours. The rights of the individuals to property in land are recognised, rules relating to inheritance and partition to such property are settled strictly as per customary law. Among the Angamis, land especially permanent terraced cultivated one, is freely sold and bought, there being no difficulty in selling a terraced field than in selling a pig or a cow. "The standard for measurement for Nagaland is not area, but the number of loads of paddy that it yields. Terraced rice land is both sold and let . . . An acre of rice land near Khonoma . . . sold as much as Rs. 600 . . . but it can be bought for about 1/3rd of that sum (also). An acre of terrace rice land lets from Rs. 3 to Rs. 9 a year according to quality, while an acre of *jhum* land can be rented for two seasons . . . for a rupee and a half . . . (though) the absence of any system of measurement renders the exact pitch of these rents a little doubtful" (Allen, B.C.:

1981: 51-52) wrote B.C. Allen, the author of the Gazetteer in the first decade of the present century. The *jhumming*, which is quite secondary in importance among the Angamis, is based on individual's clan based rights. The portion of the *jhum* land, which has not been brought under the private rights, cannot be sold except by the clan itself.

It was reported that a thousand Angami Nagas visited Nowgong to trade salt and beads in 1848. The Mezdiphema region had been producing a type of cotton, which was used for producing the famous Angami shawls, which was also bartered and was available for sale as well. The Angami farmers had special attractions to Khamkiri village (literal meaning iron tree in Lhota) near northern foothills from where they used to procure little bit of iron for spearheads, etc. They used to trade their *mithun* (bos frontaslis), cotton, shawls, occasionally ivory, with salt, dried fish, shell beads across the Angami country. They could also visit the markets in the foothills to exchange their cotton and ginger with that of minor articles such as trinkets etc. "The most of the business is transacted on a cash basis and there is very little barter. The principal trading communities are the residents of Khonoma, Jotsoma, Mozema and Visema . . . (and) will go as far as a field as Bombay . . . (for) carrying beads . . . There are no such things as village markets (Allen, B.C.: 1981: 59).

For the Nagas forest has been closely linked to their economy. Besides *jhumming* it provided them with building materials for dwelling houses, provided opportunity for hunting, bringing food as meat, and for collecting honey and edible leaves as vegetables. Ownership of forest comprised (a) individually owned forests, (b) *khel* forests, (c) clan forests and (d) village forests. The British administration appreciated the customary rights of the people in forests through the Chin Hills Regulation, 1896 and the Regulation III of the Naga Hills Jhum Land Regulation, 1946. The provisions of the above Regulations were further supplemented by the Nagaland Jhum Land Acts, 1970 and 1979. The ideas concerning property (*puckinyi*) among the Angamis vary according to the nature of property and types of ownership involved. All villages have distinct boundaries, which are normally streams or rivulets. The village territories contain terraced fields and *jhum* fields, fallow land, bush and forest lands. There is no land in the village without an owner and there is no villager without some land for certain uses. Even irrigation channels (*dzuye*) are owned by individuals, families and lineages (Das, N.K.: 1987: 133-37).

In spite of an impression of egalitarianism, inequality was reflected through unequal share of power, prestige and wealth in traditional Naga set-up. Wealth in the form of rice (for staple food and formenting beer), *mithuns*, pigs and other animals (for meat) were greatly sought after. These acquisitions were mediated through which ambitious men could acquire status of *big men* and leadership, and secure various levels of alliances. The *feast of merit* through which perishable surplus food was redistributed, had a social function to secure symbolic prestige and honoured alliances during the wars and peace. A series of a dozen such feasts were in practice among the Angamis suggesting gradual promotion of the status to the feast givers.

It is interesting to know the various circles of the people entitled for such communal feasts. There were stages of the feasts in which the people were invited in the following order: (i) one's own lineage members, (ii) clan members, (iii) clan members of the self and wife, (iv) all members of the various clans of the village, (v) the members of the clans in the village from the neighbouring villages and (vi) the entire segment of the tribe to which the person belonged. In this complicated schemes of distribution, three main sets of people received meat: one, the kinsfolk, another, the performers of various rituals and services, and third, those who had given such feasts in the past. The persons belonging to the last set were specially honoured and, in this way, the feast giver used to stake his claim of status among select '*men at the top*' through a free use of perishable wealth (Das, N.K.: 1987: 109).

Furer-Haimendorf vividly describes the institution of the sacred chiefs among the Konyaks as it existed in 1930's. "These powerful village chiefs, such as the great Ang of Mon and the great Ang of Chi, have sacred blood of the chiefs, pure and undiluted, in their veins. There can be no more exclusive community than that of the great Ang clan, for as the kings of Egypt kept the royal blood pure by marrying their own sisters, so the great Angs take their wives from their own Great Ang Clan, and it is only the children of such a union that acquire the fathers rank" (Furer-Haimendorf, C. Von, 1968: 104). Similarly Hutton reports that the Sema chiefs, who found their villages or succeeded their fathers and owned the entire land of their administered villages.

After a gap of more than 30 years Furer-Haimendorf visited the Konyaks and recorded the transformation (Furer-Haimendorf, C. Von, 1976: 326). "One of the most heart-warming experiences of my stay in Mon was the visit of Chingai of Oting, the veteran *dobhashi* (Konyak Naga chief and interpretor to the British administrators), who thirty-four years earlier had been my constant companion on my visits to villages of the Thendu group. He had clearly prospered and now occupied a modern bungalow in the district headquarters . . . had a new and attractive Ao wife and three sons and two daughters from that marriage. His new wife was a teacher and she and the children spoke English. Chingai acted as not only a valuable middle man between the administration and villages, where he had influence, but seemed to engage also in various profitable business enterprises. His house was well furnished in Western style; and his sons and daughters had received a modern education."

He ran into at Tang village an ex-insurgent turned contractor, who claimed to profit Rs. 13,000 from a road contract of Rs. 20,000. His another encounter was with a commoner, elected to the *Area Council*, in the local state administration and a protogonist of modernization, who was converted to Christianity by an Ao teacher some five years earlier. The beginning of an erosion of the authority of the Great Angs was noticeable in all the villages. The Government officials treated the chiefs with courtesy and considerations, but found it convenient to work with men of more progressive ideas, who were intent in building up their position in the system of elected village representatives. The present generation of villagers pay respect of the Angs, but the school going children were not expected to do so. These Angs were nominated by the Deputy Commissioners of the District as the *Gaonburas,* the Government recognized village headmen. He passed through a road side washing place where water was flowing out of three iron pipes, a feature unknown thirty years ago.

Further, he found the path lined with bamboo indicating that surrounding bamboos and forests were private property of the individuals, unheard of earlier in a Konyak village. Rich people maintained rice grainaries for giving on loans on various social occasions. Semi-educated young people were found to be idle even during the rush time of rice harvest. Wage labour at the rate of Rs. 15 to Rs. 20 was a new innovation. He also mentioned a former *dobhashis*'s Christian and contractor grand-son, dressed in shirts and trousers, who did not appear to have ever done any manual work and whose brother was minister in the state Government. In the village of Shillong with 637 persons with as much as 35 were employed as the government servants. That ensured the flow of cash into the household budgets, which explain the villagers' ability to buy numerous factory produced consumer goods.

The social scene from the western part of Nagaland saw the same phenomena much earlier. Zubza, an Angami village on the highway from Dimapur to Imphal, had rich farmers, poor peasants, landless labourers and wage earners in 1970's. The village had three types of peasants: (i) rich farmers—big land owners—of orchards and *jhum* lands, (ii) small land owners—terraced and *jhum* fields and (iii) the landless labourers. The rich farmers used power tillers, improved seeds, chemical and organic manures and produced surplus cereal and horticultural products for the market. Introduction of advanced technology required capital investment and entrepreneurial skills. Land had turned into a commodity and transfer on a considerable scale had created a land market. Thus, "clear-cut differences based on wealth are now emerging in some areas on account of various factors such as steady transformation in quality of land, dependence on orchards and the new crops. Various ways to diversify ways of earning money and increasing participation in the larger market economy are a result of direct impact of micro economic processes on traditional subsistence economy" (Das, N.K.: 1989: 161).

The more enterprising highlanders especially the neo-rich contractor-cum-politicians and even some bureaucrats—have bought big farm lands in the low-lying foothills for paddy and cash cropping. They themselves stay away to Kohima, Dimapur or elsewhere and assigned their less endowed kinsmen for managing the farms. On such farms invariably the *Mias* (the Muslims from Manipur valley or Nowgong district of Assam) are employed as farm hands on annual basis. It so happens that the *Mias* (or the Meiteis from Manipur, Nepalis and Bengali immigrants and even some Assamese) come annually before the plantation season to the respective land owners, who provide them with huts for their shelter; make provision for their food; and they are given implements, seeds, manure etc. for the cultivation. All these amenities are extended to the share croppers on deferred payment. When the crops are harvested the share croppers get 1/4 or 1/3 of the crops as their labour from which the advances paid to them are deducted. They are supposed to sell the paddy to the land owners at the existing market price and then they go to their native place with some sacks of grains and some amount of money with a view to returning to the same master for the next year. Thus, this exploitative cycle continues year after year (Sinha, A.C.: 1989: 207-208).

V

The Government of India invited Furer-Haimendorf in 1944-45 and Lt. Col. Graham Betts in 1948-49 for exploratory ethnographic survey of Balipara Frontier district of Arunachal Pradesh resulting in first reliable ethnography of the region (Furer Haimendorf, C. Von, 1956; Betts, U.G.: 1963). Since then Haimendorf has been visiting the region off and on providing running commentaries on the social transformation on the base of almost 'static' structure of 1944 (Furer-Haimendorf, C. Von, 1962; 1980; 1982). One of his chapters is entitled "patricians and slaves" and another one after examining the issues of "social structure" refers to "the position of slaves." One need not go in enthropogenic details over here. However, certain points need to be reiterated. Firstly, Nocte, Wanchu and Khamtis had the practice of 'sacred chiefs' almost on the pattern of the Konyak Angs. Secondly, an institution of slavery was extensively reported from all over Arunachal Pradesh and greater part of Nagaland. Thirdly, Apatanis like the Angamis were one of the few settled wet-paddy cultivators within the hills, who had developed an elaborate agrarian social structure . Fourthly, the marginal peasants on the *jhum* cultivation used to supplement their economy by hunting and collecting petty, trading and raiding neighbouring communities. Lastly, the administration except for occasional exploratory and punitive expeditions left the Arunachalis in 'splendid isolation'. The ethnographers have been reporting an idlic life of the tribal social scene as basically egalitarian with some status differentiation. However, four decades long state intervention has resulted in an extensive restructuring of the Arunachalis' life.

As early as 1962 Haimendorf had indicated the direction of change among the Apa Tanis. The former slaves began to receive cash wages at the rate of Rs. 2, surplus rice was sold against cash payment to Nishis (Daflas), shops and tea stalls were opened, the valley was linked to the Brahmaputra valley with a motor road and an administrative outpost was established among them at Zero (Furer-Haimendorf, C. Von, 1962: 154-161). He restudied the Apa Tanis in 1978 and published a suggestive title, *A Himalayan Tribe: From Cattle to Cash* (1980). In traditional Apa Tani society a man's prestige and influence depended mainly on the issue of his land holding, which could be exchanged against *mithan*. By 1970 half an acre of paddy land on an advantageous side could fetch as much as Rs. 40,000 (p. 37). Consequently, landlessness and capitalist trend in land holding were in practice along with share cropping, wage labour and land tenancy. Between the former patricians and commoners a patron-client relationship was taking shape. Though some commoners emerged as socially and politically important, the majority of the political leaders, prominent businessmen and contractors were patricians and their pre-eminence was probably due to their family fortunes.

In place of traditional *buliang* (arbiters of tribal law and the upholders of tribal justice), the Government had nominated red coat wearing *gaon buras* (village headmen) as grass root level formal functionaries. There had been a series of court cases involving land disputes. As many as 15 Apa Tanis were occupying gazetted and 342 non-gazetted government posts earning between Rs. 130 and Rs. 225 a month each in 1978. Of late education has emerged as a good investment for the Apa Tanis, who even sell their land for educating their children. It was considered prestigeous to have an educated member of the family, who could rise in business, politics or well-paid government job. Many of the patricians have turned into successful shopkeepers, businessmen and contractors. Instead of past practice of ritual distruction of one's wealth with a view to humiliating an opponent and vindicating one's honour, the Apa Tanis have acquired now the reputation of skillful enterprising traders and even wholesalers. Though *mithuns* are still owned as a measure of prestige (and as many as 1000 *mithuns* were owned by the Apa Tanis in 1978), as many as 1200 tribesmen had current account with a balance upto Rs. one lakh at the local branch of the State Bank of India in 1978.

Examining 'the economic base' of the Arunachalis, as a whole, Haimendorf makes certain observations: Arunachal has ideal conditions for slash-and-burn cultivation; but in recent years the ratio between population and available land has changed leading to the shortage of land among the Nishis and Wanchu (Furer-Haimendorf, C. Von, 1982: 37-38). However, still the problem can be solved among the Wanchu, who though shifting cultivators, had individual rights in land and could both hire and purchase land from those who had a surplus (p. 43). Change has occurred in terms of payment for *mithun* and *pigs*, which were priced at Rs. 1500 and Rs. 400 each in 1980 (p. 45). In their hours of crisis, the hillmen had to sell their own labour and turn into wage labourers (p. 49). Enterprising Apa Tanis traders reported to purchase old beads and Tibetan metals valuables from 'modernized' Nishis (p. 59) as a future investment for possible trading. Arunachalis had a tradition of having multiple wives, which still continues by the educated persons, who leave the senior and ill-educated wives, for attending to agriculture, etc. in the village and keep another, more educated one with them at the capital of the state to act as hostesses (p. 80).

As a whole wide-ranging social and political relations have replaced the former encapsulation of tiny tribal groups. Some Nishi politicians have become wealthy by doing business in the field of public transport and supply of controlled commodities such as petrol and kerosene (p. 126). The greater part of the cultivable Monpa land is either privately owned or held on lease by individuals (p. 157). Monpas are broadly divided into three social status groups: the highest (Bhapu and Sherchipa), middle (Bagipa, Tsongkapa, Tukshipa, Bonyakpa) and lowest (Merakpa and Shermu). Intermarriage among these classes are not permitted and the members of the lowest class cannot rise to become monks or nuns and work as sweepers in the monasteries (p. 160). The Buddhist communities of Kameng district referred in the past as the bridge and buffer (Roy Burman, B.K.: 1972), have shown a remarkable awareness of the outside world with rapid improvement in communication. Modern education and extension of the regular administration has led to emergence of a secular elite rivelling the clerics (p. 176). For certain status conscious Arunachalis such as the Khamtis, presence of outside ethnic groups such as Nepalese provide continuation of the old master-servant relationship in the changed situation in which slaves have been freed (Sarkar, J.K.: 1987: 189).

VI

Reviewing the writings on the agrarian scene in the region, Karna finds: (a) Broadly, the studies have failed to examine the agrarian problems in historical background which a *sine qua non* of understanding agrarian class relations in a changing economy; (b) Exaggerated importance attached to the geographical and ecological factors of agricultural backwardness has thrown the whole question of institutional transformation into the background; (c) Inherent structural impediments of the customary land tenure systems which essentially go against the interests of the tillers of soil receive very casual treatment; (d) The portrayal of the traditional social structure in terms of the harmony of interests continues throughout overlooking the role of new socio-economic forces which are at work in the country side; (e) That the problems of land reform and agrarian change have not received adequate attention is natural within the framework of arguments currently in vogue. The advocates of agricultural development in the north east will under the circumstances help the upper layer of the peasantry, since the benefits of development cannot percolate to the poorer sections as it is planned within the framework of an outdated agrarian structure; (f) The picture of the N.E. country-side as presented by these studies, is 'more mythical than real'. The peasantry no longer suffers from passivity and over-tolerance. Half-hearted reform measures instead of solving problems have forced it to 'shake off its attitude of resignation.' It has already adopted the path of resistance in different parts of the region. Unfortunately, this rural dynamics is yet to be taken into account (Karna, M.N.: 1982: 160-61).

On the basis of the above presentation certain broad generalizations may be made:

Firstly, a number of hill communities such as Khasi, Mizo, Angami, Sema, Konyak, Wanchu, Apa-Tani, Monpa had a tradition of social differentiation (Aier, L.A.: 1985), private property, individual ownership of land, forests, animals etc. Such practices, which have been accorded constitutional approval as part of the tribal customary rights, have of late eroded the claimed tribal solidarity as equalitarian system and provided impetus to social inequality.

Secondly, it were the progenies of the Khasi *bakhraw*, Mizo Sailos, Apa Tani patricians, Konyak, Sema, Wanchu chiefs and Naga *dobhashis*, who emerged first as a rudimentary middle class and then provided their communities with an incipient upper strata.

Thirdly, post-independence period in the lives of the hill communities brought in the concepts of planned development and the welfare schemes resulting in flow of substantial cash effecting traditional barter system adversely. Since secondary sector of production is not available to the hill communities in an appreciable way, most of their savings are being invested in land, turning the communal control into private property.

Fourthly, emergence of private landed property has resulted into a number of associated trends found in the laissez faire economy. Among them mention may be made of absentee landlordism, wage labour, share cropping, landless labour, agrarian tensions and exploitation. Benefits of various welfare and rural development schemes (Ao, A.L.: 1993) do not invariably reach the grass root.

Finally, in place of the traditional tribal 'notables' an aggressive set of neo-rich contractor-politician elite has emerged as the most significant power wielders among the hill communities. They have positioned themselves between their communities and the outer world as the most articule spokesmen and mediators of the conflicting interest. The real underdog among the tribals have no spokesmen as they are sandwiched between the fast vanishing traditional system and a still born welfare state.

References

1. Aier, I.L., 1985: 'Contemporary Naga Social Formation and Ethnic Identity: A Case of Development or Decay', Ph.D. thesis, M.S.S., Dept. of Sociology, NEHU, Shillong.
2. Allen, B.C., 1905: *District Gazetteer of Naga Hills and Manipur*, Gian Publications, New Delhi (Reprint) 1981.
3. Ao, A.L., 1993: '*Rural Development in Nagaland*', Har Anand Publication, New Delhi.
4. Ao, Alemchiba, 1972: 'Problems of Readjustment to a New Situation (with special reference to the Naga tribe)' in K.S. Singh (ed.) *The Tribal Situation in India*, I.I.A.S., Simla.
5. Betts, U.G., 1953: *The Hidden Land*, London.
6. Brown, R., 1874: *Report on the Exploration of the Angami Naga and Manipur Boundary*, Shillong.
7. Butler, John: Rough Notes on the Angami Nagas and the Language, *Journal of Asiatic Society of Bengal*, Vol. xiv.
8. Chaube, S.K., 1983: The Middle Class in the North East India: Retrospects and Prospects in B. Dutta Ray (ed.) *The Emergence and Role of Middle Class in North East India*, Uppal Publishing House, New Delhi.
9. Das, N.K. 1982: 'Agrarian Structure and Change in Nagaland' in K.S. Singh (ed.).
10. Das, N.K., 1987: *Ethnic Identity, Ethnicity and Social Stratification in North East India*, Inter-India Publications, New Delhi.
11. Dutta, P.N., 1983: 'The Emergence and Role of the Middle Class in the Khasi Jaintia Hills 1824-1950' in B. Dutta Ray (ed.) *The Emergence and Role of the Middle Class in North East India*, Uppal Publishing House, New Delhi.
12. Dutta, P.S., 1986: 'Some Reflections on the Changing Agrarian Relations in Mizoram 1889-1986', Seminar on Changing Agrarian Relations in North-East Since Independence, Department of Sociology, NEHU, Shillong, April 23-24, 1986.
13. Dutta, P.S., 1989: 'Estimated Differentiation in a Traditional Tribal Economy', in: *Peasant and Peasant Protests in India*, M.N. Karna (ed.), Intellectual Publishing House, New Delhi.
14. Dutta, P.S., 1992: *India's North-East: A Study in Transition*, Har Anand & Vikas Publishing House, New Delhi.
15. Furer-Haimendorf, 1955: *Himalayan Barbary*, John Murray, London.
16. Furer-Haimendorf, 1962: *The Apa Tanis and Their Neighbours*, Routledge & Kegan Paul, London.
17. Furer-Haimendorf, 1968: *Naked Nagas*, Thacker Spink Co., Calcutta (Reprint).
18. Furer-Haimendorf, 1976: *Return to the Naked Nagas*, Vikas Publishing House, New Delhi.

19. Furer-Haimendorf, 1980: *A Himalayan Tribe: From Cattle to Cash*, Vikas Publishing House, New Delhi.
20. Furer-Haimendorf, 1982: *Highlanders of Arunachal Pradesh*, Vikas Publishing House, New Delhi.
21. Goswami, B.B., 1977: 'Social and Political Institutions of the Mizos' in a Seminar on Social and Political Institutions of the Hill Peoples of N.E. India, Shillong, NEICSSR, July 4-5, 1977.
22. Goswami, B.B., 1987: The Mizos in Context of State Formation in S.C. Sinha (ed.), *Tribal Polities . . . . N.E. India*, K.P. Bagchi & Co., Calcutta.
23. Hutton, J.H., 1921: *The Angami Nagas*, Oxford University Press, Calcutta, 1968 (Reprint).
24. Karna, M.N., 1982: 'Agrarian Studies in North East India: Some Reflections', *The Eastern Anthropologist*, Vol. 35 (2).
25. Lahiri, B., 1986: Land and Land Relations in Meghalaya, Seminar on Changing Agrarian Relations in North-East Since Independence, Department of Sociology, NEHU, Shillong, April 23-24, 1986.
26. Majumdar, D.N., 1986: 'Garos in Plain Areas—A Study on the Change of the Concept of Ownership', in: *Land Reforms and Peasant Movements*, Atul Sharma (ed.), Omson Publications, New Delhi.
27. Mann, R.S., 1984: 'Research Ventures and Trends—Case of Tribal N.E. India', *Journal of North Eastern Council* (Shillong), Vol. VI (1).
28. Mathew, T. and S. Nair, 1983: 'Tribal Mode of Production in Transition', Mimeograph, Department of Economics, NEHU, Shillong.
29. Mishra, B.P., 1982: 'Kirata, Karyo Kinesis', in: *Economies of the Tribes and Their Transformations*, Concept Publishing House, New Delhi.
30. Mishra, S.N., 1983: 'Arunachal's Tribal Economic Formations and Their Dissolution', *Economic and Political Weekly*, October 22, 1983.
31. Mishra, U., 1983: 'Naga Nationalism and the Role of the Middle Class', in B. Dutta Ray (ed.), *The Emergence and Role of the Middle Class in North East India*, Uppal Publishing House, New Delhi.
32. *Report of the Land Reform Commission* (*LRC*), 1974: Government of Meghalaya, Shillong.
33. Owen, R., 1973: 'Emperial Policy and Theory of Social Change', in: *Anthropology and Colonial* Encounter, (ed) Talat Asad, Ethaca Press, London.
34. Roy Burman, B.K., 1972: 'Integrated Area Approach to the problems to the Hill Tribes of North East India' in K.S. Singh (ed.), *The Tribal Situation in India*, IIAS, Shimla.
35. Sarkar, J.K., 1987: *Society Culture and Adaptation Among Three Tribes of Arunachal Pradesh* (Khamti, Padam and Kaman Mishmi), ASI, Calcutta.
36. Singh, K.S., 1985: *Tribal Society in India*, Monohar, New Delhi.
37. Sinha, A.C., 1989: 'Peasant and Peasant Conflicts in Medziphema Block

of Nagaland', in: *Peasant and Peasant Protests in India*, M.N. Karna (ed.), Intellectual Publishing House, New Delhi.

38. Sinha, A.C., 1992: 'The North East Indian Context and Perspective of Social Science Research for 1990's', *The North Eastern Research Bulletin* (Dibrugarh), Vol. X, Summer.
39. Sinha, A.C. 1993: *Hill Cities of Eastern Himalayas*, Indus, New Delhi.
40. Sinha, S.C. (ed.), 1987: *Tribal Polities and State Systems in Pre-Colonial Eastern and N.E. India*, K.P. Bagchi & Co., Calcutta.
41. Vincent, K., 1978: *Socio-Economic Study of Bhoilymbong—A Village in Meghalaya*, The Christian Literature Society, Madras.

5

Managing the Social Consequences of Smallness

There has been a growing appreciation of the size of country since Second World War. It happened all the more so because a number of such newly decolonized countries (or 'states') were very small in size. This simply requires one to cast a glance on the size of the territory, population and resources of the member states of the United Nations Organization. Not only are they under-developed from urban and industrial considerations, but the entire quality of their life is also marked by traditionalism and a particularistic social structure and neglect of resource exploitation. This state of affairs leads us to various issues: What sort of autonomy can they have? How can they provide for their increasing population? Can they hope to maintain or even improve their standard of living? What political forms can they develop? What are the social consequences of smallness?

Criteria for Smallness

Schumacker's small may be beautiful, but it is intriguing. How to define smallness? Can it be in terms of area alone? This makes Singapore small and Bhutan large. Will it be population alone? In that case, Bhutan becomes a small state and Singapore turns out to be a bigger one. In a similar way, higher density of population of the countries cannot be indicative of their size. In case, the criteria of area, population and density are of not much use, could it be smallness in resources? Has it something to do with the geographical location or the ecological setting of the states? These are some of the issues one may keep in mind while examining the implications of smallness. However, it goes without saying that we know intuitively that Maldive Islands is a small state and Mexico is bigger one. In the similar way, in case we review the Indian scene, Maharashtra is a bigger one and Manipur is a small state. But these statements do not take us nearer to the criteria for the smallness. For that purpose, it may be rewarding to uncover the various facts of smallness such as geographic, demographic, political, economic and sociological.

Geographical and Demographic Aspect of Smallness

In case, a small country with her small population and limited resources is located in the heart of the ocean far away from the land mass, or is placed as a land-locked territory in inaccessible montane region, her remoteness will be all the more accentuated. In such a situation, diffusion of ideas and technology becomes rather belated. Because of the geographical inaccessibility, communication is affected and, thus, the community becomes insular. Size turns out to be an unavoidable compulsion and innovation becomes financially prohibitive. In this way, remoteness perpetuates itself. Apart from the above, there has been a tendency among small developing states that their crude death rate is decreasing, while the birth rate tends to be constant. This results in a surplus population year by year, straining the already limited resources of the small states.

Political Aspect of Smallness

Small states as political entities may have to be measured against the yard stick of statehood. To begin with, do the small state have a feeling of 'nationhood' and 'national' unity? Do they possess an administration to carry on the chores of the normal governance effectively? Do they have enough trained manpower to man various specialized positions in the states? Are these states financially viable? Answer to the above questions are depressingly negative. Most of the sovereign small states lack nationhood and national unity; they may not have an effective administrative structure; their requirements for trained manpower is far from satisfactory; and most of these units are highly insolvent. Given the above predicament, there are only two alternatives left of them: either to federate or integrate themselves to the neighbouring political units or accept a relatively prolonged status of clientship of various types to the more resourceful state. In another way, size and autonomy are intimately linked with each other. A small state in the above trying situation, occasionally raises real or imaginary claims and counter-claims on their neighbour's territories. It is also to be kept in mind that a small state is the biggest employer of her citizens because other viable employment generating enterprises are very few in existence.

Economic Aspect of Smallness

Small state may not be able to provide large economic specializations. In fact, some of them have specialized in the production of particular commodities. For example, Cuba and Mauritius produce sugar and their entire economy is based on sugar industry. Cuba and Mauritius are so much dependent and tied to sugar industry that they cannot gainfully introduce other crops for the sake of economic alternatives. Their own markets are so small that if sugar is not sold outside their countries they cannot consume it by themselves. At the same time, they themselves require large number of consumer goods other than sugar, which they cannot produce. The production of such consumer articles will not be economically feasible in the absence of a skilled labour force, non-availability of raw materials, lack of market for their consumption and non-existence of a sophisticated standard of industrial and entrepreneurial acumen. Such modern entrepreneurial establishments are capital intensive. These small states because of propensity to consumerism, rarely accumulate a dependable capital for industrial investment.

Sociological Aspect of Smallness

The compulsive economy of small states leads to a lower standard of life, which may have some serious social consequences. If the state is not technologically very rich, it attracts technologically skilled immigrants from abroad. This leads to inter-ethnic conflicts and various complex issues of adjustment. On the other hand, some of its own citizens who manage to acquire specialized expertise in rare trades, are not utilised by the small state themselves because complex economic and industrial diversifications are non-existent. This situation leads to what is commonly known as the brain drain to the technologically developed states from that of the underdeveloped ones. Thus, these states are denied of the services of their most talented members. Their social world is small; their mental horizon is limited; and their outlook to life and universe is past-oriented and tradition bound. Their society is particularistic and what Reisman termed as tradition directed (Reisman, D.: 1958). The particularistic population of the small states has various levels of conflicts such as between small private loyalty and impersonal allegiances, between personal roles of kinship and obligation and public role of office. By and large, primordialities are preferred to the class associations and intellectual convictions.

Sociological Approach to Smallness

Bendict Burton (Burton, B.: 1967, 45-46) identifies three distinct approaches to the study of small social phenomena. Firstly, the most significant approach among the sociologists to study small groups as parts of the larger social set-up has been known as face-to-face group or primary groups. Various scholars have examined interests, types and associational features of a small segment of a particular society. However, whether it is small or larger territorial states, the general features of primary and face-to-face groups remain the same everywhere. Thus, this approach may not be of much help to us. Secondly, the social anthropologists have addressed themselves to small scale societies or what is known as the primitive societies. Such primitive tribal societies like Birhor of Bihar are smaller in comparison to the Chinese or the Hindu and may possibly be identified at two levels. While some of the above small scale societies are composed of a series of primary groups; there are others which have a complex organization of a number of small primary groups in an interlocked large population. While Tikopia, Trobriands are examples of the former, Nuer, Tiv, Tallensi, Naga and Mizo may be identified as the latter. Thirdly, the village, peasant or folk communities have been conceived by anthropologists and sociologists as distinct from that of the large scale urban-industrial complex societies. Robert Redfield advanced the criteria of relative smallness, homogeneity, self-sufficiency and exclusiveness with that of the folk society against an urban backdrop (Redfield, R.: 1955: 4). A.L. Kroeber identified the folk (or peasant) society as 'part society' (Kroeber, A.L.: 1948: 284). Taking small scale societies as the major intellectual concern, Robert Redfield visualized about half a dozen approaches to the study of the 'little community' (Redfield, R.: 1955). Extending Redfield and Kroeber's tradition to the Indian villages, a number of studies were made on Indian villages in 1950's (Dube, S.C.: 1954; Marriot, M.: 1954). In course of time, these village studies were analysed in terms of larger Indian social structure.

All three above approaches may contribute something to the uncovering of the phenomena, the small state. However, to us, the 'holistic' approach of the sociologists and social anthropologists appear to be the most rewarding. The two disciplines have a tradition of emphasizing the organic or functional relation between parts and whole rather than an atomistic approach to the study of culture of a people. This approach argues that it is useful in some instances to think of societies as constituting social systems, with the implication that in studying the whole in this manner one is paying due regard to both the parts and the relationships holding between the parts. Such an approach is a structural approach and one of its best examples may be found in A.R. Radcliffe-Brown's *Structure and Function in Primitive Society*, 1952. Another illustration may be cited from Robert Redfield's *Little Community* (Redfield, R.: 1955), which came to be known as the classic model of an empirical and conceptual research. While the particularistic analysis of the tribal bands, families, gangs or small social segments are important, a generalized and an holistic totality of the small state is equally desirable. And only then we shall be able to uncover the uniqueness of the small states. With the above approaches at hand, certain problems are to be tackled: What are the attributes of smallness? With the attributes identified, what are the consequences of smallness? Do these attributes and consequences, typical of the small states, produce certain types of dilemma unique to these states?

Attributes and Consequences of Smallness

We have a hunch that in small states intensity of relations should be at a different level from that of the large scale societies. By that we mean a closer face-to-face relationship may have preponderance. Nearly every social relationship may serve a set of varied interests, necessitating individuals to play a number of roles simultaneously. A number of relationships may be unique to themselves and relevant only to the societies in question. Accordingly people have limited choices and few alternatives for a meaningful role performance. In the above situation, it becomes rather difficult to maintain anonymity. At the macro-level, these societies are weak and vulnerable to outside pressures. As a consequence of the above in this ascriptive social milieu, status is largely dependent on birth. There is a very small elite group, whose social base is limited. There are little chances for specialization of roles. Personal failure is invariably deemed as evil intentions of 'others' or inauspicious intervention of the non-human super-natural world. In such a situation, people have little control over their destiny and they play no significant roles in shaping the course of their future. All these lead to various sets of dilemma impartial and objective role vis-a-vis social alliance such as kinship; personal loyalties and special traditional role vis-a-vis technological expertise; membership to the group, kin, caste, and sub-tribe vis-a-vis positions in the state administrative machinery.

The Indian Small States

We feel this is an opportune time to focus on the national exercise in identifying, analysing and evaluating the exigencies of social change, economic growth and political implications of small (frontier) states in India. The Indian Union consists of 31 political-administrative units (22 states and 9 Union Territories. In our present discussion all 31 units will be referred as the 'states' irrespective of their being 'states'or 'Union Territories'). Among these states, the first six large size states contribute to more than 50 per cent of the total area as well as the total population of the Indian Union. On the other hand, 15 small units (states) together make up only 8.9 per cent of the area and about 5.5 per cent of the Indian population. In case, we consider the size of the population along with smallness in territory, we get a list of 17 states which are small. To this, if we associate the extent of these units' dependence on the Central government's financial support, we shall find that Goa, Pondicherry, Chandigarh, Dadra and Nagar Haveli and Delhi are to be excluded from the list. In case we examine the cultural distinctiveness of the states (i.e. presence of a least one-third population belonging to the scheduled tribe/caste), we come across only some states which are small in territory, population, resources, and have particularistic demographic characteristics. Incidentally, these are the states which are geographically inaccessible because of their location on the Indian frontiers. They may be identified as Andaman and Nicobar islands, Arunachal Pradesh, Lakshdweep-Minicoy and Amindivi islands, Mizoram, Nagaland, Meghalaya, Manipur, Tripura and Sikkim (Table 5.1).

These states may be classified into two sets: (1) the six states from among the members of the North-East Council and their neighbour, Sikkim, all located on the distant North-Eastern international frontiers and geographically inaccessible mountainous region; (2) the two island states scattered on the expanse of the Bay of Bengal and the Arabian Sea, posing strategic challenge of their own.

Table 5.1. Population, area and ethnicity in the small states

Unit state	Area in sq. kms.	Total population	Density of population	Percentage of scheduled Tribes
1. Andaman & Nicobar Islands	8,293	1,15,133	14	15.72
2. Arunachal Pradesh	85,573	4,67,117	6	79.02
3. Lakshadweep	32	31,810	994	92.86
4. Manipur	22,356	10,72,753	48	31.18
5. Meghalaya	22,489	10,11,199	45	80.48
6. Mizoram	21,087	3,32,390	16	94.26
7. Nagaland	16,527	5,16,449	31	88.61
8. Sikkim	7,299	2,08,843	29	38.00
9. Tripura	10,477	15,56,342	149	28.95

Some Features of Small States

It is instructive to examine the issues around the theme of development for the above states in terms of the following (Table 5.2): (i) Development potentials: col. 4: forests; col. 6: area not available for cultivation, thereby indicating that the rest is available for cultivation; (ii) Development achievements; col. 2: number of towns; col. 5: cropped areas; cols. 7 & 8: road; col. 9: small scale industries; (iii) Some consequences of development: cols. 1 & 3: urban population; cols. 10 & 11: number of government employees.

As regards the development potentials of the above states, it is to be noted that they are located on the geographically inaccessible regions. The second feature that emerges is that the most of these states are of crucial strategic significance because of their location on the international frontiers with China, Bhutan, Burma and Bangladesh. Thirdly, five of the states, e.g. Arunachal Pradesh, Lakshadweep, Meghalaya, Nagaland and Mizoram are predominantly tribal states, while nearly one-third population of Manipur, Tripura and Sikkim belongs to the scheduled tribes and there are the scheduled castes inhabiting these states.

In case we consider the consequences of the (small) size on development potentialities, the contour of underdevelopment gets all the more exposed. Apart from the various forms of natural resources such as minerals, hydel energy, etc. (which have not been examined here), two significant potentialities in the form of forests and agriculture (and incidentally both in the primary sector of production) appear to be bountiful in these states. There are states such as Nagaland, Manipur and Meghalaya which are somewhat deficient in forest resources. But paddy grown in Manipur valley and potato produced in Meghalaya do compensate this loss to a great extent. It is instructive to note that in Nagaland and Meghalaya, there has been no effort for diversification and expansion of economic activities (including even agriculture). As a result of that, there is large scale deforestation. This adverse effect of small size, absence of economic deiversification and lack of territorial mobility need special attention. Again, except Nagaland, all other states have enough areas available for cultivation, if they decide to expand the agrarian activities.

Table 5.2. Indicators of development in the small states

Sl. No.	Urbanization			Forest	Agriculture		Roads		Small scale indus-tries	Govt. employees population	Total
	Urban pcpu-lation	No. of towns	Sch. Tribe popu-lation by town		Cropped area	Not avail-able for cultivation					
	1	2	3	4	5	6	7	8	9	10	11
1. Andaman & Nicobar Islands	22.77		NA	76.6	(6)	(5)	(7)	(8)	Negli-gible	Govt. emplo-yee/total population	Gazetted/ non-gazetted
2. Arunachal Pradesh	3.70	4	20.00	61.7	2.30%	Negli-gible	5.6	0.02	.004	38.52	15
3. Laccadive & Minicoy Islands	Nil (4)	None	NA	None					Negli-gible		
4. Mizoram	11.36	2	92.71	NA	3.93%	25%	6.8	4.05	.1	NA	NA
5. Nagaland	9.95	3	39.98 (3)	18.8	6.29%	70%	35.7	9.34	.007	19.666	36
6. Maghalaya	14.55	3	60.85 (1)	33.7	8.09%	10%	24.0	6.59	.01	75.99	21
7. Manipur	13.19	8	5.36	26.9	7.32%	less than half	39.0	8.04	.06	46.33	37
8. Tripura	10.45	8	4.80 (2)	60.4	39.96%	Negli-gible	36.2	2.48	.02	74.81	35
9. Sikkim	9.37	7	NA								
10. All India	19.91		1.18 (10)	23.30	54.24%	13%	34.4	2.06	.05		

NOTES FOR TABLE 5.2

1. High because of Tura and Jowai included.
   Shillong has only 41%
   Jowai = 86.89
   Tura = 54.60
2. Represent for Agartala the State Headquarters;
   — In other towns it is negligible.
   — In Agartala the concentration is in the municipal area (MA), and every negligible is the out-growths (OG).
3. Dimapur = 13.04% These towns are arranged in order of
   Kohima = 43.64% their decreasing commercial importance.
   Mokokchung = 32.00% The more the commercial importance the lesser is the percentage of the scheduled tribe population.
4. Laccadive and Minicoy Island has no town, hence 100% rural population.
5. Figures relating to area not available for cultivation, i.e., non-agricultural use and barren land are approximate. Exact figures not available as in many states no proper survey has been made. Moreover, these percentages are of the "reporting area" which in some cases is less than the total geographical area of the state. The trend indicated by the figures, however, are sufficiently suggestive of the broad pattern and reliable to a fair degree.
6. These figures are percentage of the reported area as above.
7. (i) Col. 7 = roads in km. per 100 sq. km. area.
   (ii) Col. 8 = roads in km. per 1,100 population.
   (iii) Unsurfaced road length as a percentage of total roads will be very revealing.

Arunachal Pradesh	= 63.37%	Manipur	= 85.84%
Mizoram	= 43.70%	Tripura	= 72.86%
Nagaland	= 80.75%	All India	= 41.77%
Meghalaya	= 87.14%		

   The reason for this high score could not be ascertained as necessary figures on various types of towns is not available. This, however, needs deeper probe.
8. Figure for Assam (182.40) is very revealing, when read along with the figures from other six states fare compared.
9. Indicates percentage of Scheduled tribe urban population to total urban population. This does not exactly compare with figures indicated against the name of each state—as the all-India figure does not include figures from towns but for urban areas. The definitions may differ.

With the exception of Tripura all the states are agriculturally backward. Similarly, economic development is reflected in an appreciable way through the extension of roadways. The figures relating to the extent of roads (Table 5.2: cols. 7 & 8) appear to be misleading as they include roads made primarily for defence purposes on the international frontiers. Undulating topography forbids water and rail transportation. Even the capitals of many states are not connected even by the most primitive air services. The other indicators used to determine economic development is the existence of small scale industries. The figures available for this one are suggestive of a lower rate of economic development in all the states except Manipur and Mizoram. These two states have the averages which are above the all-India average. In the same way, small scale industries are not reflective of the actual economic development. It is because they are under unorganised sector, left to the traditional domestic units of production, more as a part of traditional style of life than as an economic enterprise.

The consequences of this economic backwardness and low development performance of these states is reflected in the low percentage of urban population. The Andaman Islands are the only exception where the population of the capital town, Port Blair, accounts for 22.77% of the population as there is little potentiality for populating the other small constituent islands. If one examines the social composition of each town in the different states under review, it may be found that in the capital and commercial towns, members of the local community (tribals) are less in number than the non-locals (non-tribals). Most of the non-local and non-tribal population in these towns are the salaried employees of the state governments, the Central Government or Corporate bodies or are traders. One of the consequences of this is reflected in the ratio of the total administrative employees to the total population. This ratio is high in these states because the only easy option open for the 'local' is to find employment in thier 'own' 'governments' (administration).

Issues Involved in Smallness

The above explication of the economic performance of the small states provides the basis for analysing the wider implications of territorial size and the contingent constraints on the overall development potentialities. Uniqueness of size may be uncovered if we view (i) the given sets of distinctiveness and (ii) the development efforts which are being made. Among the given sets of distinctiveness, the following may be examined:

(i) *Ecological Distinctiveness:* All the nine small states have a distinctive geographical location which puts serious communication constraints with their neighbours in the area and also with the other parts of the country. The montane and marine terrains necessitate special technological innovations to cope with topographical uniqueness for agricultural, industrial and infrastructural developments.

(ii) *Ethnic Distinctiveness:* This refers to the cultural insularity prevalent among the small states. These states are the homes of the demographically small tribal groups. Lack of exposure to the larger 'national' context inbreeds various sets of psychological and political apprehensions among them. Ecological inaccessibility perpetuates a type of self-fulfilling prophecy of socio-economic exclusiveness. In this way we find the ethnic groups taking pains in maintaning their specific cultural boundaries vis-a-vis the state territorial limits.

Some of these communities have their own dialects written through the Roman script for a century now. However, they have a microcosm of 'literati'. Whatever is being written in their dialects/languages is either sacred literature or romantic verse, both in a way distant from the hard realities of life. Imaginative and creative literature as reflection on the social experiences is yet to emerge. Accordingly the local literature fails to provide communication and leadership in dissemination of ideas, knowledge, and other abstract forms. Thus, even their literature contributes to their ethnic peculiarity instead of universalizing their distinct genius.

(iii) *Economic Distinctiveness:* The ecological and the ethnic factors determine the economic conditions, achievement experiences and entrepreneurial capability of the small states in a conspicuous way. 'Lack of entrepreneurship' and the absence of 'industrial culture' has resulted in the invasion of 'non-locals' trade, commerce and scondary sector activities. Thus, the local community is left with the age-old subsistence economy based on slash-

and-burn type of rotational cultivation or food gathering.

(iv) *Political Insularity:* Apart from the factors of geographical inaccessibility, social uniqueness and economic underdevelopment, extensive conversion to Christianity has conspicuously brought the realization of cultural-historical distinctiveness. This cultural complex around Christianity has been able to provide a new identity to a sizeable population of small states. This 'tribal Christian' identity is being used as a political idiom vis-a-vis the Indian national politics.

Developmental efforts are being made at various levels to cope with the problems of these states. They can be identified at various levels: (i) *State Development Programmes*: They may be enumerated as cottage industries, agro-industries, family welfare programmes, etc. (ii) *Regional Development Programmes*: This includes the various coordinational activities undertaken by the agencies such as the North-East Council for the north-eastern states. (iii) *National Development Programmes*: Among them mention may made of (a) location of heavy industrial units; (b) transport and communication network; and (c) location of energy generating units. (iv) *Defence Activities*: The presence of the armed personnel on the sensitive frontiers requires a dependable transport and communication system. It has invariably been found that the isolated frontier communities rarely require the above amenities for their immediate benefits. Moreover, the presence of the armed personnel within the neighbourhood of the ethnic groups distorts the logical local priorities crucial to the community life. Many a time, it adversely affects the local consumer economy. Notwithstanding the above, it goes without saying that the defence activities provide one of the significant infrastructural efforts for the otherwise neglected areas.

The Problems for Consideration

The analytical consideration and a thorough identification of the relevant problems of the small Indian frontier states may be summarized as: (i) the implications of the smallness on the development of each of the states in terms of their resources; (ii) the effect of the various consequential characteristic (as evidenced by the over-all performance of each state) on the re-inforcement of the factor identified as impediments to development due to smallness; (iii) implications of their size on their neighbouring states in terms of regional perspective and on the nature of their expectations from the centre; (iv) implications of their size on the social context as unique and small isolated marginal men; (v) the problems of man-power planning—especially when the small states have been 'attractive for in-migration' but have not shown an appreciable size of 'out-migration'; and (vi) to uncover the facets of resource underdevelopment and economic colonization by external exploiters.

To sum up, the analysis of the developmental strategy in small states, whether they are small sovereign states or small Indian administrative units, is fascinating in various ways. They do not appear to have enough social base for a stable politico-administrative set-up. That may be one of the reasons for frequent change in the governments in these small states. Their cultural distinctiveness and developmental requirements pose a problem of choice between particularistic ethnic-centered political culture and a desired universal economic progress. They are not in a hurry to make this choice, and, thus, preservation of the traditions and a desire to modernity remain a live issue. Meanwhile, a rudiment of middle class elite has emerged as power wielders. This assertive elite group has been raising various issues of economic exploitation, ethnic conflict and political dominance of the 'outsiders', while they themselves are equal partners of this exploitative, unequal and discriminating system.

References

Birla Institute of Scientific Research, 1979, *Centre-State Financial Relations*, Abhinav, New Delhi.

Burton, B. (ed), 1967, *Problems of Smaller Territories*, University of London, Institute of Commonwealth Studies, The Athlone Press, London.

Dahl, R.A. *Size and Democracy—The Politics of Smaller European Democracies*, Stanford.

Dube, S.C., 1954, *Indian Village*, Muoton, The Hague.

Kroeber, A.L., 1946, *Anthropology*, Harcourt, Brace and World Inc., New York.

Marriot, M., 1954, *Village India*, Chicago University Press, Chicago.

Pant, Y.P., 1974, *Problems of Development of Smaller Countries*, Oxford and IBH Publishing Co., New Delhi.

Redfield, R., 1955, *Folk Society and Culture,* Chicago University Press, Chicago.

Redfield, R., 1955, *Little Community,* Chicago University Press, Chicago.

Riesman, D., 1953, *The Lonely Crowd,* A Double Day Anchor Book.

Schumacker, E.F., 1977, *Small is Beautiful,* Radha Prakashan, New Delhi, seventh reprint.

Selwyn, P. (ed), 1975, *Development Policy in Small Countries,* Institute of Development Studies, Sussex, Croom Helm Ltd., London.

Vital, D., 1976, *The Survival of Small States—Studies in Small Power-Great Power Conflict,* Stanford.

6
The Nepalese Immigration

Territorially large societies such as India provide challenges to the analysts because of their expanse and complexity. There is another obvious dimension: whether the Indian state and the Indian society are the same. While the former has a legal, formal, and constitutional existence, the same cannot be said about the latter. The frequent cliche about the Indian society is that of 'unity in diversity', acknowledging its plurality. Looking at the situation from an entirely territorial point of view, the Himalayas, and for that matter the north-eastern frontier region, is peripheral to the mainstream. The Nepalese, nestling in the Himalayas and immigrating to the north-eastern frontier region are the focus of our present analysis. We propose to examine briefly the Indian mainstream and the north-eastern periphery. Secondly, we intend to examine the issue of the Nepalese immigrants in India and analyse its various aspects. And finally, we would like to examine the questions of identity and the dilemma faced by the Indian Nepalese. We find the Indian Nepalese with conflicting identites—as Nepalese and as Indians—which have to be resolved for a happier Indian social scene and a harmonious way of life.

Mainstream and Periphery

Among the two approaches to understanding a large state such as India, the first may be identified as politico-cybernetic-communicational, in which the key concern is with power and related concepts such as authority control, dominance, influence, coercion, surveillance, and so on. The control of the state, defined as a political system with monopoly of the use of force over its territory, over the physical and human resources and its deployment of coercive devices are considered natural. In this context, the state is presumed to be like a unicellular organism with nuclei (core, centre, and capital), bodies (territorial expanse), and outer membrances (the boundary) with stomi (border passes, ports). It is considered as a system in which a continuous surveillance by the dominant of their subordinates' behaviour, and the deployment of threats and punishments are normal ingredients (Strassold, 1980). All these are performed in terms of power, which is defined as control over communication flows, located in the state, at a point where selection is possible, decisions are made, and information is transmitted. Naturally, commands flow down from the centre to the periphery and information is demanded in the opposite direction. From this point of view, the extensive territory of India may be understood as a hierarchy of power centres branching out from a seat of ultimate decision making.

Alternatively, in the normative approach to understanding the phenomenon of state, power is substituted with a collective consensus on shared goals and values. Emphasis is placed on society, and social order is achieved through the spontaneous co-ordination of individual behaviour and not through a coercive power system. Status and prestige are peacefully and unanimously accorded to those who fill the most strategic roles in society. It is presumed that there is a central zone as a realm of values, beliefs, and emotions in the structure of society. This central zone also provides a set of activities, roles, and personnel within the network of institutions. In this way, the central zone is intimately connected with what society considers to be sacred and ideal, espoused by the ruling authority (Shils, 1961). From this point of view, larger territorial entities such as India have a number of subsystems which are organized through common and overlapping sets of values, ideals, and personnel. Needless to say the above subsystems characterize the pattern of authorities symbolized by individual behaviour.

These two approaches may appear apparently conradictory. However, as Strassold argues: "Real societies are mixure of both models; the politicological-cybernetic one strongly tied to a spatial pattern of centre-periphery, and the sociological-culturological one, which is much more volatile in its spatial reference. No wonder then that both the 'materialistic' model based on power and communication and the symbolic model based on consent and shared meaning have been subjected to analysis through spatial categories such as centre-periphery (1980: 40)."

If one examines the expanse of the Indian Union closely from the centre to the periphery from the points of view of religion, language, and political control as indicators of power structure, certain interesting patterns emerge. First, predominantly Hindu, Hindi-speaking and traditionally a Congress-supporting Rajasthan, Haryana, Himachal Pradesh, Uttar Pradesh, Bihar, Madhya Pradesh and Delhi may be identified with the core or mainstream of the Indian system.[1] In terms of political power, 40 per cent of the seats in the Indian Parliament, the sovereign authority over the Indian landmass, are controlled by them. Secondly, as associates to the core or mainstream we may identify states such as Gujarat, Maharashtra, Karnataka, Kerala, Tamil Nadu, Andhra Pradesh, Orissa, West Bengal, Tripura, and Assam. These are also predominantly Hindu (though non-Hindi speaking), but also constitute a stronghold of the Congress or some 'national' parties with a few exceptions. They control 52 per cent of the states in the Indian Parliament. Thirdly, on the outer fringe of these two zones there are states such as Jammu and Kashmir, Punjab, Goa, Lakshdweep, the Andaman Islands, Mizoram, Nagaland, Meghalaya, Arunachal Pradesh and Sikkim. These units are inhabited by predominantly non-Hindu, non-Hindi speaking communitites and have a strong tradition of regional political parties (Chaube 1984: 235-37). They elect only 8 per cent of the members to the Indian Parliament. It may not be out of place to put on record that Jammu and Kashmir and Lakshdweep are the two Muslim majority states. Punjab is the only Sikh state, Sikkim is the only predominantly Buddhist state and Nagaland, Meghalaya, Mizoram, and Arunachal Pradesh are the scheduled tribal states within the Indian Union. As a broad generalization, the first two categories may be identified with the core or mainstream, while the third zone may profitably be thought of as the periphery.

If one examines the north-eastern frontier from the mainstream it appears vague, distant, and amorphous. Physical distance from the core is coupled with the insufficiency of the communication network. There is no quick, effective, and convenient means of communication between the core and this region. In such a situation, those who go to the region consider themselves rather as pioneers, explorers, and adventures. The white-collar functionaries come to the region on punishment, occasional promotions and out-of-routine postings. Very rarely does a functionary opt for a posting in this region. And why should he? After all, no significant decisions, even those affecting the local situations, are taken in the region. Consequently, a frontier functionary, who lives a deprived and inconvenient life, plays no role in the process of decision making; rather he is supposed to obey 'orders' from 'above' and to keep on filing the information.

On the other hand, the frontier communities equally feel the core to be complex, manipulative, mysterious, devoid of sensibility, and a jungle of rules. The moment they get out of their native environment, they confront language, food, transport and communication that are uncomfortable and unfamiliar. It is a fact that the better parts of the region became part of India effectively only during the last 150 years or so. Even Assam, the traditional Ahom land, came effectively under the Hindu fold (and thus to the mainstream) as late as the seventeenth century. That is why social structure, commensality, marital pattern, and festivals are uniquely Assamese. In such a situation, the various states in the region are not in a position to identify a collective code of conduct, a shared belief, and historically transmitted traditions along with the mainstream. This picture becomes all the more muddled when we examine the issues pertaining to the Nepalese immigrants in the region, who are identified neither with the mainstream nor with the associates to the mainstream or even to the periphery or indeed any distinct territory of their own within the Indian Union.

Nepalese Identity

In the traditional view, Nepal has been on the cultural frontiers of India and China. The legend goes that a celebrated ascetic called Ne 'cherished' or 'looked after' the land known as Nepal (Ne + *pal*: the country looked after by the ascetic Ne). In ancient Indian tradition Ne was a benevolent patron saint, the guardian of Nepal

(Paterson, 1983: 126). According to another tradition the bodhisattva Manjusri, coming down from China, drained the Kathmandu valley by opening the southern rocks and permitting water to flow down to the Indian plains as the river Bagmati (Pemble, 1971: 1). The earliest inhabitants of the land are said to be Kiratas—a loose generic term for numerous tribes, who are claimed to have immigrated from Assam and north-east India to Nepal. The Newars, a literate and cultured race, came to Nepal either from India or Tibet several centuries before the Christian era. Their industry, artistry, sculpture, architecture, language, and urbanity were identified as uniquely Nepalese.

Another Indian wave of immigrants came to Nepal in the form of Lacchavi Hindu Rajputs, who introduced to classical Hindu institutions of *varna*. More urbane Newars tried to assimilate the new role among themselves and for this reason they are known as *Buddhamargis* (worshippers of the Buddha) and *Shivamargis* (worshippers of the Hindu deity Shiva). Thus, Hinduism and Buddhism mingled to co-exist in Nepal, a state of affairs epitomized by the sacred centres of the Hindu Pashupati and the Buddhist Swayambhunath temples in Kathmandu. It appears that the Kiratas were pushed to the north-eastern part of the country, where their descendants are found as Rais, Magars, Limbus, and other tribes even today.

The comtemporary usage of the terms Gurkha and Nepalese has a recent history. In the beginning of the eighteenth century, the land between the valley of Kathmandu and Kumaon was fragmented into forty-six lordships, grouped into two loose confederations. The *Baisis* (twenty-two principalities) were located in the Karnali basin and the *Chaubis* (twenty-four principalities) were in the Narayani (Gandaki) basin. These principalities were theoretically under the Mughal emperor of India, but in practice they were autonomous. The Shah family of Gurkha, a small state in *Chaubisi* and alleged to be immigrants from Chittor in Rajasthan, emerged as the strong force under their ruler, Prithvi Narayan Shah, in the middle of the eighteenth century. The Gurkhas proceeded to conquer the entire valley, defeating the Malla rulers of Kathmandu and Patan in 1768 and Bhatgaon in 1769, and the Gurkha ruler thus acquired for himself the title of 'the king of the hills'. The Gurkha forces increased their might and by 1815 they had subjugated the territories from the Tista river in the east to the Sutlej river in the west, and from the northern Gangetic plains to the high Himalayan ranges. In the course of time, the Gurkhas, or 'Nepalese', turned out to be a nation of several tribes and castes. who claimed to be the descendants of the original subjects of the Gurkhas and who speak the language called Gurkhali or Nepali.

From an ethnological point of view the Gurkhas or Nepalese can be divided into three major ethnic stocks. First the Kiratis, claimed to be the earliest inhabitants of the land, are divided into a number of largely endogamous tribes such as Rai, Magar, Limbu, Lepcha, Tamang, etc., who speak their own dialects, are either Hindus, Buddhists, or animists and are located in the north-eastern and eastern part of Nepal (Sinha, 1975: 7). They are traditionally hillmen, are fond of forests and ethnologically closer to the north-eastern tribal region of India. Secondly, the *Newars,* an urban trading and commercial stock located mainly in the Kathmandu valley and eastern Nepal, are also divided into a number of castes among themselves (Rosser, 1978). The *Newars*, who possess their own script, language, arts, crafts, and architecture, are bilingual like the *Kiratis*, since besides their native *Newari* they also speak Gurkhali. Their contribution to the Nepalese tradition is immense and they are one of the three pillars of the present Nepalese rule (Garge, 1975; Sinha, 1984:86). It is an enterprising community, spread all over Kathmandu valley, eastern Nepal, Sikkim, Tibet, Darjeeling and north-eastern India. Thirdly, the *Thakuris* or the *Gurkhalis* are the Nepalese counterpart of the Indian Hindu endogamous caste system, with their concept of purity and pollution. The Chetris, a term which is a corruption of *kshatriya*, are the rulers of Nepal and have contributed to the consolidation of the Nepalese nation. They are very proud of their Hinduism and their martial tradition. Though they are found in all parts of Nepal, they are settled mainly in the western and central regions and the Kathmandu valley. On another plane, the Nepalese can be divided into two groups (Sinha, 1975: 8): the *tagadharis* (those who are entitled to the sacred thread) and *matwalis* (those who are outside Hindu orthodoxy and are permitted to drink intoxicating beverages). While all the *Kiratis*, most of the *Newars*, and some of *Thakuris* are known as *mat-*

wali, high caste *Newar* Hindus and Gurkhas are included among the *tagadhari*.

Nepalese Immigration to India

The Nepalese presence in the north-eastern region has a long history and their role in its unification, development, and reconstruction has been crucial. It is claimed that the ancient Pragjyotish state was extended from Sunkosi (Subansri) in the east to Kushma (Kosi) in the west. Similarly, the ancient kingdom of Kamrup extend up to eastern Nepal (Dungel, 1983). Much later in the second decade of the sixteenth century the Coch king, Vishwa Singh, married Ratna Kanti Devi, the daughter of the Malla king of Kantipur (Kathmandu). It is claimed that the Coch king brought from Nepal to his kingdom a number of Brahmin priests, woodwork artisans, stone and metal sculptors and the pagoda-style temples. Similarly, Nildhwaj and Narnarain, the two Kamrup kings, were married in Nepal. Apart from their consorts they brought to their kingdom Brahmin priests, Chetri warriors, farmers, herdsmen, and artisans from Nepal and granted them rent-free land (Dungel, 1983).

It is claimed that a mountain contingent from the Nepal hills fought on the British side at the battle of Plassey in 1757. That was one of the glorious periods of the Nepalese history, as noted above, when Prithvi Narayan Shah was consolidating his Gurkha kingdom between the Sutlej and the Tista. He had a plan to attack the Coch and Ahom kings in collusion with the Deb Judhir of Bhutan. The British intervention in the Coch-Bhutan dispute on behalf of the Coch and the subsequent removal of the Deb Judhir from power temporarily contained the Gurkhas' eastward expansion. However, from 1780 to 1813 they raided Sikkim, and its south-western part, known as Vijaypur Sikkim, came under Nepalese control to the extent that the plains district of Rangpur in Bengal Presidency touched the Nepalese and the Bhutanese territories in 1813. Ultimately, the Nepalese ambitions clashed with the British, resulting in the present political boundaries of Nepal. The Indo-Nepalese Treaty of Sugauli, 1815, stipulated that the territory east of Mechi river would be taken away from the Nepalese, and it was restored to Sikkim following the Treaty of Titalia. The British arm-twisting tactics with Sikkim for the next five decades and the Indo-Bhutan war of 1864 resulted in the creation of the British districts of Darjeeling, Jalpaiguri, Kamrup, Goalpara, and Daranga.

An 88,320 acre (or 138 square mile) area of Darjeeling with about 100 persons was acquired by the British in 1835 as the site for a health resort. The Sikkim Durbar used to get a revenue of about twenty rupees in those days, and this was handsomely compensated by the British, a point which was later contested by Hope Namgyal, the consort of the last ruler of Sikkim (Namgyal, 1966). The mountainous parts of the district were inhabited by a few Lepcha, Limbu and Bhutia families. However, it is claimed that the annual revenue in 1845 from the Sikkimese Terai used to be about Rs. 50,000 to Rs. 55,000 (Namgyal, and Dolma, 1908). About a dozen headmen are named, who paid land revenue, cattle tax, timber royalty, pig tax, ferry duties on goods, and incomes from lawsuits in estate properties. By 1849, the revenue to the Sikkim Durbar had fallen to Rs. 15,878/12/6. The reason for the declining revenue was not lost sight of by the royal couple: In 1839, Darjeeling contained about a hundred *bastiwallahs* but within ten years more than 10,000 houses had settled there. People from all parts of the country flocked there. It having become a great market, the slaves and menial classes of Sikkim, Bhutan and Nepal—all—took refuge there. The Sikkim people, not being aware of or used to the usages of powerful government, used to pursue their slaves and kidnap them back from Darjeeling. And the criminals from Darjeeling sought refuge in Sikkim. These things brought about an ill-will [between the British and Sikkim] (Namgyal and Dolma, 1908).

The Nepalese were recruited to the British Indian army in a big way after 1815. They not only turned out to be a strong ally and mercenary force but also became pioneers of the British penetration into the eastern Himalayas. The British were engaged in developing the eastern Himalayan foothills for tea-plantation, an attractive proposition for the gregarious and thriving Nepalese. Moreover, in their efforts to contain the Bhutias of Sikkim and Bhutan and in a limited way even the tribes of the eastern frontiers, the British used the Nepalese as a wedge between themselves stationed in the plains and the indigenous people. Thus, they formed 34 per cent of the population of Darjeeling out of 94,712 in 1872, a proportion which had increased to more than 50 per cent of the total by

1901 (O'Malley, 1985: 41).

Between 1869 to 1907 the population increased by about three times. According to the Census of India, 1941, Nepal provided 45 per cent of foreign immigrants to India. According to the 1961 census the number of immigrants per 100 persons over the period 1931-61 averaged around 35 persons in the hill areas of Darjeeling. Needless to say, in the early period it was still higher (Dasgupta, 1985: 52).

By the middle of 1980s more than 90 per cent of the population in the hill district of Darjeeling are claimed to be of Nepalese origin. It appears that the Nepalese prefer grazing and farming in the hilly and forested areas. Their presence is noted by eloquent absence elsewhere in the tea growing districts, Darjeeling excepted. The Royal Commission on Labour in India, 1930, recorded that even in Jalpaiguri, the plains district with the highest number of Nepalese tea plantation labourers, there was a decline of 30 per cent in Nepalese plantation force between 1911 and 1921. Possibly the Nepalese were lured to the adjoining northern Bhutan as graziers and farmers, as Nepalese were immigrating to southern Bhutan in considerable numbers in those days.

Even before the British emerged as the masters of Sikkim, there were Newar coin minters (*taksharis*) such as Laxidhar and Chandrabir Pradhans, who were permitted to mine copper for coinage on behalf of the Durbar (Bhattacharya, 1980: 220-226; Sinha, 1975: 8). Sikkim effectively came under the British empire in 1889, when John C. White was appointed the Political Officer at Gangtok. White, an engineer by profession, took the job of infrastructural and economic development of his charge seriously. In his zeal for development he took the Nepalese under his wing at the cost of alienating even the royal couple. This appears to have been part of the British ethnic policy in the eastern Himalayas in the 1890's. Herbert Risley, the British scholar-administrator, wrote in 1894: "The Lepchas are rapidly dying out; while from the west, the industrious Newars and Gurkhas of Nepal are pressing forward . . . Here also religion will play a leading part. In Sikkim as in India, Hinduism will assuredly cast out Buddhism, and the praying wheel of the Lama will give place to the sacrificial implements of the Brahmins. The land will follow the creed; the Tibetan proprietors will gradually be disposed and will be taken themselves to petty trade . . . Thus, race and religion, the prime movers of the Asiatic world, will settle the Sikkim difficulty for us in their own way'' (Risley, 1894).

However, within fifty years, the British ethnic policy in Sikkim changed completely. The new Indian Union was advised by the Political Officer to encourage Sikkim and Bhutan to distance themselves from India so that a new element of Buddhism should not be added to the existing Indian communalism.

The excerpt from Risley lays bare the British ethnic policy in Sikkim. Consequently, from 1891 to 1986 the Nepalese population in Sikkim had increased phenomenally. With a view to creating a better future, they joined the movement for democratization against the feudal anachronism. It was primarily a movement by the Nepalese peasants led by semi-educated persons of lower middle class. Neither did they have any ideological sophistication nor organizational skill. They altogether lacked a sense of larger political perspective. It was a confused movement against vague targets. Their slogans, symbols and programmes were largely irrevelant to the local situations. That is why when the Political Officer of the independent India dismissed the first popular government in Sikkim in May 1949, the Sikkim State Congress leadership was thoroughly puzzled. This dismissal was, in the typical British colonial style, in utter disregard of the fact that the State Congress was practically the Sikkimese branch of the Indian National Congress which was ruling India at that time. In the new situation, Sikkim meant the Maharaja of Sikkim, and not the people of Sikkim. Thus, the administration was once more handed over to the paternalistic care of the ICS, who saw to it that the staggering feudal structure was strengthened at the cost of the democratic forces.

What resulted on the Sikkimese political scene came to be known as the democratic fraud of the *parity formula*, a concession to the feudal authority and deception of democracy to the people of Sikkim. The crown prince and later the last Chogyal, Palden Thondup, organised the Sikkim National Party, an anti-thesis of the State Congress. It is an open secret that in typical British colonial style, New Delhi encouraged the *Durbar* in its manoeuvring against the State Congress. No doubt it was a vulnerable movement because of its weak social base. In this way, what happened in Sikkim between 1973 and 1975 was neither an invasion nor a revolution. It was simply a matter of changed priority from New Delhi's point of view. The Chogyal had overplayed his limited role, gone beyond his brief, and was already nursing hopes of an international role and identity which he never had. In the new dispensation, while the Lepcha-Bhutias were recognized as the scheduled tribes with twelve out of thirty-two elective seats in the State Assembly, the Nepalese felt cheated, as the rest of the unreserved seats were declared open to be contested by any Indian citizen. By then four-fifths of an estimated four lakh of the total Sikkimese population belonged to the Nepalese and another 30,000 stateless Nepalese were waiting for formal citizenship certificates. The Nepalese leaders in Sikkim have been demanding reservation of the seats in the State Assmebly for the Nepalese, recognition of Nepali as one of the Indian regional languages and granting of citizenship to the stateless Nepalese. Though these issues have been hanging fire for nearly a decade now, the state is ruled by the Nepalese and Nepali is one of the state languages of Sikkim. It is the only state of the Indian Union in which the language has been accorded such a privilege.

Nepalese sources claim that the Dharmaraja Namgyal settled some Nepalese in the Dalimkote region of Bhutan in the seventeenth century (Dungel, 1983). However, the effective Nepalese colonization of Bhutan started with the Indo-Bhutanese war of 1864. It was the Zungta Kazi and Ha Dzongpen, the effective ruler of western Bhutan, who invited the industrious and sturdy Nepalese to clear the difficult Duars with British encouragement. Charles A. Bell, the settlement officer in Kalimpong, provided statistics on 500 square miles of western Bhutan in 1904 (Bell, 1904). According to him, the Siphchu and Sangbe Kazis had 750 and 50 houses of the Nepalese under their respective controls. The three Nepalese *thikadars,* the contractual settlers—Nandlal Chhetri, Garajman Gurung, and Lalsing Gurung—could count 800, 1,000 and 130 houses of the Nepalese in their command. Bell worked out a population of 15,000 Nepalese in the region calculated at the rate of 5.5 persons per house; an apparent underestimate, because the native Bhutanese families were always smaller than those of the Nepalese. He found the Nepalese under oppressive Bhutanese control and even then he identified four reasons for immigration. First, the land was much more abundant in Bhutan than in the adjoining British territory. Secondly, tenants in Bhutan could cultivate any unoccupied land and burn the jungle as they pleased. In fact, in view of the backward state of cultivation the situation was much appreciated by the Bhutanese authorities although extensive forests were exposed to wanton burning and grazing. Thirdly, they could brew all kinds of liquor without restriction both for their consumption and for sale. And lastly, they could cut wood wherever they desired, as there were no reserve forests in Bhutan.

Some three decades after Bell's survey, Capt. C.J. Morris undertook an extensive tour of southern Bhutanese districts to assess the posibilities for Nepalese recruitment into the Assam Rifles stationed at Shillong. He worked out a rough estimate of about 5,494 Nepalese houses from the places he could visit. However, he could not visit all areas of Bhutan, such as Siphchu, which were inhabited by the Nepalese. Thus he estimated an approximate 6,000 Nepalese houses and worked out a population of about 60,000 at the rate of ten persons per family. However, he had good reasons to believe that the correct population figure of the Nepalese in Bhutan was considerably more than the estimate. The Bhutanese system of taxation encouraged large immigrant families, as land rent was levied on each house, not on the family. Estimating the population of Bhutan as 300,000 he found more than 20 per cent of the total to be Nepalese (Morris, 1932).

There has been no formal census in Bhutan, though the authorities occasionally claim to provide the latest population figures of the country. The latest official population of Bhutan was claimed to be 1,165,000 in 1981, distributed through eighteen districts. The Nepalese immigrants are huddled in large settlements, unlike their indigenous northern neighbours, in three south Bhutanese districts. Though the state does not provide an ethnic breakdown of the population figures, it is claimed officially that 15 per cent of the total Bhutanese are from Nepal. The Nepalese, settled as peasants in large villages, provide almost the entire urban-industrial unskilled labour force of the country. They claim to contribute atleast 60 per cent of the total population of Bhutan. One may safely say that while the official population figure is patently underestimated, the Nepalese claim is equally wild. On balance it would be fair to estimate at least one-third of the total population of twelve lakh Bhutanese to be of Nepalese origin.

The Nepalese on the Eastern Frontiers

'There is a hill; send up a Gurkha' is more appropriate in the context of the seven states of the North-Eastern Council (Chandler, 1913). The first direct contact between the Nepalese and this region appears to have occurred in 1817, when 1,000 Hindustanis and Gurkhas took part in the Sylhet operation as part of the Cuttack Legion (later known as the Assam Light Infantry; Shakespeare, 1977: 6). It is claimed that one Subedar Jaichand Thakur, retired from the Eighth Gurkha Platoon, Sylhet, got settled as early as 1824 at Shillong. He is credited to have built a Radha Krishna temple at the place of his residence (Dungel, 1983). Some four decades after that Thurnton records in his memoirs that an irregular corps of the Sylhet Light Infantry consisting mainly of Gurkhas was stationed at Jowai in the Jaintia Hills during the 1862 rebellion (Thurnton, 1895: 104). The Nepalese presence was such that even before the capital of Assam was shifted to Shillong. Thurnton found, in 1867, that 'an excellent cricket ground had been formed on the smooth and level floor of a valley . . . and cricket was played several times a week . . . The Gurkhas are very fond of games like cricket and football and sometimes excelled in them (Thurnton, 1895: 153).

The story of Nepalese involvement in the consolidation of the region under the British empire is ably presented through the pages of Col. Shakespeare's *History of Assam Rifles* (1977). Whether it was Sylhet or the Shillong plateau, Naga Hills or Lushai Hills, Chittagong Hill tracts or Sadiya Frontier tracts, the Bhutan wars or the Manipur rebellion, the Gurkhas constituted half the Assam Rifles and were always there in operation. Their important role in the Assam Rifles was recognized as early as 1865, when the Nepalese *khukri* replaced the short sword which had impeded their progress through the jungle (Shakespeare, 1977: 23). It may be appropariate to inform the readers that in the course of time the crossed *khukri* was accepted as the emblem of the Assam Rifles, the custodians of the security of the region.

The Gurkhas could perform any odd and sundry job, including specialized jobs, assigned to them. Col. Shakespeare records an incident revealing the versality of the Gurkhas. It was during the Surma Valley expedition in 1871, recorded by Lord. F. Roberts, the senior Staff Officer. To begin the construction of the first bridge "he sent for the Sapper Officer . . . It would take time, the Officer said, as he first had to calculate the force of the current, weight to be borne by the bridge, strength of the timber required etc. He left to make his calculations and plans, and some of the Frontier Police came up to Lord Roberts to ask if he needed a bridge there. On hearing this was the case, the men, together with some Gurkhas of the 42nd ALI, set to at once, some felling bamboos and trees, others cutting them to required length, while others waded to their chest in the stream and drove uprights into the river bed, to which the bamboo flooring was then rapidly attached. The bridge was completed in a rough but efficient way, and was being tested by marching men over it before the Sapper Officer returned with all his calculations ready to begin his work. His surprise at seeing this unscientific but practical method of bridging can be imagined, and matters of this nature were henceforth left to those better acquainted with such work in this country" (Shakespeare, 1977: 69).

L.S.S. O'Malley, the editor of the Bengal District Gazetteers, echoed this spirit when he recorded that the Nepalese 'are a capable, cheerful and alert people, and are essentially a virile race. Though quick tempered and keen to resent an injustice, they are remarkably willing and loyal, if treated with consideration . . . Though small in stature, these Nepalese have big hearts . . . Naturally vigorous, excitable and aggressive, they are very law abiding' (O'Malley, 1985: 44). This was also testified in an intelligence report on the offical account of the Abor Expedition of 1911-12: The greater part of the striking force consisted of Gurkhas. The latter is to great extent a savage himself and remarkably well able to look after himself in the jungle, if he is encouraged to use his own initiative, and this instinct coupled with the fact that he has been trained to think makes him quite able to cope with almost any jungle man (Intelligence Branch, Army Headquarters, 1983: 33-

34). Half of the fighting force and carrier coolies on this expedition were Nepalese.

The Ex-Soldiers

Besides the Assam Rifles, the Gurkha Training Centre (GTC) and various battalions of the armed forces were stationed at and around the district towns and strategic locations on the hills. After their release from service, a number of Gurkhas settled down around these places. Besides the other agencies, the Assam Rifles alone has rehabilitated its Gurkha ex-soldiers on atleast forty sites numbering as many as three thousand individuals. Some of the sites such as Sadiya in Assam, Mantripokhari in Manipur, Aizawl in Mizoram and Mokokchung in Nagaland are as old as a hundred years. Of such sites, Assam alone has thirteen, Manipur eight, Mizoram and Nagaland seven each, Arunachal Pradesh three and Meghalaya and Tripura one each. These are predominantly Nepalese settlements, though there may be a smattering of others. Most of these residents have adapted themselves to the local situation in such a way that they are counted among the indigenous people with all the benefits, even though they have their own communities and their own way of life, speak their language and maintain their own traditions. But the Nepalese have a great capacity to assimilate themselves with the hill communities. They adopt the languages of their neighbourhood, contract marital alliances, and turn out to be an inseparable part of the local economy. In the Mon and Ao areas they have been adopted as members of the tribal communities where they are counted as legally indigenous people and secure the amenities to which the hill tribes are constitutionally entitled. It is said that a former Chief Minister of Nagaland is heavily dependent on the Nepalese electorate of his constituency from Mokokchung. So much so that his father, who was an interpreter (*Dobhashi*) in the British days, had adopted a Nepali as his son in accordance with Ao tradition. This adopted Nepali brother of the leader is claimed to be his right hand man in matters of political support.

The Nepalese ex-soldiers were encouraged to settle down in the foothills, forest fringes and in other strategic points on the frontiers. In this way certain compact pockets of Nepalese settlements in Arunachal Pradesh, Assam, Nagaland, and Manipur emerged.

These new settlers, with their peasant background and the discipline of their strict military training, acquired an image as loyal citizens with pro-establishment attitudes towards the government. With their hard work, perseverance and investment of their pensions in agriculture, they have been able to turn out their newly acquired settlements as thriving centres of prosperous peasantry. Their apparent and visible prosperity among the relatively indolent and less achievement-oriented indigenous communities attracts jealousies. There is another aspect of the ex-soldiers' presence in the region. A number of settlements is located in areas where there is considerable movement of armed forces to contain secessionist and extremist activities. The Nepalese ex-soldiers are accused of providing information on strategy and logistics to the armed forces. In such a situation, the Nepalese at times suffer at the hands of the local insurgent groups. That is exactly what happend in April 1980 in the Sagomong area in the Sadar sub-division of the Manipur Central District, when several Nepalese villages were burnt by the suspected insurgents (Sinha, 1982: 92).

Herdsmen and Farmers

As far as the plains from the Bengal Duars to the Barak Valley are concerned, in terms of Nepalese settlement, a distinct trend may be noted. The less skilful and marginal farmers and pastoralists turned to pastoral grazing on the hilly and forested tracts of the region. The Nepalese herdsmen and marginal farmers trickled down to Assam atleast from the first quarter of the present century. The Chief Secretary of the Government of Assam informed the Foreign Secretary of the Government of India on 13 May 1930 that: "The greater number of the numerous Nepali graziers in Assam are Jaisis and Upadhyay Brahmins or Chhetris of non-martial classes. Some of the Gurkhalis of the fighting classes, who have served in the Gurkha regiments in the Assam Rifles, settled down in Assam when they leave the service. During the cold weather many Gurkhalis of marital castes, Rais, Limbus, come to work as sawyers in the Assam forests. Very few of them, however, settle down permanently in Assam . . . The immigration of the Nepalese into Assam may be described as an administrative nuisance rather than a political menace." He adds that: 'As the province of Assam develops, the proclivities of the Nepali immigants for illicit distillation, poaching and avoiding payment of the government revenue will be defeated.[2]

Within a decade or so the situation changed. J.H. Hutton initiated a policy to remove the Nepalese settlers from the Naga Hills on economic and not political considerations. In his view, the Nepalese breed very fast and they would soon be eating up tracts of land in the hills badly needed by the Nagas, already themselves short of land.[3] Furthermore, an Intelligence Officer cautioned the government: "That there has been great infiltration of Nepalese eastwards from Nepal is very true and very noticeable. It is impossible for anybody who has lived in Assam, as I have for the last 16 years, not to have noticed the remarkable number of Nepalese that one sees all over the province, particularly in the Assam valley, the hill districts and the frontier tracts."[4]

In this context, the agrarian activities of the Nepalese in the Karbi Anglong and Khasi Hills districts may be referred to as representative cases. The district gazetteer records that 'the Nepalese for the most part were graziers, who keep large herds of cows and buffaloes. They have penetrated deep into the interior of the district and have established *khunties* (herdsmen's temporary sheds). Some of them have taken to cultivation also' (Dutta, 1979).

The Nepalese herdsman and farmer moves out of Nepal or its immediate eastern neighbouring Indian districts in search of new opportunities alone or sometimes in small groups of unskilled labourers. The only capital he carries with himself are his personal qualities as a cheerful, perseverant and sturdy hand, his ubiquitous *khukri* and a readiness to do anything to make a living. With this temperament, he easily combines a number of roles in himself as a dairyman, share-cropper, landless labourer, porter, smith, carpenter and even errand boy. When he comes to the easternhill tracts, he invariably locates himself away from the tribal village on an uninhabited possibly barren, forest fringe. Often he is guilty of felling forest trees, grazing and even clandestine settlements on the reserve forests.

With his frugal habits, perseverance, and industriousness he makes a difficult living for himself to begin with. His role in the local economy within no time turns out to be significant, because of his availability for any type of agriculture chores. The lonely porter of yesterday begins to be locally identified. He too feels comfortable enough to realize his physical, psychological, and social needs. His cosmopolitan social outlook, relative freedom from restrictions of purity and pollution in terms of food and drink and the prevalence of polygamy enable him easily to acquire a female partner. The number of wives a Nepali may have increases his productive capabilities not only biologically, but also in economic terms. In many cases, it has been found that the larger the family of the Nepali the more prosperous it is. An administrator with about four decades of experience in the region came to the same conclusion: 'The Nepalese . . . are phenomenally fertile people, and it is not unusual to find among them families where there are four or five wives and twenty to thirty children' (Rustomji, 1971: 141).

Artisans and Professionals

Besides the ex-soldiers and the marginal farmer-graziers, there are artisans and semi-skilled professionals and a newly emerging category of white collar employees among the Nepalese of the region. In the urban centres of the region, where caste-bound professional specialist artisans are non-existent, the Nepalese have been able to fill the role of intermediary semi-skilled professionals between the unskilled local and highly sophisticated professionals from other parts of the India. The types of work in which the urban Nepalese are engaged are new to the region. Thus there is little competition from the local indigenous communities, and unlike the rural ex-soldier and farmer Nepalese, they rarely come into conflict with the local community. The urban Nepalese lead a near-cosmopolitan life in which their expenses are in tune with their income. Being a Nepalese does not help a semi-skilled professional, who thus maintains a submerged identity and joins his Hindu, Buddhist, or Christian neighbours for social, cultural, and religious celebrations. The newly emerged white-collar Nepalese, on the other hand, are born, brought up, and educated in the region, speak the local dominant languages besides their mother tongue and remember the sufferings of their fathers. They are politically aware and culturally conscious of their status in the region and the Indian Union as citizens. As they compete for the the scarce white-collar jobs with indigenous communities for whom the positions are reserved in accordance with the law of the land, the educated Nepalese aspirants are unconsciously made aware that they do not belong to the dominant local community. What else can they do but fall back upon the Gurkha past, Hindu traditionalism, and pan-Nepalese solidarity as the panacea?

The Nepalese demographic claim in Assam has always been exaggerated.[5] There were only 1.9 per cent Nepali speakers in Assam according to the 1961 census. This figure went up to 2.3 per cent in 1971. The Nepali language ranked as the fifth major language of the state. With the exception of plains districts (Such as Goalpara, Kamrup, Nowgaon, and Cachar), approximately every fifteenth Assamese is a Nepali in the hill districts (Darrang 5.05 per cent, Dibrugarh 11.05 per cent, Karbi Anglong 6.43 per cent, Sibsagar 2.05 per cent and N.C. Hills 6.17 per cent. Dey, 1977: 91-92). While the decennial growth rate between 1961 and 1971 for Assam was 34.95 per cent, for the Nepalese in Assam it turned out to be 48 per cent. Keeping this in view, an estimated number of the Nepalese in the region inclusive of Sikkim, Bhutan, and the North Bengal may be anything between three and three and a half million. One may be reminded of the demand in the 1940s of the All India Gurkha League for inclusion of North Bengal in Assam; and later, in the confusing situation of the British withdrawal from India and partition of the country, of their claim made to integrate Nepali-speaking Darjeeling, Sikkim, and Jalpaiguri with Nepal, a proposal endorsed by H.S. Suhrawardy, the Muslim League Premier of Bengal (Deb and Lahiri, 1982: 196-199).

The Conflicting Identities and the Dilemma of the Indian Nepalese

The Nepalese are proud of their history, culture, religion, language and traditions. In their exuberance they naturally draw on the experiences of their perennial source, Nepal. Nepal is the only Hindu monarchy in the world, and maintained a shadowy sovereignty even during the British days. The ancestors of the Nepalese ruling oligarchy claim to have successfully fought the Mughal emperors, and conventional Nepalese still refer to India as Mughlan.

As orthodox Hindus, Nepalese share the same traditions with their Indian counterparts—scriptures, legendary and mythological heritage, sacred shrines and places of pilgrimage, language and script, and a host of other folk traditions. The Nepalese, proud of their Nepalese identity, naturally consider the average Indian (Hindu) to be familiar and not dissimilar to themselves. Before the present Indo-Nepalese boundaries were recognized as such, an average Nepali was vaguely aware of their existence and could cross and recross them for multifarious activities, which was considered normal. The Nepalese kings, who believe that their forefathers immigrated to Nepal from Rajasthan, had been contracting marital alliances from among the Indian princely states. The common Nepalese, subjects of the king and loyal to the royal family, automatically feel related to the common people of these ex-princely states from which their nobility brought their consorts. In their heart of hearts, the Nepalese know that they do not belong to the Indian core. However, they are equally certain that from a cultural, religious, historical, and over-all traditional standpoint they are as good associates of the Indian core as Gujaratis, Malayalis, or Maharashtrians. Obviously, from the historical, cultural, religious, and even geographical perspectives, Nepal is an associate to the Indian core.

The Indian core, it appears, accords Nepal a peripheral and not an associate status. Religious, cultural, and historical similarities provide an irritant between the two. For example, Nepal claims to be the only Hindu state in the world, while predominantly Hindu India is a secular state. The Nepalese insistence on its cultural distinctiveness from India does not provide enough scope to chart out the course of affinity. Similarly, the Nepalese historical claim to maintain an equal distance between India and China (Tibet as well) makes Indian core reluctant to accept it. Nepalese dress, food habits, caste structure, and commensality, an admixture of Buddhism even in Nepalese Hinduism, and a host of similar claims, blur the common original heritage of the two. As a sovereign state, Nepal figures in the Indian mainstream as a formal entity, which does not materially affect normal behavioural patterns and vital interests. Thus, Nepal, in spite of its historical, cultural, religious, and geographical proximity remains on the periphery of the Indian mainstream. The Nepalese—the immigrants from Nepal and those who were born and brought up in India—are accorded the same status as a peripheral community. This differential identification creates a host of problems which remain unresolved.

The actual status of the Nepalese, a large immigrant community from another sovereign state, has to be determined. How do they belong to the Indian commonwealth of cultures and religions? In what ways do their history, culture, language, and traditions become Indian? Will the efforts of the Nepalese to seek an Indian identity be construed as the extension of the genuine policies, programmes, and traditions of Nepal? What will be the economic cost and political implications of the transformation of the Nepalese into Indians? Might not the Hindu identity claimed by the Nepalese and the Indian secular political culture lead to a possible conflict of values? What will happen to those Nepalese who possess multiple citizenship as Nepalese, Bhutanese, and Indian? The Nepalese, unlike the Indians, have access to Tibet. Will the acceptance of the Nepalese as Indians in such a situation affect the Indian defence interest?

Before one tries to answer the above issues, one must be honest to accept certain reservations in India about Nepalese credentials. The leaders of the Indian freedom movement identified the Nepalese as faithful allies of the British and, even worse for the Nepalese, they were popularly known as British mercenaries. There is plenty of evidence to show that the Nepalese took sides with the British. Jung Bahadur Rana's march to Gorakhpur to help the British in the 1857 rebellion and the posting of Gurkhas by the British to contain the Congress agitators on various occasions during the British rule are two examples. However, two points must be made here. First, the Nepalese were not the only ones to be used by the British in such a way. Secondly, the Nepalese did contribute in the integration, consolidation, development, and reconstruction of the Indian state after Independence, especially the north-eastern states, a point which should not be forgotten.

Thirdly, the issue of the Indian Nepalese is intricately linked with the problems of the immigrant Indians in Nepal. Over at the least the last 200 years, the Nepalese rulers encouraged the land-hungry peasants from the Gangetic plains to clear the hot, humid, malarial, and 'negative' *terai* forests. While the hillmen from the interior and the eastern of Nepal were migrating eastwards to India, the *deswalis madesias* were engaged in turning the negative terai into the most prosperous economic bastion of Nepal. It is also a fact that the *deswalis* (Indian) and *paharis* (Nepalese) fought soldier to soldier against feudal tyranny. Both have their kinsmen across the border and share a common cultural and religious tradition. Moreover, the privileged among them were educated at Varanasi, Patna, Calcutta, and Lucknow saw little difference between Hindi and Nepali, which are both written in the same Devanagri script. Since 1960 resurgent ('rising' as they call it) Nepal has changed its priorities. Instead of a common heritage of culture, religion, and history, she emphasizes her distinct identity. In such a situation, the immigrant Indians are not only no more welcome, but they are suspected of carrying 'the democratic germs' to the monolithic Panchayat system of Nepal. On the other hand, Nepal considers herself the natural custodian of the larger Nepalese interests. And that is why voices are raised aganist real and putative problems of the Nepalese immigrants in the north-eastern frontiers of India.

The Bhutias in Sikkim, the Bengalis in West Bengal and the Khasis in Meghalaya invariably inform their visitors that most of the Nepalese have multiple identities—Nepalese, Bhutanese and Indians. Many of them are reported to have immovable property and voting rights in Nepal. It is said that Nepalese politics in India are not autonomous. Worst of all, it is alleged that the Nepalese are either passing information to, or taking orders, from Nepal. And that, it is claimed, is one of the reasons why no Indian Nepalese has risen to national stature in Indian politics during the past four decades. This atmosphere of suspicion and past reservations have to be changed into something positive. As Indians, perhaps we have to ask ourselves how far the genuine aspirations of the Nepalese have been accommodated in the body politic of India.

The Indian states were carved out on the principles of language, ethnicity, and regional historical peculiarities. The Nepalese claims for their territorial aspirations are not new and they should not be lightly brushed aside. However, too much reliance on historical background may lead one to draw the wrong conclusions. Since the indigenous communities on the eastern frontier region, such as Lepcha, Bhutia and other scheduled tribes, have been properly accommodated in the Indian framework, it is now the turn of the Nepalese. For their part, they must not leave any scope for anybody to suspect their credentials as Indians. As the dominant ethnic group in Sikkim and Darjeeling they must demonstrate their political maturity, eschew violence, rise above immediate and parochial issues, and integrate themselves into the national political structure. But much geater responsibility lies with the Indian mainstream. Some positive and sincere efforts must be made to acknowledge the Nepalese role in the body politic of India.

Notes

1. 'The world Hindu denotes a joint family of different faiths, different peoples . . . It is evolved out of the heterogenous ways of life of hundreds of tribes and communities that lived in India for ages. This form of Hinduism is a multi-centred, decentralized structure formation of the ways of life of all those people. Of course, the central norms of Hinduism are represented by the beliefs and thoughts of the Indo-Aryan groups because of the dominating role of those people in the making of Indian history. But influences of the non-Aryan communities should not be minimized. Thus, while peripheral beliefs will have no place in the religious books of the Hindus, some of these beliefs will certainly be part of Hindu practice' (Barlinge, 1986: 1-2).
2. India Office Library Records: MSS/EUR/p. 7607/1930. confidential letter No. 892.
3. Confidential File No. C125/47, Political, Assam Secretariat, Fortnightly.
4. Report No. 61/24 April 1946 of the Central Intelligence Office, Govt. of Assam.
5. The All India Gurkha League claimed thirteen lakh Gurkhas in Assam on 1 January, 1946 at Guwahati; while their spokesman in the Constituent Assembly, Capt. Dambar Singh Gurung, claimed thirty lakh Gurkhas in India. B.D. Dungel informs us that there were more than thirty-nine lakh Gurkhas in India, though he does not disclose the sources for his estimate.

References

Barlinge, S.S. 1986, 'Four phases of Hinduism'. Paper given at the seminar on 'Historical and Contemporary Character of Hinduism' at Nehru Memorial Museum and Library, Teen Murti House, New Delhi.

Bell, C.A. 1904, 'Report on special duty in connection with Bhutan'. 21st July. India Office Library and Records (IOR) MSS/EUR/F80/5C.

Bhattacharya, P.K. 1980, 'Study of a few documents on the coinage of Sikkim', in: *Sources of the History of India,* vol. III. Edited by N.R. Ray. Calcutta.

Chandler, E. 1913, *Unveiling Lhasa*. London.

Chaube, S.K. 1984, 'Cultural frame and the dynamics of federalism in India'. *Social Science Probings*, vol. I, no. 2.

Dasgupta M. 1985, 'Demographic pattern of the hill areas of Darjeeling district', in: *The Himalayas: Profiles in Modernization and Adoption.* Edited by S.K. Chaube, New Delhi.

Dev, B.J. and D.K. Lahiri, 1982, 'Gurkha politics in Assam and its neighbourhood'. *Proceedings of the North-east Indian History Association*. Shillong

Dey, S.K. 1977, *Census of India*, 1971, *Assam Series*-3, *General Report.* Guwahati.

Dungel, B.D. 1983, 'The history of the Nepalese communities in North East India'. *Sakhari Samikscha* (Nepali monthly magazine), December 1983-June 1984. Shillong.

Dutta, K.N. 1979, *Assam District Gazetteer: United Mikiar and North Cachar District*. Guwahati.

Gaige, F.H. 1975, *Regionalism and National Unity in Nepal*. Delhi.

Intelligence Branch, Army Headquarters. 1983, *Frontiers and Overseas Expeditions from India,* vol. VII, *Abor Expedition*. Delhi.

Morris, C.J. 1932, 'Report on the immigration of Gurkhas into Bhutan.' IOR/MSS/EUR/L¼PeS/12/2230.

Namgyal, Hope. 1966, 'The Sikkimese theory of land-holding and the Darjeeling Grant'. *Bulletin of Tibetology*, vol. III, no. 2.

Namgyal, Thutab and Yeshe Dolma. 1908, 'The History of Sikkim'. MSS. translated from the Tibetan by Kazi Dawa Samdup.

O'Malley, L.S.S. 1907, *Bengal District Gazetteer, Darjeeling* (1985 reprint edition), New Delhi.

Patterson, G.N. 1963, *Peking versus Delhi*. London.

Pemble, J. 1971, *The Invasion of Nepal: John Company at War*. Oxford.

Risley, H.H. 1894, *Gazetteer of Sikkim*. Calcutta.

Rosser, C. 1966, 'Social mobility in the Newar caste system', in: *Caste and Kin in Nepal, India and Ceylon,* Edited by C. von Fürer-Haimendorf. (1978 reprint edition). New Delhi.

Rustomji, N.K. 1971, *Enchanted Frontiers*. Bombay.

Shakespeare, Col. L.W. 1929. *History of the Assam Rifles* (Reprint edition). Aizawl.

Shils, E. 1961, 'Centre and periphery', in: *The Logic of Personal Knowledge: Essays Presented to Michael Polanyi on his Birthday*. London.

Sinha, A.C. 1975, *Politics of Sikkim*. Faridabad.

Sinha, A.C. 1982, 'The Nepalese in North East India: ethnicity and resource appropriation', in: *Social Tension in North East India,* Edited by J.B. Bhattacharjee. Shillong.

Sinha, A.C. 1984, *Studies in Himalayan Communities*. New Delhi.

Strassold, R. 1980, 'Centre—Periphery and System—Boundary', in: *Centre and Periphery*. Edited by J. Goatmann. London.

Thurnton, J.H. 1895, *Memories of Seven Campaigns*. Westminster.

Part II
Aspects of Change

7

*Peasant and Peasant-Conflict in Nagaland**

Can the tribal subsistence farmers, primitive agriculturists, the *Jhumias* and the terrace-cultivators of Nagaland be termed as peasants? A convenient answer will be that they represent the various shades of the 'Asiatic mode of Production'. Possibly somebody with access to more empirical data may not be happy with the above explanation. He may find Naga cultivators changing fast enough during the last hundred years to be adequately covered by the term. One may consider the massive transformation ensued during the last two decades or so, which suggest a possible shift from community to domesticity, from localized bartering to extensive cash transaction, from predominantly subsistence *jhuming* to an organized, permanently cultivated rotational cropping pattern. Simultaneously, one does not fail to note that various economic sub-systems co-exist side-by-side in the same locality with variation in the topography. Will this predominantly rural and agriculture based scenario be adequately understood by the term 'peasant'? This brief paper proposes to uncover the various aspects of the Angami economy. We have selected Mezdiphema Development Block (District Kohima, Nagaland) as a case study. It pro-

* We thankfully acknowledge the help of Mr. Vizier Angami, Lecturer in History, Kohima Arts College; Mr. Lanu Ao, Lecturer in Sociology at NEHU College of Agriculture, Medziphema; Mr. Lanu Aier, Lecturer in Sociology at Pachchunga University College, Aizawl and Mr. Binchilo Thong, an M.A. student, Department of Sociology, NEHU, Shillong. The ideas presented in the paper owe their elaboration to our frequent discussion on the Angamis with Dr. Imdad Hussain, our colleague from the Department of History, NEHU. While appreciating the indebtedness of the above persons, we owe all the limitations of the presentation.

vides us with diverse ecology, ethnic group and economy leading to conflicting situation at times. Incidentally, this is the most developed part of Nagaland, connected with the capital intensive Indian economy, which has created its own paradox of development.

There have been efforts to distinguish tribes from caste, and folk and peasant formation on social, psychological and economic bases. Peasants have further been identified as distinct culture bearing phenomenon with an intermediary position between tribal and urban contexts. There have been various efforts to define peasantry. However, we feel Soul and Wood's qualification of the peasants as 'those whose ultimate security and subsistence lies in their having certain rights in land and in the labour of family members on the land, but who are involved, through rights and obligations in a wide economic system which includes participation of non-peasants" (Soul, J.S. and Woods, R.: 1979). With a view to delimiting the peasant societies, Theoder Shanin identifies four basic facts: (i) family farm as the basic unit of social organization, (ii) land husbandry as the major means of livelihood, (iii) traditional culture as way of life of the small groups and (iv) domination of peasantry by the outsiders (from urban industrial metropolitan centres) (Shanim, T.: 1979). From these two conceptual and operational points of view, the Angami cultivators under question will be examined as to whether they constitute a peasantry or not.

The State of Nagaland is reported to have 7 districts, 21 Rural Development Blocks, 1,028 villages, 110,000 households, and 773,281 persons in 1982. It has 19 major communities ranging from highly articulate settled cultivators to the hunting-cum-primitive agriculturists of the interior and inaccessible hill tracts. The south western part of the state is known as the land of the Angami, administratively organized as the district of Kohima. This is one of the most developed parts of the State in the sense that visible urban-industrial, settled-agricultural, commercial and other aspects of economic transformation are perceptible. It is surrounded by relatively more exposed plainsmen and hill tribes of Assam and Manipur. It is divided into Tseminyu, Kohima, Jalukie and Medziphema Rural Development Blocks. Out of four, Kohima and Medziphema Blocks provide the rail-cum-road link, the life line of the State, which effectively connects the State with other parts of the country. While Kohima as the State Capital, is the hub of all the political, economic and developmental activities of the State, Dimapur, which falls under Medziphema Block, is something like the commercial capital of the State. In this way, the major parts of the Medziphema Block come effectively under the economic hinterland of Dimapur township.

Higher in the hills, Khonoma and Kohima along with Jotsema and Visema represent the traditional socio-economic setting for the Angamis. Their migration myths, history and genealogy and other cultural artefacts refer to southern direction. Again unlike other hill communities, the Angamis had a tradition of fortified villages, settled, terraced, permanent cultivation, cash transaction, long distance trade and lack of strong village chieftainship. We shall show that most of the Angami villages of the Medziphema Block were either settled, or satellites or dependents of Khonoma group of villages. This region on the north-western fringe of the Angami land was not in the centre of their profound orientation and activities. It was definitely used by the Angami to trade with the Kachari and Ahoms during the pre-British phase of their history. By bringing railhead to Dimapur the British increased the significance of the region considerably, as this point turned out to be the launching pad to the Angami land. However, it has developed by leaps and bounds after statehood of Nagaland in 1963.

The Traditional Village Structure

The region is located on the hilly tracts and foothills in the west of Khonoma and Kohima highlands. Historically the Angamis were more oriented towards south to Imphal valley. The northern section was less significant for the Angamis as one rarely finds a fortified village in it. However, the entire foothills upto Chumokedima (Samugothing) were decidely under the Angami over-lordship, who had a loose fraternal relationship with the Kacharis of Dimapur on river Dhanadiri. The marshal Angami could subjugate the Zemi and Zeliangs who were on the south western foothills of the region. They were taxed and enslaved by the Angamis. Many times Kukis were solicited by the Kacha Nagas with a view to containing the Angamis. On the north western tip of the region, a small colony of scattered Sema villages was located. In this way though the region was predominantly Angami, Zemi, Zeliang, Kuki, Kacharis, and Sema butted in from south west and northern directions respectively. Slopes of the land have been from south the north and from north west to south east. Consequently, the north western portion has been more extensively hilly, undulating and forested than south western.

By tradition an Angami village must have atleast two clans, a senior and a junior one. However, there are large villages such as Kohima which have even seven clans. The village land terraced, *Jhum* forest, grave yard, grassland and habitation, is normally divided among the clans. The clan members have their individual domestic units in the form of various land use patterns. Traditionally, the Angami had been great warriors engaged in inter-clan, inter-village and inter-tribal raids, feuds, and conflicts with a view to extracting certain revenues in kind and recruiting slaves. In spite of the casualties during such operations, as late as 1872 the density of population in Kohima was found to be 50 persons per square mile. (Butler, J. reproduced by Elwin (ed): 1969). Even today it is one of the most densely populated districts in north eastern hill region.

The villages were normally built on commanding and strategic positions at the height of about 4000 feet. All possible precautions were taken for its defence. The larger and stronger villages invariably oppressed and plundered the small and weak neighbours. Within themselves these dominant villages were something like city-states governed by the will of the warriors. In case of the villages diminishing in their denizens, the dominant ones insisted on annual tribute of cattle, fowls, paddy, cloth etc. or plundered them for the same articles and head-hunting. There used to be inter-clan, inter-village and even inter-tribal marriages. Such married persons used to act as the go-between among the villages during the feuds. Pfulise of Khonoma village belonging to Meyase clan got married to a Kachari girl, the daughter of the chief of village Kuthuria (near Dimapur) some 14 generations back (that is, sometimes in the 17th century). It is said that the groom had to pay the bride price in terms of *Phri* (a cross-breed of Mithun and cow) and goats. The descendants of the couple are still butt of jokes because of their alleged association with un-chivalrous goats.

Traditional Peasant Economy

The Angami agriculture was based on intricate and dexterous terracing of the hill slopes and indigenous water management devices. Even in 1874 they were found to till their terrace fields unlike their neighbours. (Broom, R.: 1874). The rights of the individuals to property in land are recognised; rules relating to inheritance and partition to such property are settled strictly as per customary law. Among the Angamis, land especially permanent terraced cutivated one is freely sold and bought there being no difficulty in selling a terraced field than in selling a pig or a cow. "The standard of measurement for Nagaland is not area, but the number of loads of paddy that it yields. Terraced rice land is both sold and let . . . An acre of rice land near Khonoma . . . sold as much as Rs. 600 . . . but it can be bought for about 1/3 of that sum (also). An acre of terraced rice land lets from Rs. 3 to Rs. 9 a year according to quality, while an acre of jhum land can be rented for two seasons . . . for a rupee and a half . . . (though) the absence of any system of measurement renders the exact pitch of these rents a little doubtful", wrote John Butler in the last century. The *Jhumming* which is quite secondary in importance among the Angamis, is based on individual's clan based rights. The portion of the *jhum* land, which has not been brought under the private rights, cannot be sold except by the clan itself.

It was reported that a thousand Angami Nagas visited Nowgong to trade salt and beads in 1848. The Medziphema region had been producing a type of cotton, which was used for producing the famous Angami shawls and which was also bartered and was available for sale as well. The Angami farmers had special attractions to Khamkiri village (literal meaning iron tree in Lhota) near northern foothills from where they used to procure little bit of iron for spearheads etc. They used to trade their *mithun*, cotton, shawls, occasionally ivory, with salt, dried fish, shell beads across the Angami country. They could also visit markets in the foothills to exchange their cotton and ginger with that of minor articles such as trinkets etc. "The most of the business is transacted on a cash basis and there is very little barter. The principal trading communities are the residents of Khonoma, Jotsoma, Mozema and Visema . . . will go as far as a field as Bombay . . . (for) carrying beads . . . There are no such things as village markets." (Allen, B.C.: 1981). That was about the time Krusietso, Z.A. Phizo's father, was engaged in trade between Burma and the Marwari merchants at Kohima and Dimapur. He used to buy glass beads from the Marwaris for selling them to the Burmese and buying silk from the latter for disposing of to the former on a considerable profit. Moreover, they had to pay the house tax at the rate of rupees two per house per annum; for that they began working on the construction of the road in consideration for cash payment.

The Angami Peasants and Peasant-Conflict in Medziphema

The Medziphema Rural Development Block has 111 villages recognised by the the State government as per its revenue records, besides Dimapur town and its suburb. Among them 28 are inhabitated by the Sema, 24 by the Angami, 22 by the Kacharis, 8 by the Kukis and 29 are mixed ethnic villages. Again the mixed villages have various ethnic compositions; in some of it are the Kukis and Kacharis, in others Sema and Lotha, still in others Ao, Angami, Sangtam, Phom, Nepalese and others in various combinations. However, there were 89 unrecognised villages in the Block in December, 1984. The Angami peasants own their terraced or *Jhum* land individually, produce cereal and non-cereal for their domestic consumption through the members of their own family. For other consumer goods such as cloth, medicine, stationery, cutlery, utensils etc. they depend on the larger Indian productive process. In this way, the Angamis may be given Theodor Shanin's definition of the farmer. However, the Angamis have descended in a big way to their north-western slope to Medziphema region during the last two decades or so. We have made a note that besides their famous terracing, they had been marginally engaged in *jhumming*. This was in practice where (i) land was in plenty, (ii) population was relatively small, (iii) technology was primitive, (iv) the settlement was devoid of cash economy, (v) location was a relatively isolated one, and (vi) where land ownership was communal. Slowly but steadily, the above factors have changed and that has led to permanently settled wet paddy cultivation as well as the extension of terracing.

The traditional handicrafts have given way to similar factory products. The forest hunters and collectors of the roots have lost their vocations because of dwindling forest resources. Similarly, village warriors are spared of their vocations as the raids, reprisals and extensive revengeful expeditions have ceased to be in practice. Consequently, traditional handicraftsmen, hunters, gatherers and warriors are available for more gainfully employed economic vocations. Naturally most of them turn to the agriculture and are possibly busy in raising fruits, vegetables and other cash crops by the road side, besides offering themselves as occasional agricultural labour. Some of them do supplement their budget by subsistence business.

The Kacharis were settled near Dimapur in the north since the pre-British phase of Naga history. The Angamis were on the southern hill-tops. They had a tradition not to travel/move northwards to slopes and plains during April/May, when a particular tree used to blossom. In case of violation of the belief, it was presumed that they would suffer from malaria, dysentery and other ailments. Thus, the Angamis considered the region inhospitable and unworthy of permanent settlement. However, there were small settlements such as Rezuphema, Tsphema, Pherima, Medziphema etc. which unlike traditional Angami fortified large villages, were insignificant in size and were possibly satellite villages of larger and more powerful ones. In course of time, Angami villages such as Sirhima, Pherima, Medziphema etc. were deserted by the original settlers and came to be inhabited by the Kuki, the Sema and the Lhota. After construction of Dimapur-Imphal Road, it was a continuous concern of the Deputy Commissioner, Naga Hills District to have some settlements by the road-side between Dimapur and Kohima. Accordingly Semas and Kukis were permitted to move in the region in 1930's as permanent settlers in some villages. However, a large scale colonization started only after 1963, when State of Nagaland was formally inaugurated.

The more enterprising highlanders—especially the neo-rich contractor-cum-politicians and even some bureaucrats—have bought big farm lands in the low-lying foothills for paddy and cash cropping. They themselves stay away to Kohima, Dimapur or elsewhere and assign their less endowed kinsmen for managing the farms. On such farms invariably the *Mias* (the Muslims from Manipur valley or Nowgong district of Assam) are employed as farm hands on annual basis. It so happens that the *Mias* (or the Meiteis or more appropriately *Pangal* from Manipur, Nepalese and Bengali immigrants and even some Assamese) come annually before the plantation season to the respective land owners, who provide them with huts for their shelter; make provision for their food; and they are given implements, seeds, manure etc. for the cultivation. All these amenities are extended to the share-croppers on deferred payment. When the crops are harvested, the share-croppers get 1/4 or 1/3 of the crops as their labour, from which the advances paid to them are deducted. They are supposed to sell the paddy to the land owners at the existing market price and then they go to their native place with some sacks of grains and some amount of money with a view to returning again to the same master for the next year. Thus, this exploitative cycle continues year after year.

The region has got some small and medium scale industries. For example, a sugar factory was started in 1970 with a financial assistance from the Nagaland Industrial Development Corporation. It is run during the cane crushing season between October and March every year creating seasonal employment for some persons. About two-thirds of the cane-growers are individual suppliers, while one-third of supply is made through the Sugarcane Growers Co-operative Societies. Between Semas (aboput 30%), Aos (about 30%) and Angamis (about 20%) 80 per cent sugar cane is grown and supplied to the factory. These three dominant communities are invariably absentee owners of the plots of land on which sugar is cultivated, but they hire normally non-tribal agricultural labour from Nepalese, Biharis, Bengalis and other communities. These wage-earners lead a miserable life, because of uncertain wages and payments, lack of housing, health and other basic amenities. Consequently, they do not devote themselves to work as normally owner-cultivators do elsewhere. Thus, among the many reasons for the malfunctioning of the factory this is one of the contributory factors through which inferior and irregular supply of the sugar cane is met. Here is a potential problem. While the land owning farmers expect a better income from the sugarcane they supply to the factory, they hardly provide amenities for their farm hands. Thus, a potential conflict between the masters and wage-earners has been in the offing.

The Kukis, Zemis and Zeliangs who had been by tradition shifting cultivators are emulating the Angamis and switching on to the settled cultivation on the low-lying southern portion of the Block. This is the region where Angamis feel that non-*jhum* land belongs to them. Thus, there is a potential danger of conflict. The relatively less exposed and educated Kukis in fact are selling off such land to non-Angamis or to any tribal, who can pay them well so that they can wriggle themselves out of the conflict. On the northern border of the Block, the Sema tribesmen are similarly pushing westwards from hills to the foothills. By tradition, Semas have small villages. An enterprising person can establish a new settlement and he would be recognised as the chief of the settlement. Besides the Sema tradition of a chief's son invariably establishing his own villages, there are some other reasons as well. The old villages no more provide with the resources for a comfortable living as population has grown and natural resources diminished. After the Shillong accord between the Naga insurgents and the Central Government, the surrendering insurgents were to be rehabilitated. The Semas seized upon this opportunity and started pushing on the forest land in the north-eastern side of Dimapur. The State Government of Nagaland is not in a position to arrest this process. Thus, a number of such villages have emerged lately and as many as 89 of them are yet to be recognized. Consequently, these unrecognised villages do not pay house tax (@ Rs. 5 per house) to the State Government. However, the violent conflicts between the Angamis and the Semas have occurred more than once on this patch of land and precious lives have been lost. There were eleven violent cases registered in the court of Extra Assistant Commissioner, Medziphema involving 70 villages from six tribes during 1979 to 1984 alone.

The western edge of the Block is found with the multi ethnic mixed villages consisting of Angami, Kuki, Lhota, Sema, Kachari, Mikiri, Nepalese, Biharis, etc. in their various combinations. There are new villages such as Rezuphema which are inhabited by a number of clans which have shadowy claims over the nearby land. Such areas are inhabited by three types of people. Firstly, the outcastes, drop-outs, criminals, expelled etc. migrate to such areas, where they lose their identities. Secondly, those who come from the hills in search of more fertile land with better opportunities. And thirdly, ambitious persons with some education, wealth and political contacts, drop down to these villages as political entrepreneurs. They contest elections for various offices; acquire contracts for construction work and invest in other urban interests. All these immigrants treat these villages as bonanza towns to maximize their profits and in the process they invariably end in serious conflicts with the dominant local Angamis.

To sum up, this brief paper endeavours to analyse the social formation of the Angamis. The Angamis invariably claim that they are not tribals as Konyaks could be understood. In case one goes by the operational definitions, the Angamis provide an excellent example of peasantry. However, in actual practice they advance multi-identities in the form of tribal religions, nativistic ideas etc. but among them the most effective has been the ethnic one. This brief note presents a hurried picture of the massive transformation during the span of a few decades. Naturally the Angami peasants are exposed to a number of conflicts, whose base is decidedly economic. The new economic opportunities are being utilized by the more articulate neo-rich Angami elite who appropriate better chunk of economic development in their favour. With a view to camouflaging the nature of inner contradictions and various shades of conflicts, the Angami elite have been advancing the issues of the ethnic identity in the forefront.

References

1. See, B.C. Allen, *District Gazetteer of Naga Hills and Manipur*, Gian Publications, Delhi (Reprint), 1981, pp. 51-52.
2. R. Brown, *Report on the Exploration of the Angami Naga and Manipur Boundary*, Shillong, 1874.
3. J. Butler, 'Rough Notes on the Angami Nagas and their Language', *Journal of Asiatic Society of Bengal*, Vol. XIV.
4. J.H. Hutton, *The Angami Nagas*, Oxford University Press, Calcutta (Reprint), 1968, p. 140.
5. T. Shanin, Ibid., pp. 14-15.
6. Johns S. Soul and R. Woods, 'African Peasantry', in: *Peasants and Peasant Societies*, T. Shanin (ed.), Penguin Books, 1979, p. 105.

8

The Character of Urbanization in the Hill States

The concept of political culture proposed in 1960s by the American political sociologists suggests theoretical and empirical focus on both the national and local politics to the level of urban centres. It has conveniently been divided into cultural sub-types to care for the empirical specificities. In this chapter, we, firstly, propose to examine the relevance of the concept of political culture in the context of urban India. Secondly, we should like to discern the character of the hill cities in north-eastern frontier states of Arunachal, Meghalaya, Mizoram and Nagaland. And lastly, we shall endeavour to identify the distinct urban political culture of the hill cities of the region with a bearing on the urban development and consequences. The chapter has been prepared with limited data with a view to identifying the nature of citizen's participation in the affairs of their cities. The basic premise of the chapter was examined afresh in the light of the various presentations in the workshop at Mokokchung in March 1991 (Sinha, et al: 1993).

The Urban Political Culture

Political culture, though still imprecise conceptually, provides a package of theoretical and empirical orientations to understand national politics at one and local level politics at another. Taking an inspiration from anthropological studies on national character, model personality, cultural patterns, cultural complex, cultural ethos, great traditions, etc. Edward Shils coined the concept civic culture (Shils, E.: 1961). The concept expresses British and American experiences of pluralistic culture based on communication and persuasion, consensus and diversity, a culture that permitted change but moderated it. In their seach for political traditions of five democracies—United States, Great Britain, Germany, Italy and Mexico—Gabriel Almond and Sindrey Verba gave empirical clarity to the concept. In their views political culture refers to the specifically political orientations—"attitudes towards the political system and its various parts, and attitudes towards the role of the self in the system" (Almond, G.A. and Verba, S.: 1963: 13). Lucien Pye used the concept in his study of Burma, which was followed by a series of systematic and behavioural studies in late 1960s and 1970s.

The recurrent themes in political cultural studies emphasize normative beliefs and values about various political objects such as roles, institutions, incumbents, policies, political self and so on. An illustrative list of such subjects has been provided by Knoke:

1. *Political Community*: Attachments to the political system as a whole and to other members, degree of national and local identity and belonging.
2. *The "Political" Realm*: What politics is all about; boundaries between decisions which may be made by the political process and those lying outside the polity; perceptions of the political needs of society.
3. *Participation*: Who may participate in political activity and in what capacity; political roles, including rights and obligations; the nature of leadership and constraints on elite behaviour; the proper motives of leaders and the general status of politicians; limits on mass mobilization by leaders.
4. *Power and Authority*: The bases for claiming political legitimacy; limits on the use of power; modes for transforming political power, resources into authority and influence, and vice versa.
5. "*Rules of the Game*": Proper constitutional devices for making collective decisions; the range of permissible political tactics; procedure for transfer of power from incumbents to challengers, modes for resolving conflicting interests.
6. *Political Symbols*: The value symbols of the political community, especially historical symbols; ideals and end states of the "good polity" and "good society."
7. *Scope of Government*: The range of functions which government should undertake; the proper division of labour between

the polity and the rest of society, and within the polity between government organisations, the amount of power desirable for government to have.

8. *Political Trust*: Willingness to work with various groups on collective actions, trust in representatives and in institutions to reach acceptable decisions.
9. *Issue Agenda*: The range of permissible issues that should actively be considered by the political system; means for raising new issues and ordering their sequence for consideration.
10. *The Political Self*: Personal role in politics, sense of efficacy, political ideals and means to achieve them" (Knoke, D.: 1981: 205-206).

A useful consideration may be to examine the various sub-cultural types proposed by empirical studies. In this context Knoke refers to the 'common-wealth" principle, 'market place view,' and a 'traditionalistic' (paternal for elitist) sub-cultural types found in American urban contexts. As these are far from empirically established, need for further studies are emphasized, in which orientation at the community level and perceptions at the individual levels are to be examined. A note of caution was sounded: "if individual orientations are to be measured, the communities and neighbourhoods from which samples are drawn must be carefully selected to maximise the representation of the full range of political cultures and their institutional manifestations" (Knoke, D.: 1981: 220). Perhaps it will be useful to fall back to the pioneering study of Atlanta by Floyd Hunter and New Haven by Robert Dahl at the level of power structure. Presthus' 'men at the top' control, govern, decide, manage and even appropriate urban affairs as per ethos and traditions of their respective civic cultures, possibly shared by the urban masses.

Urban Political Culture in India

In Indian context Ashraf's study of three metropolitian cities of Calcutta, Kanpur and Ahmedabad examines politics, government and grassroot participation at urban level. With a view to uncovering the facets of differential urban development in the above cities, he proposed two political cultural sub-types: the *Babu* (parasitical) ethic and *Bania* (entrepreneurial and altruistic) ethic. In his own words: "The socio-cultural and political differences between Calcutta and Kanpur on the one hand and Ahmedabad on the other are at the roots of institutional decay and development to be found respectively in the two sets of cities. These differences may be conceptualised at two forms of ethic—the Babu ethic and the Bania ethic. The Babu ethic is unenterprising, averse to risk, and also egoistic or parochial and parasitical. It seeks personal gratification in privilege and status, and depends on heredity or bureaucracy for achievements of its goals. The Babu ethic is, therefore, exploitative and encourages corruption. It is devoid of public spirit and blind to public interest. The Bania ethic (akin to protestant ethic) in contrast is entrepreneurial, altruistic and creative. It seeks solvency, self-reliance and autonomy in private life and in constructive and creative in public life. It is innovative, builds new institutions, and manages them with the co-operation of all. Self-employment and self-government are its key principles. The success of public institutions, more so of self-governing institutions, depends on the prevalence of Bania ethic. The Babu waits for others to do a job or solve a problem; the Bania does it himself" (Ashraf, A.: 1977: 184-85).

In case we endeavour to analyse the various problems confronted by the hill cities in the north-eastern Indian frontier states, the concept of political culture with its sub-types come handy. To begin with, these cities were created as the colonial administrative outposts on a subsistence tribal economic base about a hundred years back. Since then, they have grown in size and significance, but their hinterland remains at the subsistence level. Whether pulled to the city and its amenities or pushed out of the rural areas by stagnant economy, the urbanisation in these ex-colonial societies is not economically autonomous, as it is not the centre of an expanding industrial economy. In such a situation the rural migrants "are urban in residence, but rural in their lives they lead and the ideas they hold. They usually occupy the lowest rungs in the urban labour market; they often inhabit the most crowded sections of the city—their poor wages commonly used to satisfy only the most minimal standards of existence so that they can free more money for remittance to their rural homes. This urban adaptation is clearly a response to the lack of industrial expansion in the colonial city and the lack of economic transformation in rural areas" (Cox, R.G.: 1977: 126). The colonial societies, peasantry and urbanites all alike, were linked to the Western industrial nations so as to maximise the economic rule. Thus, they are no longer pre-industrial and not yet industrial societies in transition with plethora of problems at all the levels.

Among the above colonial cities, administrative cities have played a significant role. They are the residence of the state elite, they centralise commerce, crafts and other occupational specialities, and they provide political, economic and communicative links with surrounding country side. With increased population and population specialization, an urban class structure appears dependent on differential source and amount of wealth. In this way administrative cities are so much more than their rural environs that rural areas appear culturally denuded, socially deficient, and ideologically backward by comparison. The cities may still reflect the country side, but they do so with such intensity that it appears to have their own independent luminosity (Cox, R.G.: 1977: 62). They also turn out to be markets in which to convert agricultural products into wealth and services. Commerce in the city is subjected to the same state administrative control. Merchant wealth like peasant produce is either suppressed as a threat to political stability or extracted to subsidise the state. These cities are political extension of the bureaucratic state. As these cities are only bastion of state power and not a source of state power, they play a passive role in state upheavals. They are linked into an urban hierarchy based on their position in state administration, their relative bureaucratic functions and their relative civil and military size of establishments, as the local, district, provincial and capital cities.

Among the urban populace, civil and military functionaries and commercial interests are the two chief components. A lower category of menials, labourers and 'undesirable' elements such as thieves, prostitutes, criminals, etc. thrive as marginal urbanities. These sections are controlled by either formal state structure such as municipal government or informal structure such as ethnic, familial, religious or other ascriptive associations. In neither case do the cities develop as a unified community as such besides the state;

rather they remain desperate collection of different and distinct populations. The state creates buffers to cushion the antagonism directed at it in the form of informal or institutionalised social brokers such as religious notable. "They must effect a continuous balance between the conflicting interests of the state and the urban population. Should this balance be disturbed, these brokers are the first to be punished by the state or to be taken as victims of an urban mob" (Cox, R.G.: 1977: 85). The administrative cities impoverish the country side culturally and ideologically as well. The grandeur of the cities, great tradition is sharply removed from the folk traditions of the peasantry.

Travail of Urbanisation in India

The Pre-British Cities: We learn from our historical experience of the city like settlements of Indus Valley civilization. Similarly, anci-ent Mauryan and Gupta imperial cities of the Gangetic plains—such as Patliputra, Koshambi, Vaishali, Kanyakubza, Varanasi, Prayag etc. are referred in the 'historical' writing. The *Muslim* rulers in the medi-eval period of the Indian history established a network of military outposts—*Thanas*—in a very uncomplicated manner. It is claimed that forty *Namazis*, a central mosque and a central bazaar was all that needed to found a town. The urban artisans, position in such towns was as vital as that of the cultivator in his village. The artisans served as the productive base of urban economic life: wards were assigned to each craft, and its producers formed themselves into corporate bodies, usually affiliated to some religious order (Naqvi, H.K.: 1972). Several factors were responsible for the differential growth of the towns. Among them topography was a significant consideration. The highly urbanised region was the *Hindustan,* between Lahore and Benaras, and the terrain and extreme cold climate of Kabul and Kashmir did not encourage urban centres to grow. There were garrison cities with fortification all around their limits and most of the cities were governed by the *Kotwals* and *Darogas.* Within the city itself the community life went on the way of *Panchayat* system, a type of caste council for the street, exhibited by Ahmedabad even today in certain localities.

The Colonial Cities: The British established the port cities of

Calcutta, Madras and Bombay to locate factories and defend their trade aganist the local banditry and competing European companies. In course of time these cities emerged as the symbols of modernisation and technology in the 19th century. Moreover, they came to be identified as perimeter in their regions, magnets in a larger catchment area and cradles of political and social resurgence in the country (Sivaramakrishnan, K.C.: 1978). The British did take in consideration the locational advantage of the old cities such as Patna, Lucknow, Agra, Allahabad, Delhi, Lahore, Ahmedabad, Surat, etc., but they established a series of *hill stations* as sanatoria for themselves. That is how Dehradun, Nainital, Mussoorie, Shimla, Dalhousie, Muree, Darjeeling, Kalimpong, Shillong, Ranchi, Ooty, Panchmarhi, and a host of other cities were located in the hills to cater to the needs of the basically European settlers. They were uniquely British to the extent that they were created by the British almost on no man's land for the European comfort and control. These were invariably parasitic settlements with the least contact with the neighbouring native communities. For the European settlers—who were themselves second best in their own category—these hill settlements were second choice, where they could invest some of their savings in the urban estates. These hill stations lived on the borrowed lives of the British rule and saw instant decline in their affluence with the upsurge of democratic populism.

A third set of cities were accidentally created by the British in the most inaccessible regions as exclusively administrative outposts and cantonments for the armed forces. These were invariably identified with the pioneering spirits of their founders and even earned their names: Daltangunj, Abbotabad, Forbesgunj, etc. Another variety of this set was the identification of an ideal location in the heart of the communities to be governed and establishment of an administrative outpost with minimum facilities under the guard of a small armed contingent. And that is how Tura, Kohima, Mokokchung, Aizawl, Lungleh, Wokha and a host of others emerged from obscure unknown sites to administrative entities. These were the centres with the least contacts with the outside world and cut off from immediate community socially and culturally. They were neither meant for the white settlers nor for the native entrepreneurs. They simply happened to be ideal locational watching towers over the surrounding communities and were left to themselves for most of the time during the British rule.

The Hill Stations: The hill cities in the small frontier states were not evolved in the hoary past. As their hinterland did not have an economic stratification in the past; they did not pass through the experience of the classical feudal societies. Even today there is no industry as such. Thus, these cities do not have experience of either feudal or industrial structure and culture. When the hill cities were created as the colonial administrative outposts, they did not generate an instant response and participation from the hill communities, as they were established after vanquishing the tribesmen in war. The tribals had to pay capital and house tax, work as labour force for constructing road and public buildings and were conscripted as unpaid or ill-paid porters. Naturally, they kept away from the cities, as they were alien entities to be avoided as much as possible. But it was not possible to keep off them for long years because the cities were located in the tribal hinterland. Slowly, they came to realize that the "*haat*" had come to them, they better visit them to barter necessities and come back home from it before the sun-set.

The Haat Culture: The earliest experience for commercial transaction the hill tribes had before the colonial set-up, was with the '*haat*' on the foothills or river banks, where they could barter their wild products aganist their own necessities. They could travel long distance scaling the hills, fording the streams, and running across the evergreen forests with burning bamboo torches in their hands to ward off wild beasts. The merchants and their customers would shout prices, haggle around and ultimately bargain a favourable price through signs and broken bazaar language. The *haats* themselves were transitory congregations. They would begin by late morning, reach their crescendo around mid-day and by afternoon they would start thinning away. To the extent that with the sun-set they would be totally deserted by the itinerant shopkeepers and visiting customers leaving behind discarded refuse, filth and pariha dogs.

The visiting tribals would be in their best finery, ornaments and other display items such as hunting gear. They would eat condiments, rice and chillies, smoke *biris*, occsaionally drink country liquor and collect trinkets for their dear ones at home. They would meet their friends, relatives and even enemies; negotiate on settlements of disputes; contract marital alliances and even conspire against the foes. But by evening they would be once more on forest highway for a homeward journey leaving behind the *haat*. It did not belong to them; they did not belong to it; the two were two different worlds and were just the meeting points with minimum of interaction and that too without much intensity. One could feel free in the *haat*; act as care free as possible; come across a variety of novelties; shout and gesticulate with purpose and even sing and dance on way home. No doubt, one had occasions to celebrate, especially after a good bargain. But in the final analysis, the *haats* were just the meeting points, which belonged to nobody.

The British moved to the Khasi Hills in 1826, to the Garo Hill in 1868, to the Naga Hills in 1876 and to the Mizo Hills in 1890 and established district administrative outposts of Shillong, Tura, Kohima and Aizawl in the heart of the tribal territories. Before that, they had experimented with establishing administrative centres on tribal fringes located on a better communication network with the plains. The brief experiments of running the administration from Cherrapunji, Singimari, Chumkedima, Sadiya for Khasi hills, Garo hills, Naga hills and N.E.F.A. respectively were abondoned in favour of better locations in the interior. The land for the station was secured through cession, contractual arrangements, gifts, lease exchange or outright purchase. The basic mode of the land tenure had been community controlled subsistence farming known as *jhumming*. Normally, it is the lineage, clan, hamlet, village or tribe, which owns the land and controls the resources in forms of land, forest, fishing and hunting rights. At times, private ownership is recognised provided an individual invests his labour on a particular piece of land for years together.

Social Structure of the Colonial Hill Cities

To begin with, the hill cities had the Deputy Commissioner as the presiding deity with the Superintendent of Police (S.P.), Civil Surgeon of the Civil Hospital, the Post Master, the Church Pastor and the Commandant of the Assam Rifles as the significant functionaries. Taxes were levied on houses and were collected by the village chiefs on commission. Entry of the plainsmen to the hills was controlled and alienation of the tribal land was discouraged. The tribals were reluctantly induced to offer their manual labour on cash payment for various types of construction and porter's duties so that they could pay the house tax. The clerical staff of the small administration was invariably from the plains and the domestic helpers were the Nepalese and the few shops available were owned by the plainsmen—*Kaians*. In fact, these early urban centres were really 'non-tribal towns on tribal settings' (Chaube, S.K.: 1978: 56), functioning as the colonial administrative outposts, without much of urban amenities and style of life. "The station (of Tura) contains the bungalows of the few resident officials," wrote B.C. Allen in 1905 "and of the missionaries, a small jail, the public offices, the lines of the military police, a market place, and a few shops, but it is nothing more than a village and in 1901 had only a population of 1,370 souls . . . It is small, isolated and is generally thought to be unhealthy" (Allen B.C.: 1980: 24-25). The above statement might be applicable to most of the hill district towns of the British period with the exception of Shillong.

The first fifty years of these hill cities was the period of stagnation and stunting growth, but it was also marked by a slow and perceptible change such as monetisation of the economy, introduction of cash crops, regular markets, new occupations, and above all, a settled condition for peaceful farming. The first attraction of the hill tribes to the 'station' was the hospital. Then came the turn of the schools invariably run by Christian Missionaries on the grants from the government. The attitude to the Christian Church, its ceremonials and functionaries was more of amusement, curiosity and reluctant tolerance to begin with. Petty commercial interests followed the next. Slowly and slowly, a few blue coat employments were secured by the tribals. The young folk, who could get some schooling, was reluctant to return to their *jhum* fields and stayed back around the 'station' on some sundry jobs (Smith, W.C.: 1926; Mills, J.P.: 1973; Vieyra, R.B.: 1979: 113). Some well stocked grocery shops functioned at the bank for the higher bureaucrats. They were the sales and purchase depots, wholesalers, retailers, moneylenders and even salary disbursing agencies in some cases (Sinha, A.C.: 1975).

The centre of the hill city was very much reminiscent of the quasi-feudal structure in the form of establishment of the Deputy Commissioner's office, residence, club, church and his immediate associates. The barracks of the constabulary such as the Assam Rifles was away at a slight distance on a commanding hillock. In between the little shopping centre was located which had establishments owned by the plainsmen on a crude model of the contemporary departmental stores. The transportation from the plains took time to develop. When the modicum of automobile arrived, the regular bus service was operated by the plainsmen replacing old animal driven occasional carts for the higher functionaries. The little colonies of the office assistants were located close by the commercial areas on the outside. There were a number of distinctly tribal villages within the cities with agricultural land groves of trees and cattle heads with all the traditional tribal institutions. Slowly the house-owners in these villages started raising modest structures for renting out to the plainsmen working in the service sector. In course of time, the low lying space between the 'station' and the tribal villages was filled with *shanti* settlements, the veritable slum. The logic of the ever-present cheap labour, health hazard and law and order forced the authorities to extend the urban boundaries to incorporate the slums within the cities' limits. However, inclusion of the tribal villages within the town was not administrative, but a political issue, as they were governed by the customary laws (Sinha, A.C.: 1990).

The Changing Hill Cities

A number of tribals were recruited to the armed forces and the Coolie Corps raised during the two World Wars. When they came back home to their hills, they found that their lives were no more the same. In fact, the region was turned into a limited Eastern Theatre of the War in 1940s. They found erstwhile invincible British colonialists preparing to leave India as rulers. Their own hill brethren were politically more ambitious, demanding and active. By now the church, schools, markets and even hospitals were getting crowded. In this uncertainty and expectancy the hill towns still provided enough agricultural employment in and around their environs. The secondary sector of production was nowhere on the horizon, but the service sector was forging ahead as the most promising avenue for employment to the hillmen. Thus, the hill towns around mid-20th century were still something like swollen villages.

The post-independence period envisaged a total re-organization in the power structure of the hill cities. The all important British bureaucrats had gone away and the provisions of the Sixth Schedule to the Indian Constitution ensured certain legal guarantees to the scheduled tribes. The new bureaucrats turned out to be the plainsmen, more familiar, but less acceptable. The presence of the new rulers, the national political parties—was hardly noteworthy in the hills. There was emerging a rudiment of more aggressive tribal middle class. The newly introduced development and welfare schemes needed personnel and skills at all the levels. The small district administration was enlarged. A better infrastructure—roadways, buses, posts and telegraph, banks, schools—was introduced. In such a situation, the hill cities were turning into place of opportunities. New sets of business and service men emerged on the scene. The construction work introduced a floating population of masons, carpenters, skilled and semi-skilled workers and ubiquitous contractors. All these resulted in the swelling of the urban population in 1970s in the aftermath of the creation of the hill states. As a whole the unorganized urban services were manned by the non-tribals; the municipal space and urban housing were controlled by the tribals, and significant political and administrative decisions in the cities were taken by the distant plainsmen.

The sites of the hill cities were selected mainly because of the locational, strategic and administrative vantage. As the hill districts were the British creation, similarly these administrative cities were all the more a British creation. They played significant roles as trend setters in life style of the communities among whom they were located. Thus, Shillong with Khasi, Jowai with Jaintia, Tura with Garo, Aizawl with Mizo, Kohima with Angami and Mokokchung with Ao got inseparable identities of the above communities. Among all the four hill states, there were only four towns during the British period. Out of a total of 26 towns among them, as many as 19 are district headquarters and even now 5 districts do not have urban centres (Table 7.1). While Arunachal Pradesh is the least urbanised state (6.2 per cent), Mizoram is the most urbanised

(25.17 per cent) in the region, though absolute urban population is maximum in Meghalaya (Table 7.2). While Shillong is the only class I city among the four, Aizawl is the only class II city. Tura, Kohima and Dimapur are class III cities in the hill states. There are four each class IV and class VI types of towns among them and there are five in Arunachal Pradesh, four in Mizoram, three in Nagaland and a solitary class V town is in Meghalaya.

Table 7.1. Location of the cities in the hill states, 1981

Sl. No.	States	No. of districts	District towns	District without towns	District towns	Total of towns
1.	Arunachal	9	5	4	0	6
2.	Meghalaya	5	5	0	1	7
3.	Mizoram	3	3	0	2	6
4.	Nagaland	7	6	1	1	7
	Total	24	19	5	4	26

Table 7.2. Urban profile of hill states, 1981

Sl. No.	States	No. of urban population	% of urban population	Types of towns						No. of towns
				I	II	III	IV	V	VI	
1.	Arunachal	39,715	6.32	0	0	0	0	5	1	6
2.	Meghalaya	239,501	18.03	1	0	1	1	1	3	7
3.	Mizoram	122,765	25.17	0	1	0	1	4	0	6
4.	Nagaland	120,180	15.54	0	0	2	2	3	0	7
	Total	522,161	-	1	1	3	4	13	4	26

Political Culture and Civic Participation in the Hill Cities

Undoubtedly these "non-tribal towns in the tribal setting" were not established with active tribal participation. The non-tribal institutions such as public buildings, corporations, schools, libraries, clubs, etc. are considered as alien, strangers and unwelcome intruders. Civic amenities, public foras such as reading rooms, theatres, drama troupes etc. never emerged because the tribals do not need them and thus, have their own folk tradition of entertainment. If these amenities are to be given, they would like to take benefit of them. As such distant forces created the cities and provided them with some of the historical landmarks, the same paternalistic attitudes continue to be relevant. In case one asks "Whom do these cities belong" and "Who govern them," the answers are not obvious. These cities do not belong to the common citizens in the sense that they control the urban affairs; govern its establishments; plan for its development and feel proud of being its citizen. It is still, by and large, the formal state bureaucracy, which governs these cities. Luckily, by now their size is still manageable, thus, urban affairs, relatively simpler, are easier to be taken care of. But days are not far off when urban problems, such as housing, transportation, slum clearance, environmental pollution, vagrancy, intoxication, urban crime against property, ethnic conflicts, etc. will go beyond reasonable limits. These will be the heritage from setting of urbanisation without industrialisation.

The dominant ethnic groups of these cities appear to have an ambivalent attitude to the cities in which they live. It seems that in the ultimate analysis, they identify themselves less with the cities and more with the particular tribal traditions, in which urban experience is a new phenomenon. They are masters of the affairs on the exclusively ethnic platforms, but their own cities, which are decidedly ethnic plus provide an arena, beyond their past experience. The civic problems are complex and demand specific care. The relatively easy going image of the tribal elite perhaps needs updating. The common impression one gets that even knowledgeable and concerned citizens do not like to take all the possible advantages of the urban living, but in their own involvement in the civic affairs they follow the '*haat*' ethic. The hills cities happened to be there; as if the citizens do not belong to them; the cities do not belong to them; their relationship is marked by minimal level of interaction.

One may ask: What is the nature of the urban political culture in the hill cities of the region? The answer to the above leads to a larger issue: Do the hills states have a distinct political culture of their own? What is the nature of political participation of the regional tribal elite in the Indian democratic system? Have they been able to evolve their own pattern vis-a-vis to the larger Indian pluralism? Answers to these questions lead to the political economy of the Indian Union to which legally the hill tribe states are constituents and their simple technological base and over-all productive system fall outside urban industrial sector. One of the studies refers to the regional over-all development as a sponsored society (Aier, I.L.: 1985) indicative of parasitical development. The distinct urban ethic is again not identifiable, and if there is any thing positive, it is a loud and clear non-concern. The citizens of the hill cities possess '*haat*' ethic in urban affairs.

Broad Policy-frame

With a view to hammering out certain parameters for policy-makers we feel cities have to play crucial roles in the over-all development of the hill states. However, the hill cities have unique problems of their own and many common problems, which they share with other sister urban centres elsewhere. For their common problems such as slum, housing, transportation, etc. there should be solution, which have been tried in other cases. But their unique problems identified as the following require special attention:

1) These urban centres are suffocated because of missing institutional support. The main occupation of their citizens have been service either in the governmental establishments or in the petty trading. In spite of the availability of raw materials, inexpensive and willing labour, capital and even know-how, secondary sector of production cannot be started because of the laws of the land. Urban housing, slum improvement, development schemes such as sewage disposal, water works, etc. need acquisition of land for urban renewal. Thus, there is an urgent need to examine the traditional laws of the land with reference to the requirements of urban industrial centres.

2) There is an utter confusion in the management of the urban affairs in the region.While a state capital such as Shillong has municipality without elections for years together, another state capital in the region, Itanagar, is controlled by a village council. In between we have town committees in a number of hill cities such as Aizawl, Tura, Kohima, Mokokchung, etc. In most of the cases, it is the state bureaucracy, which controls the urban affairs from the top. There is no efforts for active civic participation in solving the urban problems. Thus, we feel that there is an urgent need for evolving some uniform civic administration on the basis of the functions and

size of the population. For example, as a policy the state capitals irrespective of the population may have municipal corporations as in the case of Gangtok, the capital of Sikkim. The rest of the hills cities should have municipalities or other fora, but in all the cases efforts must be made to involve actively the citizens in the management of the urban affairs on democratic principles.

3) The hill cities were controlled by the ex-officio functionaries from the top as a British legacy to manage the small administrative 'outposts' or 'stations'. The state governments are very much concerned with the genuine problems of the dominant hinterland—the rural development. At the national level, specific problems of the hill cities get lost sight of under the glare of daunting urban problems of metropolitan cities such as Calcutta and Bombay. In the process, the genuine problems of the hill cities rarely get attention. For that matter there is a need to create a forum of the civic heads of the hill cities of the states of the region on the pattern of the Council of Mayors in India. They may meet periodically to review their problems and evolve a common strategy to tackle them.

4) Our case studies suggest that there is no definite source of income to these civic bodies. The way their size is growing, the meagre doles advanced by the ex-officio bureaucratic heads and insufficient taxes will not be sufficient to meet with the growing urgency of urban development and renewal programmes. The quality of life for most of the urbanites is deteriorating day by day. It is high time our policy makers, in case they feel proud of their cities, decide upon a definite, regular and adequate amount of money for urban development and maintenance.

5) This takes us to a very sensitive and alive issue of civic participation in the affairs of the cities. The tribal hill states were created with a view to meeting with the aspirations of the constitutionally defined backward (scheduled) communities on a sound democratic principle. The same constitution guarantees certain fundamental rights to all the Indian citizens. Then, how come the State Assemblies, which zealously guard their democratic rights and privileges, ignore the extension of the same principles to their civic bodies, and tolerate non-representative bodies on the very seat of their authority? The articulate, educated and relatively wealthy

non-locals are legally not permitted to invest in their own cities and the cities do not get benefit of their income and savings. In such a situation, what may result in on the urban horizon is seen on the annual fare of civic strifes. The policy makers must decide the nature of civic participation of all the urban citizens and an effective functioning of the civic bodies within their states.

References

1. Aier, I.L. 1985, The Contemporary Naga Social Formations and Ethnic Identity: A Case of Development of Decay, Ph.D. Thesis, MSS, Department of Sociology, NEHU, Shillong.
2. Allen, B.C. 1980, *The Gazetteer of Assam, Vol X, The Khasi and Jaintia Hills, Garo Hills and Lushai Hills,* Indian reprint.
3. Almond, G.A. and S. Verba 1963, *Civic Culture*, Princeton University Press, Princeton, New Jersey.
4. Ashrof, A. 1977, *Government and Politics in Big Cities,* Concept Publishing House, New Delhi.
5. Chaube, S.K. 1978, *Hill Politics in North East India*, Orient Longman, Calcutta.
6. Cox, R.G. 1977, *Urban Anthropology,* Prentice University Press, Prentice Hall, New Jersey.
7. Knoke, D., 1981, 'Urban Political Culture' in: T.C. Clark's (ed) *Urban Policy Analysis,* Sage Publications, London.
8. Mills, J.P. 1973, *The Ao Nagas,* Oxford University Press, Bombay, Reprint.
9. Naqvi, H.K. 1972, *Urbanization and Urban Centres Under the Great Mughals,* Indian Institute of Advanced Studies, Shimla.
10. Sinha, A.C. 1975, *Politics of Sikkim: A Sociological Study,* Thompson Press Pvt. Ltd., Faridabad.
11. Sinha, A.C. 1990, 'Urban Ethnicity and Development in the Hill Cities of North East India; Seminar on Social Dynamics, Department of Sociology, North Bengal University, Rajarammohanpur, Siliguri, Darjeeling.
12. Sinha, A.C. et al 1993, *Hill Cities of Eastern Himalayas,* Indus Publishing Co., New Delhi.
13. Sivaramakrishnan, K.G. 1978, *Indian Urban Scene,* Indian Institute of Advanced Studies, Shimla.
14. Smith, W.C. 1926, *The Ao Nagas of Assam,* MacMillan and Co., London.
15. Vieyra, R.B. 1979, 'Students of Shillong' in: *Cultural Profile of Shillong* (ed) B.B. Goswami, Anthropological Survey of India, Calcutta.

9
Tipaimukh Hydel Electric Project and the Hmar Apprehensions

With the monetization of small scale barter economics, isolated tribes got integrated with the world-wide metropolitan economy. Such tribal communities got used to factory produced consumer goods within no time and began supplying cheap raw materials for the industrial sector. In the process, the communities and their habitat got all the more impoverished. A stage came in the lives of some of such communities, when their vital resources, such as land, forest and rivers were 'required for development of the region' uprooting them altogether. The chapter is a study of such an exercise undertaken at the instance of the Indian Union at its easternmost frontiers in the states of Assam, Manipur and Mizoram and the vitally affected community is the Hmar in turmoil. The chapter, firstly, traces the genesis of the project and provides statistics on it. Secondly, it introduces the Hmar as an ethnic group. Thirdly, after examining their precarious economy, social structure and issue of the efforts to improve their lot, the chapter makes some suggestions to take them in confidence. Incidentally, this is one of the regions where ethnic insurgency is on and such a time and capital consuming project requires careful considerations.

The Genesis of the Project

The river Barak passes through undulating forested tribal areas of Manipur, Mizoram and Assam before it enters the plains. It discharges a huge amount of water, often inundating the adjoining areas and causing considerable loss of property. With increased pressure of population on land and extensive deforestation in the encatchment areas, unrestrained flooding has become a recurrent phenomenon. Thus, there have been continuous demands for controlling the flood and harnessing the river water for irrigation and generation of electricity. In this context, the first serious efforts were made six decades back after the 1929 large scale floods in the region. However, the problems of the Barak valley generated genuine concern only after the independence of India, when a number of river valley projects were undertaken for construction. A site at Moinadhar in Silchar district was suggested in 1954, but on the basis of the geological report, prepared in 1956, the proposal was dropped on May 27, 1957. Immediately, another proposal to construct a low earthen dam at Naraindhar was initiated, only to be rejected in 1964 on the ground of an unfavourable geological report.

In April, 1974, a suggestion was made to examine the possibility to accommodate the entire dam within the narrowest gorge portion itself, where the rock conditions were likely to be most favourable. Such an ideal site was identified at Tipaimukh, 500 metres downstream of the confluence of the Barak and the Tuivai. The Project Report for the Tipaimukh High Dam on River Barak, prepared by the North-Eastern Investigation Division of the Central Water Commission, 1984, envisages the submergence of an area of 291.5 square km and 303.2 square km at EL 175 metres and EL 178 metres, respectively. In both the situations, there will approximately be 180 square kms submergence in the Barak Valley, about 30 square kms in the Tuivai, 53 to 60 square kms in the Irang and 32 square kms in the Makru river valley. The submergence of the culturable land is claimed to be negligible, as the entire area is mainly mixed jungle with bamboos. It is estimated that 31 villages with 1310 families and 743 hectares of garden land will be affected by the submergence. A state-wise break-up of the submergence has been suggested in Table 9.1.

Once the technical, financial and administrative decisions are approved, it will take eleven years to complete the project at a cost of Rs. 1,078 crores.* There has been provisions for acquisition of

---

* The estimate has gone to Rs. 1,300 crores. *The Telegraph*, Calcutta, August 10, 1990.

land, fruit trees and other properties at a cost of Rs. 1445.95 lakhs. While there is a provisions of Rs. 7.74 lakhs for environment and ecology, Rs. 390 lakhs have been set aside for rehabilitation measures. There will be substantial loss of property at the project site, which has been shown in Table 9.2.

Table 9.1. State-wise break-up of the submergence: Suggested

S. No.	Type of land	Manipur	Mizoram
1.	Forest land	113.32	9.54
2.	Uncultivated private land	109.79	12.20
3.	Private land	30.10	1.59
4.	Cultivable land	25.95	1.08
5.	Gardens	7.20	0.23
	Total	286.36	24.64

Table 9.2. Details of the anticipated loss of property from the Tipaimukh project in two states

S. No.	Types of land	Rate of compensation per hc. in Rs.	Manipur		Mizoram	
			Area in ha.	Amount in Rs.	Area in ha.	Amount in Rs.
1.	Forest	4,375	11,332	4,95,77,500	954	41,73,750
2.	Uncultivated land	5,250	10,979	5,76,39,750	1220	64,05,000
3.	Private land	8,750	3,010	2,63,37,500	159	13,91,250
4.	Cultivable land covering ginger, paddy etc.	8,750	2,595	2,27,06,250	108	9,45,000
5.	Garden areas	8,750	720	63,00,000	27	2,36,250
6.	Crop compensation	2,835	648.75	18,39,206	27	78,545
7.	Compensation for fruit trees	approx.		3,87,14,000	–	7,90,000
8.	Buildings					
	(i) Govt/Semi Govt	875.00	No 566	4,95,250	304	
	(ii) Private	437.50	1006	4,40,125	–	2,66,000
	(iii) Temples/ Churches	17,500	4	70,000	1	17,000
	Total			55,28,50,581		1,43,02,795

The Site of the Project

The proposed dam will be located at Tipaimukh in the Tipaimukh sub-division of Churachandpur district of Manipur state, though a small area in Mizoram on the western bank of the river will also be affected. As per the extraordinary Manipur Gazette No. 196-E-64, dated November 12, 1969, there were 30 villages in the sub-division. At least 22 of them located on the Vengai ranges were inhabited by the Hmars, a Kuki-Chin tribe, and were under the Thadou Chiefs' by tradition. Some of the villages, such as Loibol, have a mixed population of Hmars, Thadous and Bengalese. On the other hand, the villages across the river in Mizoram are also inhabited by the Hmars. In this way the project site will decidedly be Hmarland and Hmars will bear the brunt of the construction, colonization, resettlement and rehabilitation. Thus, it is imperative to have a detailed discussion on the Hmar society, economy, politics and ethnic aspirations. As an appreciation of the above problems, the Brahmaputra Flood Control Board, Gauhati initiated a number of studies on the themes related to the Project so that the minimum damage to the environment and community is caused and the maximum benefit is drawn from it. For that matter a high power committee decided on June 26, 1989, in New Delhi, to postpone the implementation of the project for two years and examine the various aspects of the project thoroughly on the basis of the experts' reports. The Union Minister of the Water Resources called a meeting of the Members of the Parliament from the North East in August, 1991 in Delhi and informed them that the Centre had decided to sanction Rs. 1,316 crores to the project for implementation in future. An initial expenditure of Rs. 16.2 crores for building infrastructure was approved for 161 feet long rock filled dam at Tipaimukh and generation of 1500 MW of hydel electricity.*

The Affected Community: The Hmars

The Hmars, a group of hill tribe living in Manipur, Mizoram, Tripura, Assam and Burma, belong to the Kuki-Chin community. The Mizos count them as one of their five major clans along with

* *The Telegraph*, Calcutta, October 10, 1991.

Lushai, Ralte, Paite and Pawi. The Hmars represent an earlier wave of westward migration upto Chittagong Hills and, thus, were also known as the Khawthlang (the westerners) by the late migrants to the Barak Valley such as Lushais (now the Mizos) and Thadou Kukis. Before the British annexation of their territory in 1872, it is claimed that the Hmars were settled in an extensive area from upper Burma to Tripura hills. The British labelled them into six administrative segments. Then they were variously clubbed among the old Kukis, Chin-Kukis, Mizos etc. Till 1950s, there was pressure from the Mizos from the Lushai Hills district of Assam on the Hmars of adjoining district of Manipur to merge themselves in Mizoram. The Mizo Union, a political forum of the Mizos, held its meeting at Senven village in Churachandpur district of Manipur in 1947 with a view to launching a movement for integrating all the Chin-Kuki communities under the proposed autonomous Mizo Hills district in Assam. It was also proposed that the above autonomous district would not be acceptable to the Mizo Union without an integration of the all Mizo-speaking communities. A number of leaders of the Movement were arrested by the Manipur Durbar. But the Mizos of Lushai Hills accepted the Autonomous Mizo Hills District in Assam without getting their brethren from Manipur integrated with them. The Manipur Hmars felt let down and decided to float their separate forum in 1950s, known as the Hmar National Union.

The various Hmar clans got inspired and began to assert their distinct identity away from Kuki, Mizos, Naga, Mikirs and others. They realised that their biggest problem was their fragmented location on the international boundary between India, Burma amd Bangladesh and provincial boundaries of Tripura, Mizoram, Assam and Manipur. In between, two salutary developments occurred; the almost 100 per cent conversion of the community to Christianity through indigenous efforts and a very high rate of literacy through the efforts of the Christian missionaries. They are divided into more than two dozen clans and a number of sub-clans. Many of a time their clan names coincide with the village settlements.

The Hmars and Their Culture

The first step to divide the Hmar community began in 1832

when the British confirmed Gambhir Singh, a Meitei prince, in the possession of the tract eastward of Jiri river (Pudaite, R.: 1963: 30-31). In 1868 the Lieut-Governor of Bengal directed the Deputy Commissioner of Cachar to induce the Mizo Chief Sookpilal not to attack the tea plantations in the plains and give up the captives in his custody. For that an annual money payment was offered to him and the other two chiefs of the Sonai and Tipai, and an annual return present in kind from the chiefs was expected as acknowledgement of allegiance (Mackenzie, A.: 1979: 299). For the Lushai expedition of 1871-72, Tipaimukh, the junction of the Tipai and the Barak, was selected (Tuivai-water + alien = alien water). The Hmars called it Ruong le-vai-suo—the confluence of the Barak and Tui rivers and it was selected as the advance base of operations, and by December 15, 1871, the greater portion of the Cachar Column had collected there.

The British dealings with the hill communities, such as the Hmars, began with the establishment of a chain of marts around the hills. *The General Administrative Report*, 1873, shows that there were three markets on the northern foothills of the Lushai hills: Tipaimukh (the mouth of the river Tuivai) on the confluence of the Barak and the Tuivai, Sonai bazar on the Sonai River and Changsil on the Dhaleswar river. The Tipaimukh bazaar (Latitudes: 24°.13' longitude: 93°.3') was visited by the hillmen from the remote southern villages with a view to selling natural rubber juice. Because of over-tapping many of the rubber trees died out within a few years, leading to decline of its supply to traders at Tipaimukh. In January, 1877, there were five Manipuri traders located in the market and 111 *mounds* of rubber was brought to it. The rent collected from them was divided among the Poiboi, Longkam and Chunglena chiefs (Anonymous, 1978: 41: 55).

The *maharaja* of Manipur ascertained the willingness of the Lushai chiefs, Poiboi and Longkam, to have friendly relations with the Kabui Nagas of North Eastern Manipur and proposed to send a deputation to Tipaimukh for that matter. Though the Deputy Commisiioner of Cachar allowed the deputation to proceed to Tipaimukh, he feared that Chunglena Chief Lalbura might resent the fact of being overlooked in the overtures. In fact, some members of the deputation went to Tipaimukh, and even beyond, and secured a positive response from the above Chief in 1877. However, the Chief Commissioner of Assam objected to the Deputy Commissioner's involvement and denied his intermediary role between the Lushai Chiefs and the Manipur Durbar (Mackenizie, A.: 1979: 162).

It was reported in 1877 that there was scarcity of rice in chief Sookpilal's village and the same was supplied by the Cachari traders. These markets increased in their size and importance but their growth was checked by the extraction of rent by the Chiefs. The Government storehouses were also opened at Tipaimukh and Gutermukh besides the traders mart during the famine of 1881-82. In January, 1883, Thangkoyame, a Kuki chief, raided Tipaimukh to plunder and took a captive away, and that was the year the market was temporarily closed. The chiefs implored the British authorities to reopen the mart the next year. The bazaar remained opened during 1985 to 1887 with only three shops. The Eastern Lushais (Hmars) raids continued and increased in 1887, reducing the business to be at a standstill. Since August 1888, trade had ceased and the bazaar had been abandoned (Anonymous: 1978: 55).

The Christianity Among the Hmars

It is reported that Mr. Watkin B. Roberts, a missionary at Aizawl, printed the Gospel of John in the Mizo language and sent out its copies to different chiefs through the Government mail carrier. One of such copies was received by Kam-Kholun, the Chief of Senvon village in south-western Manipur. The Missionary was invited to preach to the villagers, which he did in January, 1918, leading to the conversion of two young men from the village. This was followed by the enthusiastic missionaries, who undertook educational, literary and the Bible translation work seriously. Slowly and steadily, a network of rural church-run schools was established. Within less than seven decades, 90 per cent of 150,000 Hmar (Pakhuongte, R.: 1983) population was reported to be Christian, belonging to the Evangelical Free Church of India and other Churches. This apex body of the Hmar Christians, under its various nomenclatures, was engaged in sectarian disputes in 1950s and 1960s with other Christian missionaries working among the Mizos.

The Institution of the Chief

Piangzathang Gaite, the President of the Village Chiefs Union, Churachandpur, counts Thadou, Paite, Zou, Gante, Simte, Vaiphei, Lushai and Sukto, besides the Hmars, as among the constituent units of the Kuki-Chin commonwealth (Gaite, P.: 1990: 3). The village land in the Kuki-Chin communities is controlled by the hereditary chief. In fact, all the village land belongs to him and it is he who allots the plots of *jhum* land to the individual families. While the individual families are landless in terms of ownership, they are not a landless community at the village level. Formerly, the chiefs used to receive a fixed amount of paddy annually, known as the *Buhsun* from every family and one pectoral part of a four footed animal killed in the village forests. The chieftainship was held in only certain clans such as Sailo, Thadou, etc. The Manipur Government had enacted a number of laws with a view to regulating land revenue, house-tax, chieftainship, land compensation and agrarian relations between 1947 to 1980.*

In spite of the above laws, the chiefs continue to be in control of the village land. They continue to give the land to the individual cultivators on the payment of a fixed measure of paddy and collect house tax and land compensation in lieu of the land taken over by the Government. Keeping in tune with the changing times, the chiefs themselves demand abolition of the institution after adequate compensation to them. Their counterparts in Tedim Area of Burma were paid compensation in 1940 and Mizoram in 1955. But an apprehension was raised in the case of tribal chiefs of Manipur that a change in traditional customary land relations might lead to the Government take-over of the tribal land, which would result in loss of land to the non-tribals.

A queer situation has developed among the Hmars. Their traditional Thadou chiefs were forced to leave their villages and migrate to Churachandpur around 1960 after an inter-tribal clash. They

* Among them mention may be made of the Hill People Regulation, 1947, Village Authority in the Hill Areas Act, 1956, Armed Forces (Assam and Manipur) Special Powers Act, 1958, Land Revenue & Land Reforms Act, 1960, Hill Areas (Acquisition of the Chief's Rights) Act, 1967. The Hill Areas District Council Act, 1971, Municipalities Act, 1980, etc.

have formed the village chiefs union and kept on filing memoranda to the various functionaries in the administration. On the other hand, most of the villages have got their village councils elected and regulated their land relations and village affairs without reference to the absentee chiefs. Though they are respected, the chiefs are no more paid their customary *Buhsun* by the Hmar commoners. As the chiefs had never cultivated or worked for their maintenance, they find it difficult to maintain themselves in their traditional villages. Thus, they were forced to migrate to areas like Churachandpur, where they could get employment other than agriculture. Thus, a conflicting situation arose in which both the chiefs and the village councils are staking their claims on the compensation to be paid in lieu of the land acquired for the project.

The Hmar Economy

It is a mountainous and forested country between Imphal Valley in the east and Cachar plains in the north-west. Accordingly, the rivers flow to the east and north-west. Except Barak, none of them is navigable as they contain long stretches of rocky pools with uneven depth of water. The Hmar society basically consists of subsistence farmers who draw all their economic resources from the land, forest and water bodies. A village settlement belongs to a clan or a number of clans which exercise control over the communally acquired landed property. By tradition the Hmars are *jhumias*—slash burn type of rotational cultivators. Every year the village authorities open a large unit area of village for cultivation. The vegetation is felled in the months of January-February and is burnt in March. Seeds are sown in the burnt up vegetational ashes in the month of April and they are harvested in November-December. Normally, a *jhum* plot is left fallow for five to ten years before it is cultivated again. Because of the continuous *jhumming* and burning of the vegetation, hill slopes have been eroded and top soil washed away, leading to environmental degradation and silting of the river (Pakhuongte, R.: 1983: 17).

They grow rice, maize, beans, ginger, cucumber, vegetables, cotton, sugarcane and various seasonal fruits. Because of the undulating topography, their agriculture has limited assistance from the animals and it is also a technologically simple society. As the population pressure has grown on the land, the *jhum* cycle has been reduced to the minimum, resulting in depletion of forests and wild life. Thus, of late, hunting of the wild animals and collection of roots, fruits and leaves from the forest have largely lost their economic significance. There are streams and other water bodies in the region and the Hmars are excellent fishermen, but fishing is done entirely for domestic use. Similarly, the cattle head and fowls are kept more for consumption at the domestic level than for sale. The Hmars are a verile and an enterprising community, who used to travel long distance for trading in the past. They used to grow orange and export them as Sylhet orange before 1947. Of late many of them have taken up trading as a vocation and shifted to the urban areas of Churachandapur, Imphal, Aizawl, Kolashib, etc., and are reported to be engaged in what is known as silent trade in electronics, garments, etc. Of late, the Government has been sponsoring coffee plantation, horticultural activities in fruit and vegetable production, pisciculture, poultry, piggery, etc. as a part of integrated rural development schemes. One thing is heartening that the church takes interest in the economic prosperity of its members and encourages new economic activities among them.

Originally, most of the Hmar villages had single clans and, accordingly, all the landed property, forest, wild life and water bodies within the boundaries of the village were clan controlled resources. Again, these clans were further divided and most of them had their distinct dialects. Coming of Christianity and its literacy programme in Roman script led to evolving of a common language. In course of time, the Thadou chiefs, who were almost sovereign in their territories, came to control the resources of the Hmar villages. Any commoner who would disagree with the chief had no place in the village. In such a situation, he had to leave the village before he was ex-communicated or punished otherwise. Secondly, a criminal, such as a murderer, may move to the shelter of another village chief. Thirdly, because of the economic compulsions, such as drought, pestilence or barrenness of the land the villagers were forced to seek shelter in other villages. Fourthly, population pressure on limited *jhum* land at times forced some villagers to migrate. And lastly, some moved from one settlement to another in search of better hunting prospects. In such situations a mono-clan village turned out to be a multi-clan village. Certain clans claim to be brothers, such as Pakhuongte, Darngawn and Benzang and, thus, they work in close associations. Similarly, Ralte and Pakhuongte had interchanged their past associations on claimed past incidents, which still bind their offsprings into close ties.

The Hmar Village

It is claimed that in the olden days, the Hmars used to live in large stockaded villages on strategic locations at the hill tops. With the coming of the British, inter-tribal and inter-clan conflicts came to be minimized. Thus, the village settlements got dispersed and were laid on in regular rows along the ridges with their kitchen gardens in the backyards. There are a number of villages named after the clans, indicating that they were founded by the respective clans and that they had been inter-marrying among themselves. However, most of the villages are multi-clan and some are even multi-tribal entities, consisting of 20 to 500 houses (Pudaite, R.: 1963: 35). The large villages are divided into sections (*Vengs*). At the grass root level, the *veng* loyalty is stronger than the village loyalty, which is subservient to tribal loyalty. With the weakening of the institution of the village chiefs, the village is governed by an elected village council, in which all the *vengs* are effectively represented. The Village Council administers the land at domestic and clan levels; manages the church and school; collects the revenue for the state; maintains law and order and has of late been undertaking the government sponsored development and welfare schemes. With the eclipse of the youth dormitories (*Bounzawl* or *sier*), students association (HSA) and youth association (HYA) have emerged as significant forums of opinion leaders.

While the hunting and fishing rights of the villagers on the village forests and water bodies are unrestricted, the land is controlled by the clans in the absence of the chiefs. The various plots or sites are conventionally used by the members of the various clans, in which clan elders allocate individual units of land to the families on the basis of their needs. Every village has atleast one family of blacksmiths (*Thirsu*) to manufacture agricultural and domestic tools. He is paid a basket of rice every year from every family for his services. Similarly, every village has a village crier (*Tlangseam*) to make public announcements and inspect public utilities. He is paid in kind annually a basket of rice from every household.

The Hmars are strongly patriarchal. The father is the head of the households and his orders are obeyed. It is he, who represents the family interests in all public fora, directs the family affairs and provides for the members of the household. It is ideal for the wife to raise children, cook meals, look after the home, tend domesticated fowls, pigs, etc., and bring firewood from the jungle and water from the water sources. The children, even when they grow up, respect the father as the patriarch. A henpecked husband, known as the *Thaibawi*, is not respected and is the butt of numerous jokes. The Hmars have a joint family system, which is claimed to be peculiar to them (Pudiate, R.: 1963: 40). Polygamy is rare, but divorce is simple and easy to secure provided the husband pays the wife Rs. 40 and takes her to her parent's house. The boys marry the girls of their own choice with the consent of both the parents. The parents arrange the bride price, ranging between Rs. 240 and Rs. 320 on the basis of the bride's clan, and offer a feast to the clansmen. The boys bring their brides to their parents' house and continue to stay there till they have many children. Customarily, they move out to establish their own home only when they have children of their own, who are of marriageable age. Their new home is jointly built by the entire family. The domestic work is divided on the basis of age and sex and everybody helps in agricultural activities. While fishing nets, hunting gears, agricultural implements, etc., are to be provided by the men, the women maintain their kitchen gardens, domestic fowls, piggery, etc., and other domestic chores such as clothing, cooking, cleaning, washing, etc.

The Movements for Hmar Identity

An inter-tribal conflict started in 1959-60 between the Kukis and the Hmars in Thongalpak area, western part of Manipur, on the refusal of the Hmars settled in Kuki villages to contribute to the Kuki fund, raised by the youth. This led to physical violence and burning of the Hmars' houses by the numerically dominant Kukis. In the process, many Hmars were killed allegedly by the Kukis. In retaliation, the Hmar-dominated Tipaimukh area rose in violence and houses of some of the Kukis settled among the Hmars were burnt. It is alleged that a large number of Kuki youth volunteers fortified themselves at Zaikul river island with arms and food. This fort like hillock is within the Barak stream, separated from Manipur side through a small stream which gets dried up during the summer. The Kuki youth wanted to attack the Hmars from stockaded Zeikul with all advantage of its strategic location, but their intention came to be known to Hmars. Immediately, a large number of Hmars surrounded the fortified location. It was summer and the river stream had dried up. The Kuki volunteers were forced to starve inside the stockade; when they ventured out for water, they were fired at. In the process a large number of them were killed. The Government of Manipur sent a team of social workers to the site under armed guards for negotiating peace among the warring tribes. After a prolonged negotiation the violence was stopped. But, an unwritten clause of the negotiation was the exchange of the settlers from the Kuki region to the Hmars and a vice versa. It is claimed that all the Hmars left Kuki villages and migrated to the Hmar region. Similarly, the affected Kukis from the Hmar villages were removed and settled even around Imphal. That was the occasion when the Thadou Kuki chiefs deserted their hereditary chieftainship behind in the hands of their tenant Hmar commoners, who invariably elected their village councils to run their affairs.

A little before this incident a Hmar youth, Rochunga Pudaite, born at Sonvon in south western part of Manipur, applied for scholarship from the scheduled tribe quota, but he insisted to identify himself as an Hmar. As Hmar clan was enumerated under Mizos and was not recognised as a separate tribe, his application was rejected. He approached Pandit Jawaharlal Nehru, the then Prime Minister of India, who directed him to Kaka Kalelkar, the then Chairman, Commission for Scheduled Castes and Tribes. And that is how Hmar was included in the list of the scheduled tribes. Among others, along with Rochunga Pudaite, Rev. Rualneikhum Pakhuongte, a student at Allahabad, former principal of Sielmet Christian College and presently Executive Secretary of the Evan-

HMAR HILLS DISTRICT

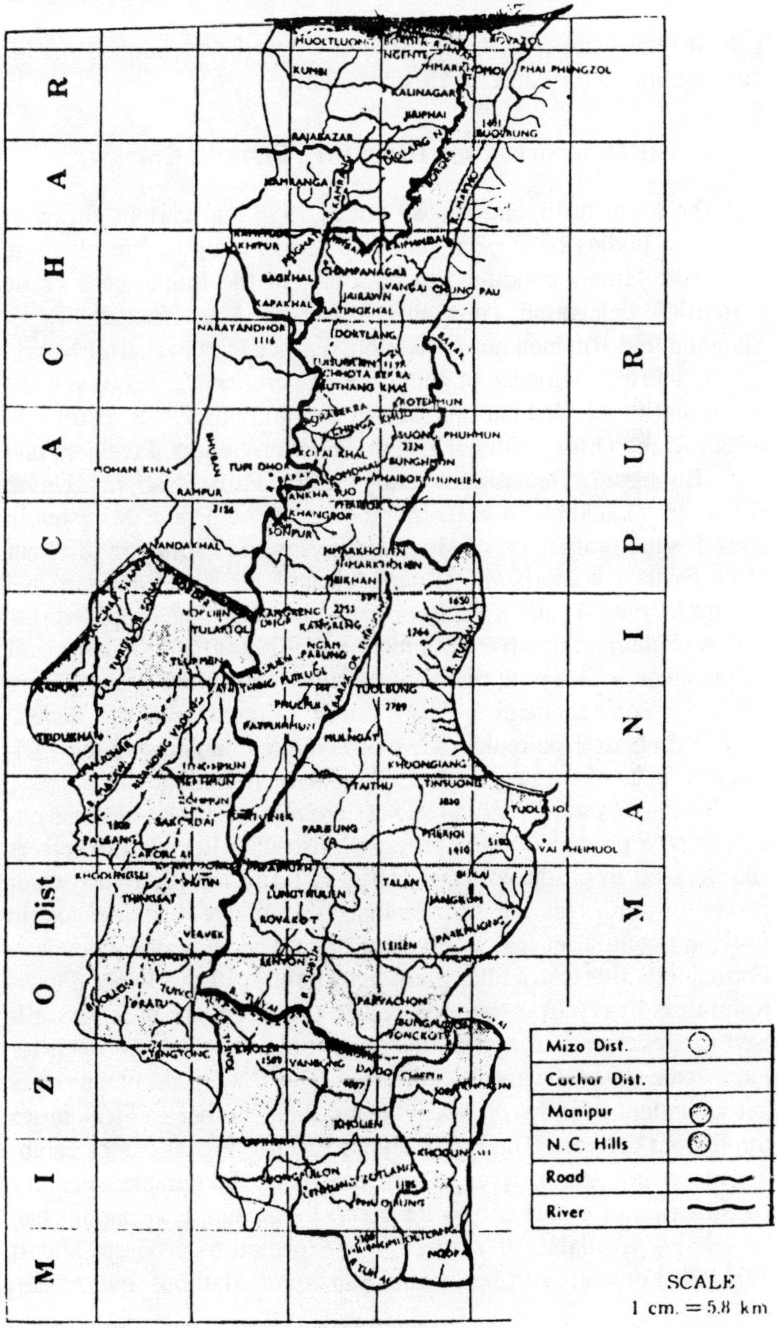

SCALE
1 cm. = 5.8 km

gelical Free Church of India, Shillong, may be mentioned for his contribution to the cause of Hmar solidarity.

The Demand for the Hmar Hill District Council

The Mizo insurgency broke out in 1966 and various forms of extremist bodies have been functioning in Manipur. But all these years, the Hmars continued to be a part of the Indian democratic system. A delegation, consisting of Messrs S.K. Hrengchal, J.C. Sengluia and Rualneikhum Pakhuongte, met Pt. Jawaharlal Nehru, the then Prime Minister of India, on November 10, 1960, at New Delhi and demanded carving out an autonomous Hmar district on behalf of the Hmar National Union. Dinglien Sonete, President and T.K. Buongpui, General Secretary of the Hmar National Union (M.A. & T) addressed a memorandum to the Prime Minister in 1968 for the unification of Hmar territories and formation of Hmar Hills District comprising 'Hmar-Majority' areas of Manipur and Assam (Senate, D and T.K. Buongpui, undated). The proposed district was claimed to have a population of 120,000 within an area of 4,400 square miles with two sub-divisions, four block development units, 20 constituencies in the District Council with the district headquarters at Tipaimukh (see map). While enumerating the various resources of the proposed district, the memorandum stated:

Hydro-Electric Works: "A vast amount of hydro-electric energy can be produced in the proposed district. Almost all the rivers can be used to produce electric energy. There are such vast water power resources in the district that rainfall over the area could provide potential energy equivalent to several thousand kilowatts. Fortunately, this district has great potentialities of this water power. Rainfall is heavy over the area. When the rivers are properly utilised for generation of hydro-electricity, the way would be open for large-scale development of industries. The Barak and other rivers get abundant supply of water from their numerous tributaries throughout the year. The Barak Hydro Electric Works can be established on the Barak river. There are many favourable sites for construction of a dam across the river. Large supply of labour can be cheaply available. If started, it is expected to generate atleast 1,00,000 kilowatts of energy and can serve Manipur and Assam apart from the district itself. The power project, when properly undertaken and executed, will be quite ambitious. It will provide employment opportunities to the unemployed masses and offer suitable jobs to the jobless. Income or royalty received from the project will add to the district funds. The proposed Hmar District has a lot of such unexploited natural resources".

The ZNC, ZORO, ZOMI and HPC

The Zomi National Congress (ZNC) was founded at a convention at Daijang in Churachandpur district on January 21, 1972, with Tungnung Gougin, an ex-Havildar of the Assam Regiment and former lecturer of the Sielmat Christian College. Its objectives were "to inculcate a sense of *Zomi* nationalism among the people of *Zoland* for this purpose, to organize a political platform from the village level." Similarly, its political aims were claimed to be the liberation of all the *Zomis* from India and Burma. The objective of complete independence was modified in 1983 to resolve that all *Zomis* should live together under one administrative unit with the protection and care of the Indian Union. The current objectives of the ZNC in Manipur appears to be separation from the state or atlest greater autonomy for the district within the state under the Sixth Schedule of the Indian Constitution. The ZNC is an important component of the *ZORO* (*Zomi* Reunification Organisation), the other component of which is the People's Conference of Mizoram. The ZNC leadership believes that Burma is in for disintegration and the *Zomis* should join the Indian Union in the larger interests. This ambiguous ultra patriotic affirmation on the part of the ZNC is fraught with international complications beyond the ethnic level in the region.

The *Zomi* is the collective name by which some of the Kuki-Chin tribes of Churachandpur district prefer to be known. They are found in all the districts of the state of Manipur and, at the same time, are the most fragmented among the Manipur tribes. Though they have been able to evolve Paite, the language of the most numerous tribe among them, as the *lingua franca*, they speak different languages as their mother tongues. This gets reflected in the fact that there are as many as 38 Baptist Christian denominations in

Churachandpur town alone. Similarly, among the Hmars in the above town, there are eight denominations. This ethnic fragmentation gets reflected at the political level also in terms of a variety of organisations: Paite National Council (PNC), Gangte Tribal Union (GTU), Hmar National Union (HNU) and Hmar People's Federation (HPF). In the light of the above, the collective identity of *Zomi* undoubtedly holds attraction to the politically conscious section of the tribes men. This has acquired further urgency in the last few years in view of the politically unsettled affairs and repression of the ethnic minorities in Burma.

In such a scenario, the formation of ZORO in the third week of May, 1986 at Champai in southern Mizoram appears to be logical. This convention was attented by some delegates from the Chittagong Hills tracts of Bangladesh and Chin state of Burma, besides delegation from Manipur, Assam, Tripura and Mizoram. The ZORO leaders of Churachandpur organised training camps for their volunteer force known as the ZORO Revolutionary Volunteers (ZRV) in the border areas. However, in the diverse background, the ZORO movement appears to be ambitious and of late it has shown signs of less acceptance.

At the swing of the pendulum is the Hmar People's Conference (HPC), organised locally by the end of 1988 with the avowed objective of carving out an autonomous district council in Hmar-inhabited northern Mizoram. With a view to achieving its objectives quickly and impressing the urgency of their demand they have raised an armed wing, the Hmar Volunteer Cell (HVC), with H. Darangeur as President and H.L. Biekhlien as the Secretary. The HVC is a well-knit organisation under seven commanders and subdivided into sections. The volunteers are trained in arms, ambush, and physical endurance at the hide outs scattered in the wooded terrains of Churachandpur. They have started a "monthly levy" of Rs. 50 from each trader, five percent of salary from each government employee and Rs. 10 from every family. The HPC, which is non-committal of being either an underground or an insurgent organisation, started its agitation in March, 1989, through *bandhs* and road blockades. They are claimed to be in league with the Naga guerillas and the Boro hardliners. It is reported that the 300 strong HVC has been asked by its parent body to start violence as a reprisal against the 'atrocities' on the Hmars committed by the Mizoram Armed Police (MAP). It may be pertinent to point out that activities of HPC may pose serious problems for the proposed Tipaimukh Dam Project, as the area happens to be the centre of their operation.

The Hmars in Tripura, Cachar and North Cachar districts of Assam and Manipur insist on retaining their own mother tongue. Even in Mizoram while the Raltes have forgotten their language completely and switched on to Lushai (Mizo), the Hmars in Mizoram are bi-lingual. They speak Mizo, but have also retained their own Hmar language vigorously. The church has produced educational, devotional and theological literature in Hmar language. The Hmars in North Mizoram were regrouped along with others around the road during the insurgency. Many of them, moved to Aizawl town, got educated, employed in the Government and other agencies and occupy high positions. Many of them are very rich by Mizo standards. In fact, Hmars are one of the most numerous along with Lusheis among the Mizo elite, who occupy positions of power, wealth and prestige. Incidentally, they are the people, who are opposed to a separate Hmar identity, because the larger Mizo identity is instrumental in their upward mobility. On the other hand, unemployed youth and compact Hmar villages, even from northern Mizoram, insist on separate Hmar identity, and they would like to join hands with their brethren from across the state boundary to carve out a separate Hmar district.

The Mizoram administration under Congress (I) rule pursued the HPC activists even up to the Hmar villages within the Tipaimukh sub-division. The Hmars presumed that to such acts the then local member of the Manipur State Assembly (MLA) and a Minister in R.K. Jaichandra Singh's cabinet and a Congress (I) man, Mr. Ngurdinglien, was a party. Consequently, he was defeated by Mr. H.R. Hrangkhawl, who became a Minister in the cabinet, headed by R.K. Ranbir Singh. It is commonly believed that H S A, H.Y.A. and the Sinlung Society took part in electioneering in favour of the non-Congress forces during the last election for the State Assembly.

In the changed political scenario of 1990s the Mizoram Government took the initiative for a dialogue with HPC. Thus, the two sides met at Aizawl on July 30, 1990 to find out a solution to the Hmars' demand for an autonomous district. Though the meeting ended without findings a mutually acceptable solution, they agreed to continue their dialogue and there is a marked decrease in the hostilities between the two sides. The two sides reportedly reached an agreement to establish Sinlung Hill Development Council, to introduce Hmar language as the medium of instruction at the primary level, and rehabilitation of the militants and those who were subjected to violence* in the last week of September, 1993.

Grounds for the People's Apprehensions

The Hmars have a tradition of self-sacrifice and hard work for the cause of others, known as *tlawmgaihna*. It implies an ideal act for an individual to be public spirited and useful in the cause of the community, which is necessarily the Hmars, or at the most the Kuki-Chin tribes in some special situations. On the other hand, the rest of the human beings are known as the *vai* the alien, outsiders or simply non-Hmar 'others', a term originally used for the Bengalese/Assamese of the Barak Valley. The Hmars will not like to work under a *vai*, who is considered to be a sly and clever person. The Hmars are a hard working people, who will happily take manual labour and petty trading once the occasion arises. But they will not prefer to work as cobblers, barbers, washermen, sweepers, rickshaw-pullers, etc., which are considered to be demeaning. Because of the old tradition of *jhumming*, in which one's daily needs and requirements are satisfied on the produce from the field on a continuous basis, they have no concept of a home economy as such. That is one of the reasons why a petty official or a white collar employee does not plan his domestic budget for the month and spends most of his earnings soon after receiving the salary. A sense of sacrifice for the community, culturally based distance from the outsiders, avoidance of so-called demeaning professions and lack of a domestic budgetary planning may provide key considerations for future welfare schemes.

At the community level one of the most ticklish issues will be

---

* The *Indian Express*, Bangalore, October 2, 1993, p. 10.

the conflicting claims between the Hmar commoners and the Thadou chiefs for the cash compensation in lieu of the land acquired for the project. While the customary laws favour the chiefs' claim, the operative part associated with the use of the land is in favour of the Hmar community. In the absence of an official public statement pertaining to the extent, effects, benefits and compensation amount derived from the Project, the region is full of rumours of all sorts, which have generated fear of losing the most precious asset of the community—land—and apprehension against an uncertain future. The Manipur administration must make the legal position clear about the conflicting claims on land compensation at the earliest. At the same time, the appropriate authorities must organise reasonable publicity through the mass media about the intent, extent, damage, advantages and projected targets from the Project so that fear and apprehensions may be minimised.

The Hmars of the Tipaimukh sub-division apprehend, and rightly so, that the better part of their cultivable land, orchards and most of their level ground will either be submerged under water or will be acquired for township, colonies, or other types of constructions. Their fields for paddy, cotton and chillies, slopes for the pine apples and orchards of orange, guava, and jack-fruit will be lost for ever. The Hmar *jhumias*—cultivators are totally at a loss to know their future once their land is lost and their activities associated with land come to an end. The Project has a rehabilitation scheme for the evacuees and the affected families, but what are the alternative jobs available to them, at what remuneration, for how long and on what qualifications have not been stated. The Hmars fear that most of the jobs thus generated will be technical in nature, which will require special skill, an expertise, which they do not possess. Thus, a large scale non-tribal but skilled personnel will be stationed for the Project. This scenario leads them to the secondmost precious asset they have—the women folk. It is generally believed that a relatively better qualified and higher salaried *Vai* immigrant will entice their women folk in marital alliance leading to a possible ethnic tension and conflict.

It was openly said in the region that their own fields were not flooded; their undulating hill land will not be irrigated and they could as well do without electricity; then why should they loose their most precious asset, the land? They are obviously uncertain, diffident and vague about the benefits from the electric power, emergent township and expected new jobs. Their opinion leaders, who are equally ignorent about the benefits from the Project, were found playing a negative role. They measure every step sponsored by the Government through an ethnic barometer. In their view, the Project is a non-tribal conspiracy to steal the tribal land for the benefit of the non-tribal plains men and townsmen. They shoot out a number of questions: Will the Government establish a polytechnical institute at Tipaimukh to train the Hmar youth in various technical skills required for the Project? Will the Hmars be given priority in the jobs generated by the Project? In case the promises made to them, provisions made in the scheme of this Project and rehabilitation and welfare proposals are not carried through for the benefit of the community, is there any future course left to them?

The above issues touch upon another dimension of the conflict: local versus outsider's (regional or national) interests. In some way or another the Hmar experience tells them that even the good intentions of the Government are rarely implemented in their favour. Similarly, in regard to the compensation to be paid for their property, rehabilitation of the evacuees and welfare of the affected families, they feel that in the absence of a reliable watchdog body, the State Government may not implement the provisions and the Central Government will be too distant an agency to meaningfully implement the above decisions in favour of the affected tribesmen. In such a situation, they would like the Government to take them in confidence. For that matter will the Government consider creating a watchdog body consisting of representatives of the significant Churches, for example, the Evangelical Free Church of India (EFCI), Independent Church of India (ICI) and Evangelical Assembly Church (EAC), the local M.L.A., the local M.P., Chairman of the Sinlung Society along with the General Manager/Chief Engineer of the Project? Such a body may play a constructive role in favour of the Project as such and the affected community. Furthermore, representatives of the Hmar Students Association (HSA) and the Hmar Youth Association (HYA) may be associated as special invitees as and when the situation demands.

The Hmars argue that if the Tipaimukh Project is being constructed in the national interests for the entire North Eastern Region, as its direct and indirect benefits will go to all the states in the region, why should not the various state governments—specially Mizoram, Manipur and Assam—agree to integrate the scattered Hmars into one unit? This has reference to the movements for the integration of various Kuki-Chin communities into one unit and also carving out an autonomous Hmar district under the Sixth Schedule of the Indian Constitution. They argue that only in such a situation the evacuees from the Project site will be rehabilitated elsewhere in the Hmar areas and the affected villages will plan for economic benefits from the Project. In that case the Hmars may not be forced to spend their energy in various forms of agitations and take up the challenge of reconstructing their scattered economy.

The Hmar region was known for its horticultural products such as orange, known as the Sylhet Orange during the Pre-Independence days. Even today pine apples, jackfruits, guavas and other seasonal fruits are grown in the region. Cash crops, such as ginger, cotton and chillies are cultivated. Plantation crops like coffee and rubber are proposed to be introduced. In the absence of viable agricultural activity the local people may be trained to take up fruit preservation and canning, poultry and piggery, meat processing and ranching, rubber tapping and coffee processing works with active institutional financing. In this context, a system of ranching with cattle rearing and meat processing may generate employment, suit the local temperament of hunting, provide protein to their diet and may be marketed in the region itself.

The Tipaimukh hydel project presents contradictions at various levels: between the needs of the plains and the hills, between the perceptions of the state administration and the micro-level tribesmen, between the demands of developed and urbanised plainsmen and the relatively isolated small communitites and between the proponents of development and exploitation and the supporters of survival and preservation. The divided and fragmented frontiers community of the Hmars is a poor match to the mighty state structure, capital investment, scientific skills and above all, the lack of national concern for a small vibrant community. Moreover, the Hmars have taken up arms against the state and spurned even award of amensty. In the given situation, it appears that they have been taken for granted by the technocracts and policy makers. And that's why no efforts appear to be made to take them in confidence. One only hopes that the better experiences of the Swarnrekha Multipurpose Project, Bihar and Gandhmardan Bauxite mining in Orissa may not be repeated on the eastern frontiers.

References

1. Anonymous, 1978, *The Lushai*: *1878-1889*, Tribal Research Institute, Aizawl, reprint.
2. Gaite, P. 1990, *Chiefs Union, Churachandpur District Manipur State*, Churachandpur.
3. Mackenzie, A. 1979, *The North East Frontier of India*, Mittal Publications, New Delhi, Reprinted from 1884 edition.
4. Pakhuongte, R. 1983, *The Power of the Gospel*, Shillong.
5. Piangzathang, 1990, *Hereditary Chieftainship and Village Land for the Chief Minister*, Manipur, Churachandpur.
6. Pudaite, R. 1963, *Education of the Hmar People*, Seilmet, Manipur.
7. Senate, et al. Undated *Memorandum to the Prime Minister of India*, possibly, 1968.

10

Communication and Development

The Indian communication scene presents one with perplexing paradoxes. The national government and the various state governments desire to use the New Information Technologies (NITs) for developmental purposes. Thus, unchecked import of communication hardware and software is not permitted and their indigenous production is encouraged. This production is left in the hands of private entrepreneurs as well as a few of the state-owned companies. While broadcasting, telecasting and licensing of the software are under the state control, print media, cinema, and other audio-visual software are left in the hands of private entrepreneurs, speculators and innovators. In this way, the Indian communication scene almost parallels to the Indian mixed economy, where a complete co-existence of all possible contradictory tendencies is possible. What is non-existent in this complexity of rules, regulations and laws is a sound communication ideology, from which policy statements, state communication strategies, specific programmes and definite decisions might have logically followed. In such a situation, we have noted that the Indian communication scenario may fruitfully be understood by the producerism-consumerism model. To a great extent this model is based on the market situation, which, in theory and practice, is a part of the world electronic market.

Advertising is an inseparably necessary component of the dynamic world market. With a view to optimum dynamisation in the world market, national and cultural peculiarities are to be harmonised. This market harmonization can be achieved through the trans-border satellite technology. This is necessarily dependent on the privatisation of television, on which "prime time" viewing hours for the mass audience entertainment is ensured. Television was introduced in India more than 30 years back in a modest way. Almost for two decades it was for the metropolitan clients and experimental purposes. Since 1982 Asain Games in Delhi the national government extended telecasting antennas to the farthest nook and corner of the country through the satellite system. Initially, large number of television sets were imported and the popular western commercial serials, films and other software materials were welcomed from abroad. Side by side, the indigenous producers came up with their own products with a claim that their products were more suited to the needs, temper, technology and idiom of the Indian masses. In this way, within less than five years, even the most isolated Indian territory was hooked to the national and indirectly to the world communication market. Thus, the New Delhi Communication Moghuls are all set to conquering the "backwardness" and "primitiveness" of the Indian masses in general and north-east in particular through the television medium. And that becomes clear when one takes a note of the North Eastern Council's (NEC) recent decision to distribute 5000 colour televisions sets to the villagers free of cost.*

I

The Video Scenario in the North East

The video came to the North Eastern Frontier Region in a big way in 1982. Now it is found in the state capitals, district towns, rural market centres and even in the villages. As there is no distinct communication policy at the central level, it was presumed that with the opening of the new telecasting stations, the remote areas will be linked to the national mainstream. Certain efforts are decidedly being made in this context. However, as a by-product of it, a large number of illegal, unlicensed, and unauthorised software are being used in the region. With a view to uncovering the video scenario in the north east we decided to undertake an extensive survey of the phenomena. As it is largely an illegal and unauthorised operation, its spread, extension and coverage require

* *The Statesman*, Calcutta, September 1, 1986.

maximum amount of data for authenticity. We evolved a technique of snow-ball in which we tracked it down from the metropolis to the state capitals, then to the district towns, from there to the sub-divisional towns and from there even to the villages. Then there have been some sort of touring video operators in the rural areas. With a view to getting a clue of their functioning four sets of questionnaires (one, video librarians; second, video parlours; third, the electronic shop owners, and the fourth, for the video viewers in general) were evolved and administrated in four states of Manipur, Nagaland, Meghalaya, Sikkim and the Assamese metropolitan city of Guwahati.

North east is geographically isolated, infrastructurally backward and is predominantly a tribal region. It is located on the international border and this is one of the two meso-regions in the country, which is land-locked. Sikkim on the Chinese and Nepalese frontiers, Meghalaya on the Bangladesh and Nagaland and Manipur on the Burmese borders in our study provide a very different picture from that of the national scene. These states are not only ethnically distinct, but are also the homes of small ethnic groups, which are not only isolated on the undulating topography, but technologically backward. They speak a number of small dialects and languages in which there is a relative lack of written literature. Though efforts have been made to produce films in Assamese, Manipuri, Nepali and Khasi, as a whole, there is no film production centre in the region worth the name. The software produced elsewhere in the country are screened in the region, which may not be upto the best liking of the masses. Possibly, this is the one reason for the clandestine trafficking in English cassettes from across the international borders. There is another aspect of the video boon in the region. The tribals of this region do not pay income tax. The national government is extending liberal financial aid to the states of the region for their socio-economic development. An appreciable amount of this state sponsored investment finds channellised to a new category of contractor-entrepreneur-politicians. This newly emerged neo-rich class has been able to control a good amount of what is known as the 'black money'. A chunk of this is being spent in acquiring VCRs/VCPs as the items of entertainment, display and luxury.

The video technology has opened up a new vista on the economic and communication horizon of the region. A number of persons, who were looking for an opportunity to earn money and make investments in a paying proportion took advantage of it. Even some of the state governments and the banking system came forward with financial assistance. However, all persons engaged in the video business cannot be termed as the *videopreneurs*. A typical 'videopreneur' is one who undertakes business risks either in the video libraries, video parlours or the video related electronic shops and any 'mix' of them, makes it a profit making proposition, sustains its growth atleast for sometimes and serves as a model for others to be emulated. However, a 'videopreneur' is not necessarily a successful and profit making individual. His main attributes are outgoing, risk-taking and a sort of electronic missionary, who has an intense faith in the efficacy of the video technology. He creates an atmosphere in which video-related hardware and software turn out to be the talk of the town.

All the video parlours in the region fall in the category either of unpredictable and subsistence nature or stable and licensed videopreneurs. The electronic shops are either in the category of stability or entrepreneurship. However, the video libraries are mainly in the domain of the subsistence business. They tend to be a stable business, when it is coupled with other associated business. In itself, it is a new, an unsure and an uncertain investment. Thus, while electronic shops are sound business and commercial prepositions, video libraries and video parlours are largely risk-involving business propositions for the north east frontier region of India.

The video viewers of the region prefer Hindi commercials in the cinema halls and the English commercials on the video. The local language films are not in a big demand and X'rated films are not preferred publicly in the cinema halls or on the video. Normally, friends are preferred for the company in viewing a film on the video. Two-fifth of the viewers' support the government taxation on the video operation and establishments. It is strongly felt that the video affects the social intercourse and it is realised that the traditional forms of entertainment will be adversely affected. Our viewers prefer foreign technology so far the video hardware is concerned.

The Hindi cinema halls and English video parlours are going to co-exist atleast for sometime in the region. Certain inadequacies in the national television programmes have helped popularise the unauthorised video operations all the more. While radio continues to be an important aspect of mass media., other traditional audio-visual media are loosing to the video. As a whole, the video is taken seriously in the north east region. It is considered to be a revolutionary technology, a boon to the developing countries, instrumental in changing social relations, with a high educational potentiality, generative of black money, beneficial to the business community and a menace to the individual privacy. However, it is a fact that it could as well be an aid to the social development of the region.

Implications of the Video Penetration in the North East India

The video as an important category of the New Information Technology (NITs) is a transitional culture, which cannot easily be contained within the national boundaries. Our communication media present a 'mixed' situation in which producerism-consumerism is the main determining factor. To the extent that state appears to be facilitating the demands of the producers and consumers at a subsidised rate. However, after making the above statement loud and clear, one must not loose sight of certain obvious national priorities, on which there is a national concensus. Among them mention may be made of secularism, socialism, democracy, social non-discrimination, uplift-ment of the disadvantaged section of the population, rural development, industrialisation, universal education, basic health care etc. One of the reasons for the state control on the radio and television is their use for social development and economic transformation which are in keeping with the above priorities.

Coming to the video, possibly the flow of the hardware from across the national frontiers can be controlled to a great extent. But it is difficult to control the external flow of the software, specially when there is no linguistic barriers. Television and video are very strong audio-visual media. Their viewing can go to the extent of an addiction to the population, to which they are newly introduced. Their impact on the masses can be contagious. Our study of the video penetration in the region confirms to the national expectation. The video is considered by the viewers to be a potential aid to social development. However, our data suggest that this potential is not being harnessed. Possibly no adequate steps have been taken at the level of the software. When we are talking in terms of the lacking state communication ideology as the guiding factor becomes clearer by the chaotic video situation in the region. We have stated above that certain state governments in the region provided financial assistance to the unemployed graduates for starting video parlours, which were to be banned by the same state(s) within a few months, when there was a public outcry against the videos. Apparently, no care was taken in providing the financial assistance as nobody obviously bothered as to what would happen to investment and investors in the banned video parlours. Was it because of the lack of will, concern, expertise, experience, an ideology or a policy?

As a whole, the video has been acquired as a luxury item by the emerging neo-rich urban middle class. It is also obvious that the unaccounted black money is being invested in acquisition of VCR/VCP possibly at the cost of some other essential domestic items. Its impact in the rural areas is not that pervasive, but some disturbing symptoms are discernible. In the absence of a positive, direct and purposeful outlet, its exploitative, negative and debased aspects catch the attention of the simple rural people—and specially the younger folk—easily.

There has been an apparent division of the video related work among its various sets of operators in the region. As a whole the video hardware business is controlled by the relatively large scale family-oriented professionals and experienced non-tribals. The software dealings are, by and large, the domains of inexperienced, small scale, subsistence and some stable tribal business men. Atleast some of the entry points of the video material unlike the other parts of the country, are located on the difficult mountainous and forested tribal tracts on the international boundaries. These entry points are obviously controlled by the local videopreneurs, who are naturally linked with the national and international electronic smuggling network.

At the level of the mass media, it can safely be said that the video has no impact on the print and radio media in the region. It is feared that the traditional communication media such as folk dances, devotional performances, drums, village criers, etc. are being adversely affected. As there is a lack of software video materials in the local languages, the video viewers are turning more and more to the English language. The content, quality, technology, cinematography, treatment of the theme and overall English language software appeal more to the young mind of the region. Thus, English films are preferred on the video. Unlike the reports from the other parts of the country, the largely English medium video has not affected the Indian languages cinema adversely. In fact, the largely Hindi medium cinema halls are having their houses full as usual in the region. In this way, the Hindi cinema halls and the English video parlours are co-existing in the region and in fact both of them are having good business. However, we would like to make a note here that though there is a persistent demand from an influential segment of the regional population for recognition of Manipur, Mizo, Khasi and Nepali languages by the Central Government, there is no demand from the video viewers for the software in these languages.

The video can be turned into an obedient and useful slave of the mankind. Its potentials for harnessing the cause of social development and economic growth are recognised. It can also fruitfully be used as a teaching aid in the educational institutions. Illiteracy, ignorance, superstitions, religious intolerance, communal and ethnic tensions, rural development, rural industrialisation, removal of social disabilities from the weaker sections etc. are some of the state sponsored programmes in which video can fruitfully be used. Perhaps without waiting for the evolution of a distinct communication ideology on the part of the state, those who are responsible for implementation of various welfare programmes can come forward and utilise the availability of the video for social transformation. The NITs as the gift of science to the humanity is neither a blessing nor an evil. It is their social use, which will turn them into useful or useless devices. The Indian national government believes that the video is a positive developmental device and that it is the reason such a huge investment is being made in it. Let us avail this opportunity for a positive cause by entertaining ourselves with a healthy, meaningful and constructive software.

A last warning in this regard is to be sounded. India is a plural society, in which various ethnic, linguistic and religious communities form an intricated tapestry. Some of them are very small, underdeveloped and isolated. However, they are very proud of their languages, traditions, cultural values, and an overall image. The national approach to the video software has to be sensitive to the requirements, appreciation and acceptance of all segments of the Indians. The video has to be innovative enough to gauge the needs, moods and temperament of the people. And only then, it will remain a healthy medium, free from debasement and perversion.

II
The Messaging Needs and Implications

The Post and Telegraph Department was created by the British administration as an adjunct to effective administrative control over Indian people. The department was run on the cost-benefit consideration. However, it was also established 'to serve the people' (those who could afford to). The department was rather slow in adopting new technological innovations. But it did increase its network to the length and breadth of the country and with the dawn of independence, the department was geared to the cause of the national priorities and programmes. As a government department, it slowly turned out to be one of the biggest employers of unskilled and semi-skilled persons. With the massive emphasis on rural development and overall demand for social transformation, the department did try to modernise itself technologically to meet the ever increasing demands on it. As a whole this modernisation phase in the department is largely based on technological transfer. No serious efforts are being made to ask whether the technological transfer fits in the national policy of self-reliance. In fact, its adoption is based on the principle of trickling down benefits from the top and what is known as technological diffusion.

So far North Eastern region in general and Meghalaya in particular is concerned, it is not only inaccessible from transport, communication and telecommunication point of view, but it is also economically at a subsistence level. By tradition, the vital resources—land, water, forest and even minerals—are controlled by the community, in which technological investment is minimal. The British introduced monetary system on this fragile base some 150 years back resulting in a very limited cash transaction. A limited number of 'locals' were employed in the government service, Christian mission activities and petty trading. In this way, till middle of the 20th century it did not have a sound and effective economic support base for the state sponsored efforts for infrastructural modernisation and overall social transformation.

The Indian independence brought in a new situation through the constitutional safeguards for job reservations in the various sectors for the scheduled tribes and large scale financial investment through the successive development plans. This process led to a disequilibrium in the communal ownership of resources leading to an emerging middle class and a set of neo-rich contractor-politicians as effective spokesmen of the communities. It is they, who articulate the community demands as per their perceptions. These articulate neo-elite—the modernised traditional leaders or the contractor-politicians—are bound to use the telecom amenities to further their hold on the community at the cost of the common tribals. Further access to modern technology may provide stimulus to widen the gap between the masses and the elite.

The Khasis of Meghalya in particular are well-connected with the world outside because of Shillong—their cultural and political capital and one of the most cosmopolitian towns of the region. About a decade back the Central Government decided to extend railways to link Meghalaya with an effective and cheaper transport system. In the peculiar ethnic-political scenario of the state, the neo-rich contractor-politician elite successfully opposed the extension of the railway line (which might have broken their relative isolation and insularity) to the state. The same elite demands a reliable telecommunication and air link to Shillong (which may increase their contracts with the outside in a selective way). They rarely raise the issues around the nature of development, but they do demand an access to a reliable telecom service for development and modernisation of the backward region. One may raise the question how and for whom is the state sponsored technology in general and telecom in particular helping the process of development in the state.

Starting in the last quarter of the 19th Century as a cart tract, the present Guwahati-Shillong Road (NH 37) used to have a horse-driven *tonga* service between Shillong and Guwahati for the British Officers. Since then this road, turned into a double lane National Highway, has become the lifeline for the supply of the essential consumer commodities to the capital. Similarly, all the district and sub-divisional towns are linked with metalled roads. However, with only 16.40 kms roads for every 100 square kms and 3.17 kms of road for every 1,000 Meghalayans, it is definitely insufficient.

There will be no second opinion on the need for an effective, reliable and comfortable all-weather surface transportation to the state, as most of the goods, articles and common man use these roads. It is a fact that in a topographically undulating and land-locked state such as Meghalaya, the cost of road construction and maintenance is higher. Besides importing the consumer goods from outside the state, local horticultural and mineral products may reach the markets for a better price. Health care and educational facilities may be made available to the needy without much delay. As better transportation leads to better awareness for alternatives, these roads may help the community to generate alternative sources of livelihood.

Among the audio visual media, radio is known in the state for a long period of time. We have noted above that it is largely used as a means of entertainment (which is in itself a very important aspect), much less for information and the least for development and educational purposes. The need of hour is to reorient this scenario and introduce a more balanced treatment to the various programmes. It must be used effectively as a vehicle to bring about change. The question should be raised that should the government owned media such as radio and television spend most of their time and programmes on entertainment? At the same time since the bulk of the population continues to be illiterate, audio-visual inputs are to be improved for better acceptance.

Among the audio-visual media television is a very powerful means of communication. Within five years since 1982 it has spread to the every nook and corner of the state. Along with it has come the video boom, which is undermining the conventional means of entertainments such as folk dances, theatres and cinema.

Violence prone and cowboys type Western feature films are mostly screened on the video anywhere for private or commercial viewing. At times uncensored pornography and blue films are also screened, which is causing irreparable damage to the younger generation. Though Khasis are producing video films, need of the hour is to produce aesthetically sound films acceptable and attractive to the young people. There is no television studio at Shillong to produce software in the local language on the local themes. The two television relay stations at Shillong and Tura relay national programmes for the Meghalayans. In a study of television coverage in Meghalaya (Sen, M.: 1988: 167) we found the viewers' disinclination to the national programmes. Like radio, it is largely taken as a means of entertainment followed by information and this medium is taken seriously by very few viewers for its role in educational and developmental purposes. Now that the state government has decided to introduce 630 community television sets, should it not think of producing or helping those agencies which are competent and willing to produce educational and development oriented programmes in local languages? However, it goes without saying that continuous exposure to the national programmes through television does diffuse some elements of national programmes to the distant places leading to the national integration.

We have done the content analysis of the banners of the two most read newspapers (an English and a Khasi) in Meghalaya. Our analysis gives a confused picture of the purpose behind the publication of the two newspapers. They do not provide entertainment, but even the information they give are lopsided, least educative and development oriented. Besides their claimed purpose of providing information and political education to the readers, the newspapers may have their latent functions, which are unstated and even our analysis did not enlighten us very much. So far the larger public is concerned, the newspapers are read for political gossip, 'contract tender' information, black-mailing some persons, etc.

Between the postal and telephone departments, postal service continues to be more reliable. For the limited requirements of the Meghalayans, it continues to serve their purpose in terms of providing mails and postal stationery within a reasonable time limit (though of late it is complained that postal stationery is not available in the post offices quite frequently). There were negligible complains against the postal department, as nobody expects it is to deliver the mails urgently considering the overall transportation system.

It is the post office, which books the telegrams for onward transmission. They still operate on old Morse type of mechanical devices for transmitting the messages. In the ecologically hazardous topography such as Meghalaya, there is frequent landslides during monsoon months leading to quite frequent traffic disruption. In such situations telegrams are sent to the T.D.O., Shillong through the ordinary postal mails for onward transmission. This entails undue delay in reaching the message to the addressees causing further problem of reliability.

There is another dimension of the postal communication. It is considered to be a public utility service, which is for years now running on loss. Many believe that the postal deficit is mainly because the government does not introduce pricing policy of its stationery and services as per the cost. "That the average cost of postal service should be cheaper than entertainment costs makes a mockery of the economic priorities. That some of the postal rates are unrealistically low in the context of the steep erosion of the money value can be seen from the price of postcard, which since May 15, 1974, has remained static at 15 paise . . . cost of providing this service has increased . . . today is about 58 paise. At the present rate of staff escalation (30% per annum) the position in 2001 A.D. would be: population 101 crores, traffic (ordinary mail)—Rs. 2,114 crores, working expenses—Rs. 4,000 crores, revenue at the present rate of tariff Rs. 1,072 crores and deficit of Rs. 2,932 crores".[1]

In such a context of low postal rates when finance will be in a permanent state of deficit, the service will tend to adjust itself to rising costs by pruning its operations or reducing frequency or duration of various services such as mail collection, delivery or counter services. However, such efforts in economising operations may evoke popular dissatisfaction and resentment. In the North Eastern Postal Circle itself, the year 1987-88 showed a deficit at Rs. 1486.93 lakhs. At the national level with Rs. 557.5 crores revenue and Rs. 770.12 crores expenditure there was an annual deficit of Rs. 216.43 crores in 1986-87.[2] In such a situation, a radical departure from the present tariff policy is strongly recommended.

In spite of the mounting losses, postal service is still considered, and rightly so, a device to ensure a balanced rural development. We are informed of the new norms for opening of the new post offices.[3] It is proposed that the population of the village should not be less than 5,000 in normal areas and 2,500 in hilly, tribal and backward areas. For the purpose of identification of a tribal area, it has been laid down that only areas identified as tribal for purpose of implementation of projects would be considered as such. The hilly areas should be identified as such by the Hill Area Development Programme. The permission limit of loss is fixed at Rs. 2,400 a year in normal areas and Rs. 4,800 a year in hilly, backward or tribal areas. Similarly, the stipulated income from the post office should not be less than 50 per cent of its anticipated cost in normal areas and 25 per cent of its cost in backward or hilly areas. In such a situation, the overall annual financial district deficit will increase for the national postal service.

Telegrams

Our findings suggest that the predominant purpose of telegrams sent is that of official and domestic crisis and they are sent in handwritten English language. It is a time consuming process, which delays the message and does not work properly. Cost, language, education and socio-psychological factors were not seen as problems. As a whole, it was considered to be desirable, but unrealiable device for sending the messages on time to a distant place. The messages are sent to Shillong, Tura, Guwahati, Dibrugarh, Imphal, Calcutta and upto Bombay, but it is predominantly regional in character. They universally desired that the telegraph office should be located within a distance of 5 kms in their locality. It appears that the cost and the number of telegrams to be sent are not related. For example, even then the price of a telegram is reduced to a ridiculous less than a rupee per message, there is no considerable increase in the number of telegrams to be sent from Nongpoh, because they have to locate the situation and the individuals for such a messaging.

Telephone

The persons who use the postal mails most and send the maximum number of telegrams out of Nongpoh are private businessmen, administrators and bankers. Similarly, though the telephone exchange functions far from satisfactorily, out of the seven agencies using it most frequently, first six are private business and commercial establishments and the seventh and the last one is the administrative head of the area Sub-Divisional Officer, Nongpoh (Civil). Persons associated with agriculture, voluntary social service, political parties, educational institutions are conspicuous by their absence. Then the valid question: 'Who is going to talk to whom and for what purpose?' in case rural telephone is installed in Meghalaya need to be answered.

The Problems with the Existing Telecom in the Region

The problems can be identified at three levels: accessibility, reliability and credibility of the service. By and large rural folk interacts more at interpersonal levels. Most of their relatives, friends and associates with whom they work are normally available within a walking distance. They prefer to walk to the place for a face-to-face interaction. Moreover, the special services available to urban centres, which might be made available telephonically, are not present in the rural areas. On the other hand, the telecom installation is invariably located in an establishment owned by the government, from which the common man has learnt to keep a distance. It is normally considered as an item of luxury for administrators, affluent, educated and wealthy businessmen. There is another aspect of basically illiterate rural folk's reaction to telecom: how to reach it? How such will it cost? Whom to and what to talk? Thus, the impression is that telecom is not for common man and a common service and it is an exclusivè preserve of the elite. And it is one of the reasons that only .34 persons out of 100 who possess the magic wand of telephone in India.

That the messages sent through the telecom transmission will certainly reach the destination is not normally accepted proposition in the region. The rural consumer approaches a telecom device in a desperate bid such as an accident, a calamity or a disaster, or stickness has befallen on him. He finds that the telecom staff and office works between 10 a.m. and 4 p.m. and in between the operating staff on duty is in the habit of going for a cup of tea or refreshment, which may range from a few minutes to even hours. Even if the telecom station is open and the staff is on duty, it is very likely that the mechanical system might be out of order for days together. Then comes another problem. Even if the message is accepted, it may take time to get the line. In not infrequent cases, the telegraphic message is routed through postal service taking any time between 3 and 7 days to reach its destination. Invariably, by then the urgency to use the telecom is over.

The national average of the fault rate per 100 telephones per month is 24.35. The highest fault rate in the country is recorded in Assam (47), which is very closely followed by N.E. region with 46.5 and then West Bengal (39.65). The main reasons for the poor performance in these areas compared to all-India figures is said to be old, worn-out cables, old telephone instruments and worn-out exchanges. Some states such as Assam and N.E. region in particular are also prone to natural calamities like heavy rain and floods. There are a number of hilly areas, where faults in the external plants are frequent. Due to financial and resource scarcity, only 12 per cent lines of the total installed capacity as on March 1988 and those exchanges, which have outlived their average prescribed life on April 1990 will be replaced during the Eighth Plan period, 1990-1995.[4] Thus, the customers have no prospect of a reliable telecom service even after 1995.

The Maitland Commission was aware of such a situation. While enumerating various possibilities under 'Quality of Telephone Service' a hypothetical similarity to Indian scenario was described: "Country—A low income economy with a telephone penetration of less than 1 per 300 population.

Service . . . very poor and under present operating conditions is deteriorating from day to day . . . Lack of spare parts drastically reduces the traffic capacity . . . . causing bottlenecks and unreliable service . . . countrywide only 49% of manual long distance calls are connected the day they are booked. Five minutes to obtain a dial tone in the busy time of day. . . 22% of lines in the country out of service . . . 80% of faulty lines . . . out of operation for more than one month. 50% of faults were due to local cable networks, 45% to subscriber plant and 5% to switching equipment" (I.T.U.: 1984: 114). In such a situation, the worst casuality is the reliability of the telecommunication system.

The problem of reliability gets further complicated by the quality of service provided to the common customers. Again this may be seen from two angles: mechanical and human. So far telecom machines located in the rural areas are concerned, they are old ones, manually operated, providing an inferior quality of service as a whole. Not infrequently it is difficult to get through the line. While conversing, it is a common experience that the line gets crossed, jammed or simply goes silent. Then comes the human aspects. The telecom operating staff very much like their machines lack social credibility. In spite of all the rules to check the inefficiency and lodge a complaint against misbehaviour, they are invariably unattentive to customers' complaints and unresponsive to even queries. In such a situation, telecom suffers from a serious credibility gap.

The Role of Telecom in the Process of Development

The role that telecom plays in development has remained obscure because of difficulty in measuring its impact. Such difficulties arise because besides point-to-point benefits, telecom generates immense indirect benefits to the users and local economy, which is difficult to be measured statistically. In addition to the direct benefits to the users, its social benefits are likely to contribute to improve the quality of life in rural areas. These emphasis reflect current concern with equity, decentralisation and self-reliance. To achieve these goals, developing nations such as ours must pay greater attention to rural human development (Hudson, H.E.: 1984). Otherwise lack of access to critical information can place the rural residents at a major disadvantage, and can impede the improvement of rural social and economic conditions. However, the provision of telephone service for rural users is not a remunerative proposition in itself. As it is considered to be a socio-economic need of the bulk of the population residing in rural areas, it has to be provided on a subsidised basis.

Our data indicate that, by and large, rural population interacts locally, say within a radius of 50 to 75 kms and at most within the district for most of the purposes. Unless and until telephone service is made available in all the villages within the sub-division or district, it is difficult to expect higher calling rates (Murty, B.S.: 1984: 24). It is imperative to expect certain level of infrastructural, economic and administrative activities to reach for expecting an appreciable rate of even indirect benefits. "Although telecommunications can be used on occasion as a substitute for transport, their effectiveness in co-ordinating the movement of goods in reducing inventories, in finding the best markets for produce and so on depends on the adequacy of the transport system. The same is true of the role of telecommunications play in emergencies. The telecommunications link between patient and doctor will not fulfil its purpose unless transport is available to move the patient to hospital or to deliver drugs and other supplies" (I.T.U.: 1984: 10). And only the telecom infrastructure plus other complementary infrastructures can together lead to more economic growth and more effective social service delivery.

Back to Shillong, the N.E. Telecom Circle has drawn an ambitious plan to achieve certain targets fixed in terms of B.S. Murty's proposals. Out of a number of telecom devices, they have decided to instal Multi-Access Rural Radio (MARR) system at 50 locations in Manipur in 1988 and another 200 locations will be linked up next year. In this way, 75 per cent of the proposed hexagonal Village Cluster Cells (VCC) in the state will be covered. Similarly, by the end of this year, 10 each villages around Shillong and Tura will be lined with the help of MARR system. For that matter village sites have been identified, antennas at Shillong and Tura are fixed and actual operators in the respective villages as agents of the telecom department willing to make device available to the users are being identified. In this way, a beginning has been made in the state of Meghalaya. However, it was surprising that the Chief General Manager, N.E. Telecom Circle at Shillong did not appear to be aware of the SBRNT experiments.

It was encouraging to note that the Indian Prime Minister included "Mission Better Communication" as one of the five elements of his 'Technology Missions' for the modernisation of the country. His technology adviser, S. Pitroda maintained that "car telephones (proposed to be installed in Delhi) are mere gimmicks and we have no need for such a (tele)phone system, which would cost Rs. 75,000 a piece. For every three car phones we can have one rural (telephone) exchange, which should be the focus."[5] Further, he informed that the Union Government had taken up a plan to instal one rural digital exchange with 80 lines, per day from April 1988 for a year. Under this plan 250 such exchanges would be set up all over the country and the cost per phone to the government would be about Rs. 10,000. Expressing his resolve to set right the urban bias in telecom, he maintained, "The need is not to increase the (tele)phone density, but to give a thrust on the accessibility of communication for rural masses . . . . we realize that the modernisation process has to relate to the larger sections of the community."

Enumerating the various performances of the N.E. Telecom Circle in the year 1988-87, M.N. Shukla, the C.G.M., informed that the Telecom Board had taken a decision not to instal any more electromechanical or old technology equipment in this region.[6] He exhorted the telecom employees in the spirit of Pitroda's quoted above, "The modernisation of service puts a certain responsibility on the officers and staff working in this circle. Firstly, the outlook of every day should simultaneously undergo a change: to think modern and to tune oneself to the new situation, thus, making the process of modernisation total. Everyone will also need to develop the skill to handle the modern technology. My advice to the staff is not to be left out from the alround change taking place but to plunge whole heartedly in it".

As a whole, the telecommunication (i) provides information; (ii) plays a vital role in emergencies and health services; (iii) increases efficiency of public administration, commerce and other economic activities; (iv) assist in national integration, self-reliance and political stability; (v) reduces regional disparity within the country; (vi) helps shrink distance; (vii) can reduce need to travel, and (viii) facilitates better use of existing transport facilities. However, full utility of rural telecom can be realized only when most of the villages are telephonically linked and other associated infrastructural amenities are extended to the area. Though its indirect and imperceptible impacts take time to be felt, the measurable economic impact of the use of telecom channel in an area such as Meghalaya will depend on two factors: (i) the increase in information flows achieved by telecom in comparison to other communication networks and (ii) the extent to which new messages change economic agents' opinion of the probability of events (i.e. the social receptiveness of the rural folk to new information).

III

We conclude firstly, that the Meghalayans depend on interpersonal channel of communication by travelling to or sending messengers through automobile transportation; 70 to 90 per cent messages are transmitted within the district and the state; 20 to 80 per cent messages are sent within the North Eastern region; and less than 5 per cent messages are sent beyond the region within the country and abroad. Secondly, as no viable and autonomous centres of industry and commerce have emerged in the area of our study, the felt messaging needs are predominantly for individual urgencies, administration and small scale business; the existing telecom infrastructure suffers from serious problem of accessibility, reliability and credibility of the service. Thirdly, because of its strategic location, a reliable telecom will have an impressive demand in future provided; all the villages in the sub-division, district, state or region are linked telecommunicationally; supporting secondary information sectors such as education, health care, industries etc. move in to take advantage of telecom; and laws of land are liberalised to encourage interaction at social, economic and industrial levels. And lastly, access to telecom amenities may affect the social equilibrium widening the gulf between the elite and the masses.

Notes

1. 'Cheap Postal Tariff at What Cost?', *The Hindu*, Sept. 20, 1988.
2. *The Annual Report*, Postal, 1986-87.
3. *The Telegraph*, Calcutta, October 24, 1988.
4. *Ibid.*
5. *The Telegraph*, January 3, 1988.
6. From 'G.M's Desk' *Netnews*, Vol. 4, No. 2, July, 1988, The House Journal of the N.E. Telecom Circle, Shillong.

References

1. Hudson, H.E. 1984, *When Telephones Reach the Village: The Role of Telecommunication in Rural Development*, Ablex Publication Corporation, Norwood, New Jersey.
2. I.T.U. 1984, *The Missing Link*, Reprint of the Independent World Wide Telecommunications Development.
3. Murty, B.S. 1984, A Phone in Every Village, Department of Telecommunication, Govt. of India, New Delhi.
4. Sen, M. 1988, "Social Aspects of Mass Media": A Study of Television Coverage in Meghalaya", M. Phil. Dissertation NEHU, Shillong.

11

Structural Imperatives of the Indian Core and the North Eastern Region[1]

Among the many attributes of such as Indian state one is territoriality, which is in itself a geographical concept indicating a variety of features. However, another significant attribute of the state may be identified in terms of population, which is a multitude of communities co-existing in the given territory, organised themselves into the state for political purposes. A student of social behaviour may like to examine the quality of community participation at the various levels with reference to the state. Keeping that in view, the chapter, firstly, examines the concept of region as such and its various attributes. Secondly, after briefly describing the North-Eastern region as a distinct one, we have endeavoured to explicate the concepts of core (centre/mainstream) and frontier (periphery/margin). Thirdly, we propose to examine the evolution of relationship between the Indian core and the North-Eastern peripheral region. And lastly, after briefly commenting on the quality of the existing relationship, we suggest what should be the pattern of interaction between the two in future for a meaningful participation in the activities of the Indian State.

A region has location; it has its areas; and it has its limits. It is conceptually a short hand way of describing the variable characters of an area dissected deliberately from the extensive land mass. Thus, the broadest possible definition of the region may be given "as an area of specific location which is in some way distinctive from other areas and which extends as far as that distinction extends."[2] In this way, the region is an artificial intellectual construct to uncover the physical and socio-cultural attributes of the world.

Thus, it may be single-factor formal area within which homogeneity prevails or a much-factor functional area in terms of several inter-related and interacting phenomena. Since a region is identified as such on the basis of some chosen criteria, such a regionalisation should have utility as well as validity. Among the significant factors on which a region is identified, mention may be made of physiography, ethnicity, social, political and economic systems, language, religion, degree of mobility, urbanisation, cultural-historical evaluation and many more. The experts divide the world as per their speciality and the demands made on them. Thus, we have climatic regions, resource regions, cultural, religious and linguistic regions as well as geo-political regions. Accordingly, a number of approaches may be identified for studying the region. Elsewhere[3] we have examined (i) geographical and ecological, (ii) economic, (iii) culture-area/trait complex, and (iv) administrative, legal and political regions adequate enough for uncovering the extensive Himalayan region. A combination of the above approach may be able to uncover the various facets of the North-East (Frontier) region.

The northern highlands of Arunachal Pradesh is, in fact, the eastern extension of the great Himalayan arc. The eastern limit of the Indian Union with Burma is formed by the Purbanchal, extending from Namcha Barwa (on the north-eastern extremity of Arunachal) to Arakan Yoma on the border of Burma and Bangladesh. The north-western end of the region is secured by the Gangetic Delta, which separates the Mikir-Meghalayan plateau from that of the Rajmahal hills in Bihar. The central part of the region is the low-lying plains of the Brahmaputra and the Barak. The communities have moved in and out of the region since time immemorial. The migration of the communities across the international borders from the North and North-East to the region has been significant. To the extent that anthropologists such as John H. Hutton[4] and Robbin Burling[5] have shown the cultural linguistic links between this region and south Asian peoples.

Because of the geopolitical disadvantages, the region has achieved an integrated insularity. Its overall underdevelopment is an aspect of the larger scenario of unequal and uneven development in the various parts of the Union. In 1960's Sen Gupta and

G. Adasyuk[6] termed this as an economic region of incomplete formation within a meso-agricultural zone of rice-maize-market-gardening and horticultural products. Chaube and his associates also examined 14 indicators of such an incomplete economic formation.[7] Undulating topography and tribal concentration appear to have gone together in the region. Arunachal, Meghalaya, Mizoram and Nagaland out of the seven units of the region have about 80 per cent scheduled tribal population.[8] This concentration of the tribes in the hill states is significant because only 3.57 per cent of the total Indian and 11.43 per cent of the scheduled tribes were found in the region in 1971. Their distribution is also differential in the sense that only 6 persons per sq. km. were found in Arunachal Pradesh, while 186 persons per sq. km. in Assam against the regional figure of 77 and the national figure of 177 in 1971.

II

A casual visitor of North-Eastern Region from the other parts of India is baffled by the remark: When did you come from India? This may be heard in Mizoram, Nagaland, Manipur, Meghalaya and lately in Assam. The other side of the coin is the reception meted to the visitors of these frontier states to the Indian metropolitan cities, where they are asked to produce their foreign passports to establish their identities. Ignoring the mischief mongers, it is worthwhile to consider the confusion created by the genuine mistaken identities. While the former set of Indians after postponing their cultural, religious, caste and linguistic 'superiority' for the time being find the 'backward' tribals ungratefully not identifying themselves as Indians, the latter find themselves lost in the crowded mainstream because of unfamiliar language, food and complexity of communication. And invariably when not properly recognised, they tend to conclude that the statements made in favour of national unity, secularism, non-discrimination etc. are just oral platitudes. One may cancel these stray experiences as exceptions in a huge country like ours. However, such incidences may also be taken as symptomatic expressions of the complex relationship between the Indian core and the north-eastern frontier region. Not only from academic but even from practical point of view, certain questions in this context demand our attention: where is the Indian core or mainstream and what should the frontiermen do with it? In other words, what does it symbolise for and how should the frontiermen identify themselves with it? What is India after all? Is it just a 'state' or is there an Indian society? In that context, what does it mean to be an Indian? How does one normally behave as an Indian?

It needs no efforts to identify the Indian Union as a state consisting of 31 administrative units of states and territories. By its own admission, it is a plural society, where multiplicity of race, caste, religion, language etc. are logically recognised. One may also recognise India like any other 'state as a complex interaction between the spatial (concrete, communicational and other locational objects) and analytical aspects (such as social and behavioural). From purely a legal point of view, the Indian society should coincide with the human multitude within the political boundaries of the state. Naturally, this Indian society in typical Durkheimian approach to social structures may consist of material referents such as human resources, transmitted commands, coercion etc. and symbolic and mental referents like consent, fear, persecution, resistance etc. In such a situation, it is but natural to express distinct peculiarities of the national phenomena in terms of bi-polarities like rich and poor, urban and rural, dominant and subordinate, bourgeoisis and proletariat, developed and underdeveloped and mainstream and periphery. With a view to uncovering the locational and behavioural aspects of the above phenomena, the issues around the concept of core (centre/mainstream) and periphery (frontier) in Indian national context may profitably be examined.

Some scholars presume 'state' to be unicellular organism with a nuclei (centre, core, capital), bodies (territorial expanse), outer membrances (the boundaries) and the stomi (ports, border posts etc.). It is also considered as a system in which a continuous surveillance by the dominant of the subordinates' behaviour and deployment of threats and punishments are normal ingredients.[9] All these are performed in terms of power, which is defined as control over communication flaws, located in the state at the points where selection is possible, decisions are made and information is transmitted. Through this politico-cybernetic model of state the extensive territorial entity of India is nothing but a hierarchy of power centres branching out to a seat of ultimate decision-making power. Naturally, commands follow down from the centre to the periphery and information travels in the reverse direction.

In the normative model as opposed to the politico-cybernetic model of state 'power' is replaced by the concept of collective concensus on shared norms and values. Emphasis is placed on society, considered to be a commonality of immaterial elements such as images and moral codes. Status and prestige are peacefully and unanimously accorded to those who fill the most strategic roles in society. It is presumed that there exists a central zone as realm of values, beliefs and actions in structure of society. This central zone also provides a set of activities, roles and personnels within the network of institutions. In this way, the central zone is intimately connected with what society considers to be sacred and ideal espoused by the ruling authority.[10] From this point of view, the large territorial societies such as India have a number of sub-systems such as polity, economy, status systems, ecclesiastical and kinship systems etc., which are organised through common and overlapping set of values and personnel. Needless to add that the above sub-systems characterize the pattern of authority symbolised by the individual behaviour.

III

In case one examines the expanse of the Indian Union closely from its capital to the frontier regions, some interesting features may be noted. Firstly, the core of the Indian Union may be identified with Delhi, Uttar Pradesh, Bihar, Madhya Pradesh, Rajasthan, Haryana and Himachal Pradesh. This is predominantly a Hindi speaking, Hindu area which had traditionally been a stronghold of the Indian National Congress or other national political parties. Needless to add that 40 per cent seats in the Indian Parliament belong to this zone. Secondly, an associate to the core may be identified with the states such as Gujarat, Maharashtra, Karnataka, Kerala, Tamilnadu, Andhra Pradesh, Orissa, West Bengal, Tripura, and Assam. These states are non-Hindi speaking, but predominantly Hindu areas either under the Indian National Congress or other 'National Political Parties'. Incidentally, about 52 per cent seats in the Indian Parliament are controlled by them. Thirdly, at the outer fringe of these two zones, we find Jammu & Kashmir, Punjab, Goa, Lakshdweep, Andaman Islands, Mizoram, Manipur, Nagaland, Meghalaya, Arunachal Pradesh and Sikkim. These are the frontier states mainly inhabited by non-Hindu and non-Hindi speaking communities, and have a strong tradition of regional political parties. They elect only about 8 per cent of the Indian Paliament. It may not be out of place to put on record that Jammu & Kashmir and Lakshdweep are the only Muslim majority states; Punjab is the only Sikh dominant state; Sikkim is the only Buddhist dominant state and Nagaland, Meghalaya, Mizoram and Arunachal Pradesh are the tribal states within the Indian Union, which are all located on the periphery. For the purpose of broad generalisation, the first two categories may be identified with the mainstream, while the third zone may profitably be termed as peripheral to the core in various ways.

We feel this is an opportune time to focus on the national exercise identifying, analysing and evaluating the exigencies of social change, economic growth and political implications of small (frontier) states in India. The Indian Union consists of 31 political-administrative (22 states and 9 Union Territories). In our present discussion 31 units will be referred as the 'state' irrespective of

Table 11.1. Population, area and ethnicity in the small states: 1971

Unit State	Area in sq. km.	Total population	Density of population	Percentage of Schedule Tribes
1. Andaman & Nicobar islands	8,293	1,15,133	14	15.72
2. Arunachal Pradesh	85,573	4,67,117	6	79.02
3. Lakshdweep	32	31,810	994	92.86
4. Manipur	22,356	10,72,753	48	31.18
5. Meghalaya	22,489	10,11,199	45	80.48
6. Mizoram	21,087	3,32,390	16	94.26
7. Nagaland	16,527	5,26,449	31	88.61
8. Sikkim	7,299	2,08,843	29	38.00
9. Tripura	10,477	15,56,342	149	28.95

their being 'state' or 'Union Territories'). Among these states, the first six large states contribute to more than 50 per cent of the total area as well as the total population of the Indian Union. On the other hand, fourteen small units (states) together make up only 8.9 per cent of the area and about 5.5 per cent of the Indian population. In case, we consider the size of the population along with smallness in territory, we get a list of 17 states which are small. Goa, Pondicherry, Chandigarh, Dadra & Nagar Haveli and Delhi are in fact structurally and behaviourally parts of their neighbouring larger states, hence they are to be excluded from the list. In case we examine the cultural distinctiveness of the states (i.e., presence of at least one-third population belonging to the scheduled tribes/caste), we come across only some states which are small in territory, population, resources, and have particularistic demographic characteristics. Incidentally, these are the states which are geographically inaccessible because of their location on the Indian frontiers. They may be identified as Andaman & Nicobar islands, Arunachal Pradesh, Lakshdweep Minicoy and Admindivi Islands, Mizoram, Nagaland, Meghalaya, Tripura and Sikkim (Table 11.1).

These states may be classified into two sets: one, the six states from among the members of the North-East Council and their neighbour, Sikkim, all located on the distant North-Eastern international frontiers and geographically inaccessible mountainous region; two, the two island states scattered on the expanse of the Bay of Bengal and the Arabian sea, posing strategic challenge of their own. It may be noted that they are located on the geographically inaccessible regions. The second feature that emerges is that most of these states are of crucial strategic significance because of their location on the international frontiers with China, Bhutan, Burma and Bangladesh. Thirdly, five of the states, e.g. Arunachal Pradesh, Lakshdweep, Meghalaya, Nagaland and Mizoram are predominantly tribal states, while nearly one-third population of Manipur, Tripura and Sikkim belongs to the scheduled tribes and there are the scheduled castes inhabiting these states.[11]

IV

It appears that the first of the two above-mentioned approaches is closer to the empirical reality of the inter-relationship between the Indian mainstream (or the core) and the north-eastern frontiers (for the present, we shall limit our discussions to the north-east region only). These frontier states are tenuously linked to the centre (or the capital), where the strategic elites are located, significant decisions are taken, commands are transmitted to the peripheries and informations are demanded from them. The key terms, which qualify the relationship between the two are 'power' legitimacy, authority, rules, compliance etc. Such relations are formal, mechanical and legal, which sprang up because of some historical accidents, but they are sought to be of paramount significance. The pattern of this relationship smacks of colonial attitude of the past, to which a paternalistic vaneer of development and planning for the backward regions has been added by the new rulers. Possibly, it would have been ideal to look for a 'moral' concensus of shared 'norms and values', commonality of ideal images and moral codes, a realm of beliefs and actions and over all a set of sacred national objectives as the common heritage of the core and the periphery. Perhaps only such a common commitment will inspire confidence in the future and only then the real and imagined injustices supposed to be inflicted on the frontiers would set right.

The north-east frontier is vague, distant and amorphous to the mainstream. It is said to be the land of the naked, head-hunting and exotic peoples. Even the famous Kamakhya temple is mythologically associated with magical power to convert the humans into birds and beasts. The bulk of the mainstreamers are oblivious of the frontier states. In case they could locate them on the map, all they know is the territories and not the communities. Physical distance from the core is coupled with the insufficiency of the communication networks. There is no quick, effective and convenient (the least comfortable) means of communication between the core and the region. In such a situation, those who go to the region, consider themselves something of pioneers, explorers and adventurers. The white collar functionaries come to the region on punishment, occasional promotions and out of routine postings. Very rarely a functionary opts for posting in this region. And why should he do so? After all no significant decision, even the one, affecting the distant local situations, is taken in the region. Consequently, a frontier functionary, who lives a relatively deprived and inconvenient life, plays no role in the process of decision-making; rather he is supposed to obey the orders from the 'above' and keep on filling the informations. All such funtionaries who come to the region on brief sojourn have their powerful patrons, links and well-wishers in the core. That is one reason why they do not behave normally. Either they mark their time in nothingness or indulge in acts beyond their normal behaviours. In the context, studies have shown that there is a distinct change in the behavioural pattern of the Brahmins from the plains, when they travel to and stay longer in the frontier hill regions[12] of even Uttar Pradesh Himalayas.

The frontiermen equally feel the core to be complex, manipulative, mysterious, devoid of sensibility, a jungle of rules and a convenient contrivance of some crafty authority. The moment they get out of their native environs, they confront language, food, transport and communication, etc. as uncomfortable and unfamiliar. "There are historical reasons for that. What is called "Indian Great tradition" by some sociologists hardly penetrated into these difficult border terrains during pre-British times. Neither were these included administratively into any pre-British Indian empire. Later, these were conquered by the British, but were excluded from regular administration and opportunities of free contact with the plains. Neither the Indian Railways nor the Indian national democratic movement reached out to these areas."[13] It is a fact that the better part of the north-east frontier become parts of India effectively only during the last 150 years or so. Even the Ahom land, better part of the Brahmaputra valley east of Kamrup, came to effective Hindu fold (and thus to mainstream) as late as the 17th century. That is one of the reasons that social structure, commensality, marital pattern and festivals and feasting are unique to Assam. In such a situation, the various frontier states adjoining the Brahmaputra valley, are not in a position to identify a collective code of conduct, a shared belief and historically transmitted traditions along with their Western neighbours. On the contrary, they are afraid of an unequal social system of the mainstream. Many of them believe that if absorbed in the mainstream, they may be mistreated as the untouchables and reduced to a beast of burden.

By tradition the hunting and pastoral frontier communities consider the settled plains agriculturalists as inferior breeds. They do not accept the natural barriers by temperament, and the political boundaries are least acceptable arrangement of relationship for them. Individual attainments such as physical powers, swordsmanship, archery, hunting, riding etc. coupled with an element of defiance are the prized ingredients of their behaviour.[14] Such communities are not only located on the geographically inaccessible tracts, but are also part 'societies' in the sense that a section of their kith and kin are located on the 'other' side of the legal boundaries. Linguistically, culturally, socially and even economically they are separated by an artificial 'divide', which they had never really recognised as such. In fact, the above overlapping sets of loyalties naturally provide an alternative mode of behaviour in their hours of distress. Explorers, adventurers, fortune-seekers, fugitives from the law and other types of men fired with an imaginative scheme rush to the 'frontiers' from the core to make quick monetary gains. Thus, a number of bonanza shanty towns emerge, where, in fact, nobody rules and the 'business' as usual is secured through an unwritten code of violent conduct, through which a tenuous working equilibrium is attained.

Against this background, the various types of the Bengali ethnocentricism (and thus Hindu, which represents the mainstream) and actual historical claims relating to script, language, cultural attainments, political awareness, contributions to the economic development etc. in terms of the region, are seen as efforts of the mainstream to dominate the peripheries. And naturally a situation emerges between them which can be understood only in terms of dominance-subordination syndrome. Here, one would like to share the apprehension of a distinguished scholar: "In their eagerness to subject themselves as 'nationalistic', 'progressive' and 'secular' many social scientists have been vocal in condemning the loyalties to such entities as religion, caste, language and region somewhat indiscriminately. But it will be useful to keep in mind two points here. First, the human need is not only for impersonal ties with entities such as political parties and bureaucratic state on the one hand and for privatised ties provided by primary groups such as family and kin-group on the other but also for immediate structures and processes which blend and balance the two. In a country like

India such ties are often provided by caste, religion, language and region, which are often labelled as communal, parochial, and anti-national. But these loyalties and ties need not be so dismissed. Second, there is qualitative difference in their loyalties and ties between different levels and contexts. These can co-exist and one need not displace the other."[15]

V

It may not be out of place to mention A.G. Frank's concept of metropolitan and peripheral economies in terms of the marginalised so-called primitive communities. Similarly, Samir Amin's proposition of unequal regional development and consequent exploitation of the peripheries by the urban industrial metropolitan mainstream may be relevant.[16] The mainstream with its superior techno-economic organisation and decisive control on the resources tends to logically extend its economic infrastructure to exploit the peripheries. The emergent peripheral petty middle class tries to collaborate with the dominant metropolitan elements with a view to sharing the "benefits of development", but they come to realise within no time that the collaboration is to their disadvantage. Thus, more aware they are of the exploitative nature of the metropolitan control, more defiant they become in their dealings with it.

In this complex spectrum of relationship between the centre's dominance and frontiers' defiance can there be certain shared values, ideals, ideologies and objectives for a corporate living? India is a plural society and a participative democratic state. We claim to have a tradition of unity within diversity. The Indian Union is a confederation of sub-nationalities, with regional centres for certain decisions and their implementation. However, it is also a fact that the political centre and regional sub-centres have not been able to develop a system of shared functions to the best satisfaction of everybody. No sensible Indian would like to weaken the strength and effectiveness of the centre in terms of undertaking and implementing strategic decisions. At the same time, it will be desirable and healthy tradition to increase a sense of participation, belonging, and unity of purpose with regards to the national ideals, values, and objectives among the regional sub-centres. This can only be done by encouraging them to take their own decisions keeping in view the national ideals. Only then a chain of politico-cultural sub-centres will emerge in the frontier regions, which may project ver-ile traditions and observe the local shock-waves. It is high time to realize that the Indian Union does not belong only and even mainly to the mainstream and the frontiers are to be ruled and subjugated and treated as supplicant. It must also be borne in mind that frontiers do not need paternalistic proppings, but a recognition that they are trusted to take significant decisions affecting national life, and that they are able and capable to contribute to the national common-wealth as equal and proud partners.

References

1. The paper is heavily drawn from author's publication, "India's Outer Darkness', *The Statesman*, Calcutta, March 4, 1984 and his presentation, "The Conflicting Images of the Indian Core and Periphery" at Ranchi University, Ranchi, on April 13-14, 1985.
2. De Belj, J.J. 1971, *Geography: Region and Concepts*, John Wiley and Sons International, p. 5.
3. Sinha, A.C., 1984, 'Managing the Social Consequences of Smallness', in: *North-Eastern Region*, (ed) B.L. Abbi, C.R.R.I.D., Chandigarh, pp. x-xvii.
4. Hutton, J.H., 1968, *The Sema Nagas*, O.U.P., Bombay, Reprint; *The Angami Nagas*, O.U.P., Bombay, Reprint, p. 969.
5. Burling, R., 1965, *Hill Farms and Padi Fields*, Prentice-Hall, Englewood Cliffs, N.J.
6. Sen Gupta, P. and G. Sdasyuk, (ed), 1968, *Economic Regionalization of India*.
7. Chaube, S.K., Sunil Munshi and Amlendu Guha, 'Regional Development and the National Question in the Northest India', *Social Scientist*, No. 37.
8. Ahmad A., 1982, 'The Linguistic Pattern of North-Eastern Region', First National Symposium of Language and Social and Regional Identities in India, organized by Centre for the Study of Regional Development, Jawaharlal Nehru University, New Delhi, Nov. 8-9, 1982.
9. Strassoldo, R., 1980, 'Centre-Periphery and System-Boundary: A Culturalogical Perspective', in: *Centre and Periphery: Spatial Variation in Politics*, (ed) Jean Goattmann, Sage Publications, Beveraly Hills, London.
10. Shills, E., 1961, 'Centre and Periphery' in: *Logic of Personal Knowledge;* Essays presented to Michael Polayi on his birthday, London.

11. Sinha, A.C., 1984, *'Studies in the Himalayan communities'*, Books Today, New Delhi.
12. Berriman, G., 1968, *Behind Many Masks*, Correll University Press, Ithaca.
13. Guha, A., 1982, 'National Development and India's Northeast Region: Some Conceptual Aspects in a Historical Perspective'. Seminar on Regionalism and Nationalism, Dibrugarh University, Dibrugarh, November 1982, p. 9.
14. Lattimore, O., 1962, *Studies in Frontier History: Collected Papers: 1929-1958*, Oxford University Press, London.
15. Oommen, T.K., 1984, *'Insiders and Outsiders in India: Primordial Collectivism and Cultural Pluralism in Nation-Building*, Working paper-Panel I, XVII, All India Sociological Conference, south Gujarat University, Surat, December 1984, p. 18.
16. Amin, S., 1980, *Class and Nation: Historically and in the Current Crisis*, Monthly Review Press, London.

Epilogue

1. The British administered the North Eastern tribal region indirectly under their paternalistic care. Even then, as it is now, the region symbolized everything for a distant frontier. The lush green forests, inexhaustible timber, tea plantations, wild animals, torrential rains, devastating floods, exotic traditions, vigorous folk dances, ferocious and feuding tribes, unreliable means of transportation and communication, etc. were the popular attributes of the region. The relatively small and isolated tribesmen of yesterday are now trying to find meaning in the newer entities such as Arunachal Pradesh, Meghalaya, Mizoram and Nagaland. In a way, the region is no more as distant and isolated as it used to be a quarter of a century earlier and it is on a transition from its subsistence mode to the universal good of the market economy. Of late the various state-sponsored dispensations such as the armed forces, cash transactions, electoral processes and electronic media have reached to its farthest nooks and corners. A new urge to catch up with the latest trends from the metropolitan centres has taken over the region.
2. The present anthology of essays is a modest effort to delineate the structural compulsions and emerging pattern of change in the region. Among the former unique geographical unity with its magnificent isolation, rich natural resources such as forests, rapid conversion of tribesmen to Christianity, emerging inequality on an egalitarian communal base, prevalence of small scale social world and massive dose of immigration from within the country and across the international boundaries may be enumerated. Dimension of agrarian conflicts, unplanned and haphazard urbanisation, apprehensions from large

scale development projects on the social base of small tribal communities, onslaught of the mass communication media and differential perception of the Indian mainstream and the North East Frontier region may be mentioned among the significant aspects of change. The presentation in the book may be seen in the perspective of social transition.

3. The geographical unity of the region highlights its isolation from the main Indian land mass. This isolation inbreeds a sense of helplessness in the presence of daunting natural obstacles. Modern technology must be used to minimise the infrastructural obstacles and human sufferings. Frontier character of defiance may not be directly confronted, rather it may be moderated and made use of in a positive way to eradicate ubiquitous poverty and human misery. Undoubtedly, improvements have been made in increased and effective communication to the region from the national capital. However, much is desired and in this context the corridor mentality must be replaced by a sense of sharing the transport network across Bangladesh. Efforts must be made to persuade Bangladesh to open up two alternative routes to North East region to provide axis to; Delhi-Calcutta-Agartala-Guwahati, and (ii) Chittagong-Aizawl-Imphal-Kohima-Guwahati.
4. It must be understood by everybody concerned that natural resources such as forests are not inexhaustible. The forest cover and wildlife of the region have taken centuries to evolve on a fragile ecological system. Once it is disturbed, it may cause incalculable consequences for the living beings. The dilemma between the ecological preservation and resource utilisation for development may be solved by selective use of resources as an aid to developmental process. There is a need for a grassroot environmental awareness movement in the region so that issues around environmental preservation may be highlighted. At the same time, a network of forest co-operatives with membership of beneficiaries of the local customary right-holders will go a long way to a balanced environmental heritage.
5. Regional religiosity is a patent force, which cannot be wished away as obscurantist, anti-secular and anti-development. It is a fact that animism among the tribes is on decline. Hinduism and

Islam are being modernised with the help of scientific and technological kitbag and knowhow. The various sects of Christianity have found favour with different communities of the region and the Christianity as a whole is on ascendency. It is imperative that tribals' ethnic defiance, territorial identification, missionic zeal of Christianity, and world-wide support network may be used for enriching the variety of the Indian society and improve upon the quality of human life. If not properly articulated, the unique attributes of the region mentioned above may cause an embarrassment to the already belaboured and fragile secular fabric of the Indian state.

6. Emerging inequality among the communities with relative equalitarian experience of the past is a world-wide phenomenon contributed by the capitalist path of market-oriented development. The North Eastern scenario is no different from that of the general pattern. We have noted above the emergence of middle class in the form of a contractor-politician nexus causing havoc to the age-old tribal corporate living. At the sametime, as a bi-product of their conversion to Christianity, a vocal and assertive tribal intelligentsia with an intensively human face has emerged. This tribal intelligentsia, who are capable of giving a lead, may identify the ways and means to end the exploitation of their brethren by re-interpreting their customary practices and re-examining the legal provisions.
7. The North East region is notorious for different types of dissenting and insurgency movements, vis-a-vis the Indian state. Such movements and search for a meaningful identity by the various tribes are inseparable issues. Most of the tribes of the region represent a stage in their developmental sequence, which may conveniently be referred as 'small scale societies'. These tribes are engaged in a continuous process of searching for a meaningful, competitive, comparable and convenient identity with a view to competing with the various Indian-sub-nationalities. This unending search frequently leads them to social and ethnic fission and fussion in the form of social segmentation and sub-division and also occasionally emergence of larger identities such as Naga, Mizo, Adi, etc. It may be noted that while creation of Nagaland and Mizoram as states exhibit

the solidarity at the state levels and fulfilment of a meaningful and larger identity, has the creation of Meghalaya and Arunachal Pradesh led to similar achievements and claims? While it is apparent to understand Naga and Mizo identities, there is no similar Meghalayan and Arunachali identities at the pan-tribal levels. But then why did the various tribes in Assam such as Bodos, Karbis etc. are demanding for statehood?

8. The regional resources have limited capacity to feed unlimited migrants. Of late, the demographic boom has taken up swing in the region. The apparent lower density of regional population has to be seen in terms of carrying capacity of the land and it cannot be compared with intensively cultivated lands in the plains. Besides the natural population growth in the region, large scale foreign immigration from Bangladesh and Nepal have added to the ethnic conflict. In the past, while the Bangladeshi immigrants have attracted considerable attention, the Nepalese immigrants got easily merged in the regional ethnic melting pot. Unlike the other immigrants attracted to the plains and towns, the Nepalese preferred the geographically inaccesssible location in the region and strived hard to develop them. As their fate is irrevacobly linked with the ethnic policy of Nepal, they are engaged in defining their identity vis-a-vis the Indian state. With immigration, the analytical description of geographical isolation, forest resources, religiosity, social inequality and ethnic identity as given background of the region comes to an end.
9. Among the aspects of social change, the most perceptible is that of the agrarian tension. The traditional tribal agriculture is shifting towards a settled, intensive and plough cultivation. It also means a change from the past communal ownership to the private proprietory rights in landed property. The constitutional guarantee to the tribal customary laws in the hills ensures that the land invariably remains with the tribesmen, who are now educated, absentee land-owners, white-collar employees or businessmen. Thus, agrarian scene has now new phenomena of landlordism, absentee ownership, share cropping, landlessness and agrarian tensions. This is taking the shape of inter-ethnic conflict, as the landless agricultural labour is invariably non-

local and non-tribal immigrant. Though the agrarian tensions are mounting in the region, the tribal states of the region have not been able to pass land reforms acts to ameliorate the hardship in the agrarian sectors.

10. It is a fact that urbanisation is a new phenomenon in the region, but the rate of urban growth in post-independence period for the tribal states is rather alarming. These British administrative outposts of yesterday have turned into ethnic melting pots with a variety of problems of their own. As the small states do not influence the national economic and political processes in a decisive way, the urban problems of these cities also get lost in the maze of administrative procedures. In the absence of an appreciable industrial base, these hill cities are expanding on the basis of service sector besides being the administrative centres. With their expansion in size, urban problems are posing new challenges. These non-representative non-tribal towns on tribal hinterland are almost entirely controlled by the bureacracy far from popular representation. They have their regional flavour, which may be termed as the *haat* culture against the *Bania* ethic of Gujarat towns and *Babu* ethic of the north Indian towns.
11. For a prosperous agriculture, floods need to be controlled and water for irrigation is to be channelised. Urban and industrial sectors require electricity for their smooth functioning. For that among many things, powerful hydel projects are being erected on various sites in the encatchment areas of various rivers in the region, which are invariably inhabited by the tribesmen. Location of such large scale power projects such as the Tipaimukh Hydel Project on river Barak on the borders of Manipur, Mizoram and Assam among the Hmars will cause immigration of skilled men from elsewhere to the construction site, displacement of the tribal farmers, construction of resettlement colonies, emergence of new townships, flooding of the fields, forests and villages and consequent loss of property. The resultant benefits from the project are vague and distant and affected people have all types of apprehensions. It appears that there is a lack of communication between the local affected community, state Governments, central Government and the

project implementation agencies. It is desirable that a dialogue is opened with the local community and their genuine apprehensions are removed for harnessing the hydel power.

12. Among the various sets of infrastructural facilities, an effective communication network through electronic and telephone system is the most effective way to remove the regional isolation and inclusiveness. These two will decidedly affect the traditional communication media prevalent in the region. The electronic medium through television and video sets has not only brought the new form of entertainment, but it has also made available a new range of knowledge, informations, skills, education and even occupations. Similarly, availability of telephones even to remote rural areas has opened up new possibilities of growth and service sectors etc. However, it has been found that the Indian states lack an effective communication ideology and that's why the television software is entirely left in the hands of the private operators. However, a new set of 'videopreneurs' and 'television mavericks' has emerged on the scene. The impact of electronic medium on the region is yet to be measured, but nobody has any doubt that it does influence the regional mind in a decisive way.
13. The book makes an effort to uncover the given structural constraints and aspects of the social transformation of the North Eastern region. However, it is a dialogue between the Indian core and the North Eastern Frontier region. One hopes the Indian core appreciates the unique problems of the region and takes the region in confidence. Similarly, the Indian core expects the regional support on the national objectives. These are some of the minimum expectations from one another. However, the region lags behind in many aspects. In case we decide not to leave environment as an exclusive preserve of the botanists, tribes to ethnographers, religion to theologions and politics to investigative journalists, research priorities, planning procedures and decision-making processes must be coordinated. With a view to that, the following perspective may be kept in mind: i) privatisation of the communally owned resources, (ii) environmental resource exploitation and ecological preservation, (iii) a viable industrial policy and role of

science and technology in social transformation, (iv) infrastructural planning and problems of migration, and (v) primordial linkages and modernising role of the church. After all most of the problems of the region originate in the perceived threat of marginalisation of the regional identity at various levels. The resolution of the above issues will go a along way in the right direction.

Author Index

Subject Index